Snafu

Perspectives on the

'Accelerated Age'

Peter Deegan

ISBN-10: 0-9969279-8-0
ISBN-13: 978-0-9969279-8-7

Cover Design by Jasser Membreno

Pitcairn Press is an imprint of Cinenovel®

Pitcairn Press

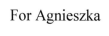
For Agnieszka

PETER DEEGAN

CONTENTS

Acknowledgments

ACKNOWLEDGMENTS

Sincere thanks to my wife, Agnieszka, and our children for their support and encouragement. I am very grateful to my editor and writing coach, John O'Keefe, for his gentle guidance and tireless enthusiasm. And my thanks to Jeff Buchanan at Pitcairn Press for all his patient help and support.

Chapter 1

ABOUT SNAFU:

Perspectives on the 'Accelerated Age'

The Merriam-Webster dictionary defines snafu as "a situation marked by errors or confusion." The word is believed to have originated in the U.S. Army during World War II.[1] As well as a cynical comment on the inefficiency of the military, it seems intended to mock the Army's love of acronyms. Snafu has survived into this century, but it isn't used much these days.

The definition doesn't capture the depth of the word, which lies in the acronym it comes from—"situation normal, all fucked up."[2] If you use snafu with the acronym in mind, it changes a polite criticism about a commonplace screw-up into a sarcastic jab at the conventional wisdom. That's what this book is—a jab at the conventional wisdom—specifically, the part that underpins our socio-economic values.

In 1958, the conventional wisdom held that production and consumption were the guiding forces of Western civilization, even at the cost of inequality and social deterioration. This was the diagnosis of John Kenneth Galbraith in his book of that year, *The Affluent Society*, in which he coined the expression "the conventional wisdom."[3] Since then, economic growth has declined and inequality has increased, yet the conventional wisdom has remained largely unchanged. We still worship production and consumption. In 2014, another unconventional economist, Thomas Piketty, revealed the simple formula behind inequality: "r > g." In his book *Capital in the Twenty-First Century*, the sequel to Karl Marx's *Das Kapital* we didn't know we'd been waiting for, Piketty wrote: "When the rate of return on capital ["r"] exceeds the rate of growth of output and income ["g"]... capitalism automatically generates arbitrary and unsustainable inequalities that radically undermine the meritocratic values on which democratic societies are based."[4] Piketty thinks this is what the 21st century holds for us—though his book, which quickly became a bestseller, may help overturn the conventional wisdom.

Snafu doesn't describe every social "situation" that's "fucked up"—just those that seem "normal." For example, it doesn't fit "situations" that are truly appalling, like slavery, torture or persecution, because they are so far from "normal," even in an ironic sense of the word. And it doesn't fit violent crime or terrorism because "situation" suggests something arranged by those in authority. Yet, Snafu does apply to war, not only because the word arose in a wartime context, but also because war is violence "arranged" by a state or someone with more-or-less legitimate authority over combatants. So, I look at war and examine why "arranged violence" is so persistent. I do that towards the end of the book.

Snafu best fits situations that are fucked up in ways that might not be obvious, like politics. Wait a minute—isn't that a rather obvious fuck-up? It is—yet what's not obvious is how and why politics became that way, given that democracy isn't supposed to be a snafu. In 1776, the United States had no aristocracy and no great disparities of wealth or privilege. Its founders wrote a constitution based on principles of liberty, equality, and the common good. Yet, less than a hundred years later, around 1870, the U.S. entered the "Gilded Age"[5]—an era of staggering inequality that made the Declaration of Independence seem like a cruel joke. Sometime in the mid-1970s, a new Gilded Age began, and it shows no sign of ending. What went wrong with America's political system? How did such a carefully designed democracy become such a mess? This is the first snafu I look at.

Nothing much happens in society without money. In 1922, Henry Ford wrote: "Those who believe that the people are so easily led that they would permit printing presses to run off money like milk tickets do not understand them. It is the innate conservation of the people that has kept our money good in spite of the fantastic tricks which the financiers play—and which they cover up with high technical terms."[6] Ford was right that there's something odd about money. As recently as 2008, "the people" saw the monetary system blow apart, yet they stood aside while politicians put it back together the same way, then printed "money like milk tickets." Why didn't they react as Ford would have expected?

We pay for society with taxes. Taxes are supposed to be as certain as death. And they are—just not for everyone. Why is that? How do corporations and the rich manage to dodge taxes? And why will the latest amendment to the U.S. tax code, a law that's supposed to raise revenue, instead raise the federal debt by about a trillion and a half dollars?[7]

Then there's work—the engine of social progress. In 1930, John Maynard Keynes predicted that, in 2030, we'll only need to work fifteen hours a week to earn a living wage.[8] Yet, the forty-hour week has persisted for more than seventy years. Many of us need to work longer than forty hours a week, while others can't find enough work. What has happened to work since Keynes made his prediction?

In addition to politics, the social systems that tie together money, taxes, and work are economics and law. These are big systems—too big to examine in this short book—so I deconstruct only a single aspect of each one.

They call economics the "dismal science."[9] It is dismal, but it isn't a science. There's a joke that, in the physical sciences, three rules explain ninety percent of behavior while, in economics, ninety rules explain three percent of behavior. There's a lot of ideology in economics—nowhere more so than in the theory of markets. Society seems to be ruled by markets. So I examine them and chart the extraordinary life of an innocent metaphor—"an invisible hand."[10]

When we think of the law, we also think of order, even if we're not talking about criminal law (which I don't). Is the law as orderly as we imagine? Around 1862 in England, they began to allow ordinary people to register companies. We all know something about companies. But what did the lawmakers know when they designed the legal framework for them? How good was that design, and what has happened to it since then?

The last snafu I consider is "reality"—the way we see the world. Our relationship with the world is partly instinctive and partly learned, sometimes rational and sometimes emotional. If we examine reality, we find that it's shot through with contradictions. These contradictions affect the way we arrange things and the ways our arrangements become snafus. So, in some ways, reality is at the base of a pyramid of snafus. I examine reality after I look at the other snafus.

The purpose of this book is to challenge the conventional wisdom. I don't offer solutions to the snafus I examine. To work, any solutions would have to be collective. And anything collective starts with a discussion. My contribution to the discussion is the question I pose in the last chapter and the answer I suggest. I ask: "Is snafu as good as it gets?" I try to answer that question without making predictions, because predictions are like monkeys with typewriters. If the monkeys type long enough, sooner or later one of them will type something coherent; in the meantime, they type gibberish. I look at the past instead of the future, even though I know that history doesn't necessarily write any better guide to the future than the one we get from the typing monkeys. But here's the thinking:

The snafus I write about—and the conventional wisdom they helped shape—largely evolved during a two-hundred-year period that started around 1776 and ended around 1976. The dates are just indicative, and the duration isn't exact. I call this the 'Accelerated Age,' because the speed at which society developed during this period was not only fast but kept getting faster. And the West dragged the rest of the world along with it (that's the reason this book is about the West, not the rest). The start of the Accelerated Age coincided roughly with the start of the Industrial Revolution, which unleashed the energy that powered it. It also coincided with the birth of the United States, which developed in tandem with it, dominating the second half of the Accelerated Age. America became the epicenter of the social systems I examine (that's the reason this book is mainly about America). But the changes that occurred during the Accelerated Age were planetary in scale. They were so profound as to close off many of our options for the future—with the result that some things in our future are practical certainties, not predictions. More about that in the last chapter.

My perspectives on the conventional wisdom are a bit like looking at pictures from an angle to try to see into the shadows. As you read this book, I hope you'll get the sense that the pictures overlap—the shadows too. When you finish the book, you might consider adding snafu to your active vocabulary. It's such a useful word—though I wish there were fewer uses for it.

---

[1] The first use of the word is thought to be in 1941 or 1942. There is an interesting discussion on the origins of the word here: https://english.stackexchange.com/questions/68954/researching-the-real-origin-of-snafu. See also: https://en.wikipedia.org/wiki/SNAFU.

[2] *Merriam-Webster*, s.v. "snafu," https://www.merriam-webster.com/.

[3] "Because familiarity is such an important test of acceptability, the acceptable ideas have great stability. They are highly predictable. It will be convenient to have a name for the ideas which are esteemed at any time for their acceptability, and it should be a term that emphasizes this predictability. I shall refer to these ideas henceforth as the conventional wisdom": John Kenneth Galbraith, *The Affluent Society*, rev. ed., (London: Penguin Books, 1999), 7 and 8.

[4] Thomas Piketty and Arthur Goldhammer, trans., *Capital in the Twenty-First Century*, (Cambridge: Harvard University Press, 2014), 1.

[5] The name comes from the novel by Mark Twain and Charles Dudley Warner, *The Gilded Age: A Tale of Today* 1873. Project Gutenberg, 2008 https://www.gutenberg.org/ebooks/3178. It is generally taken to refer to a "period of gross materialism and blatant political corruption in American history during the 1870s": *Merriam-Webster's Encyclopedia of Literature* (Springfield: Merriam-Webster Inc., 1995), 463. Some definitions extend the period to around the end of the 19th century, see: *Dictionary.com*, s.v. "Gilded Age," www.dictionary.com/.

[6] Henry Ford, *My Life and Work*, in collaboration with Samuel Crowther (Garden City: Doubleday, Page, 1922), 60.

[7] The exact estimate by the CBO is $1,414 billion: Congressional Budget Office, cost estimate, the Reconciliation Recommendations of the Senate Committee on Finance (November 2017), https://www.cbo.gov/publication/53348. See also: Jugal K. Patel and Alicia Parlapiano, "The Senate's Official Scorekeeper Says the Republican Tax Plan Would Add $1 Trillion to the Deficit," *New York Times*, December 1, 2017, https://www.nytimes.com/interactive/2017/11/28/us/politics/tax-bill-deficits.html.

[8] John Maynard Keynes, "Economic Possibilities for our Grandchildren," in *Essays in Persuasion* (New York: W. W. Norton, 1963), 358-73, available at http://www.econ.yale.edu/smith/econ116a/keynes1.pdf.

[9] Scottish writer, Thomas Carlyle, coined the expression. In an article published in *Fraser's Magazine for Town and Country* in December 1849, he wrote: "a dreary, desolate, and indeed quite abject and distressing [science]; what we might call... *the dismal science.*"

[10] Adam Smith, *An Enquiry into the Nature and Causes of the Wealth of Nations* (1st ed., 1776) edited with an Introduction, Notes, Marginal Summary and an Enlarged Index by Edwin Cannan (London: Methuen, 1904), Book IV, Chapter II, p. 456, paragraph 10, Kindle, http://oll.libertyfund.org/titles/237.

Chapter 2

ABOUT POLITICS:

Snafu's Power Law

In May 2017, when we first began to worry that two chubby crazies, with bad suits and worse hair, might nuke the world, Barak Obama made a surprise return to the limelight. He was photographed frolicking on a luxury yacht in the British Virgin Islands with Richard Branson, a smarmy English billionaire.[1] The story was a momentary distraction from the first wave of tensions on the Korean peninsula.

When Obama left office, many of us were willing to give him a C+ (even though his fondness for execution-by-drone was hard to look past).[2] We'd long known the answer to the only insightful question Sarah Palin ever asked: "How's that hopey, changey thing working out for ya?"[3] Despite his mediocre report card, it was sad to see Obama board the gravy train (yacht) to post-Presidential riches, much as Bill Clinton had.

Obama is still a standout among his recent peers when it comes to statesmanship. Let's face it, the bar is set pretty low. Although every President is going to end up looking good next to Donald Trump, don't forget that, thanks to Kenneth Starr (now himself discredited),[4] we have enough information about Bill Clinton's penis to draw a picture of it. And, before we get wistful about what might have been if Trump had lost, it's worth remembering that Hillary didn't seem to be joking in 2010 when, as Secretary of State, she floated the idea of taking out Julian Assange of WikiLeaks with a drone strike.[5]

Alan Greenspan got it right when he wrote in his memoir: "Anyone willing to do what is required to become president of the United States is thereby barred from taking that office. I'm only half joking."[6] Unusually frank for him, though he could have left off the second sentence.

Greenspan's disillusionment with Presidential politics began when he worked on the 1968 Nixon campaign. Appalled by Nixon (and, it seems, some of the five other Presidents he worked for), Greenspan appears to have remained sanguine about his George Washington High School alumnus Henry Kissinger. He and Kissinger were still tight in 1980 when they tried to get Ronald Reagan to appoint Gerald Ford as his Vice-President (and themselves to senior Cabinet posts).[7] Yet, Kissinger is no less odious than Nixon was. Between January 1969 and January 1973, he executed Nixon's order to secretly bomb Laos and Cambodia. These illegal bombings killed, maimed or made homeless around six million people, mainly civilians.[8] In the midst of this, Kissinger told the Washington Press Club: "Power is the ultimate aphrodisiac."[9] So, at least it was good for his erectile function. And, as a bonus, they gave him the Nobel Peace Prize in 1973.[10]

Before Trump, George W. Bush was God's gift to comedians. "W" was funny in the same way that a bad horror movie is funny, except it wasn't a movie. Bush started the most expensive wars in history.[11] The first to look for Osama Bin Laden in Afghanistan, a country he'd left. The second to look for weapons of mass destruction in Iraq, a country that didn't have any. He borrowed the money, while cutting taxes for the rich and benefits for the poor.

In eight years, Bush ran up a debt of 5.849 trillion dollars,[12] presided over the biggest financial bubble since the Gilded Age,[13] enriched the "military-industrial complex,"[14] accelerated the collapse of the American middle class, and mangled the English language. Then there's the small matter of the number of people killed in his "War on Terror"[15]—1.3 million and counting.[16]

These days, Bush spends a good deal of his time at his Texas ranch painting portraits of wounded veterans. He put sixty-six of them in a book called *Portraits of Courage*.[17]

Proceeds from the sale of the book go to his "Military Service Initiative,"[18] which aims to help service men and women. Who knows—somewhere behind those beady, unfocused eyes—there might be the beginnings of a conscience.

Perhaps W's greatest sin is one that's still unfolding—the Trump presidency. After W, American voters accidentally pressed the pause button. They'd intended to "fast forward" to something much better, but the Obama presidency was little more than a freeze-frame that drained the hope and turned it to anger. The result, with a little help from Putin,[19] was Trump.

What do you call it "when the middle class, finding its hopes frustrated by economic instability coupled with political polarization and deadlock, abandons traditional ideologies and turns, with the [approval][20] of police and military forces, to a poorly-defined but emotionally appealing [nationalism],[21] immediate and direct resolution of problems, and intolerance for dissent?"[22] With a couple of substitutions for words I had to look up, that's how Chuck Anesi defined "fascism" in his 2008 synthesis of various academic interpretations. Fascism is a word that carries a lot of bad freight. It would be easy to dismiss Trump as a fascist. It would be only half-right. He doesn't really have an ideology beyond opportunistic self-interest, though he flirts with nationalism and racism. He has tapped into something that seems to be taking him on a journey like the one Benito

Mussolini took.

In 1961, President-Elect John F. Kennedy revived the metaphor of America as a "city upon a hill."[23] Then Ronald Reagan used it, and it stuck.[24] How did America get from that "hill" to Trump's "swamp"? Before we consider that question, we need to ask: Was America ever really "a city upon a hill"?

Ganesh Sitaraman seems to think so. He's a legal scholar (sometimes called "Elizabeth Warren's brain," having worked as her aide).[25] In 2017, he wrote a book called *The Crisis of the Middle-Class Constitution*.[26]

Unlike most constitutions, which arise out of class struggle, the U.S. Constitution is what Sitaraman calls a middle-class constitution. He explained what he meant by this in a March 2017 interview with Rebecca Rosen of *The Atlantic*: "When the founders looked around, they thought America was uniquely equal in the history of the world. And I know that seems crazy to say, but when you think about it, it makes sense. If you imagine in the late 18th century, America is a sparsely populated area, just on the coast of the Atlantic, with some small towns and cities, and lots of agrarian lands, and it's really at the edge of the world because the center is Western Europe. It's London, it's Paris, and when Americans look across the ocean at those countries, what they see is how different it is. They see that there's a hereditary aristocracy, something that doesn't exist in America. There's feudalism, which doesn't exist in America. There's extreme wealth, there's extreme poverty, neither of which really exists in America. As a result they don't need to design a House of Lords and a House of Commons, they don't need a tribune of the plebs in order to make their constitution work."[27]

Sitaraman's equality thesis involves airbrushing three groups out of the American family portrait: Native Americans, African Americans, and women. He mentions them in passing, though not enough to let them get in the way of his argument. Yet, there is something to his theory that the United States began as an unusually equal and prosperous society (at least for white men). In 2012, Peter Lindert and Jeffrey Williamson analyzed the data and concluded: "It appears that the colonists had far higher incomes in 1774 than previously thought, on average probably greater than England, the richest country in Europe."[28] And "… free American colonists had much more equal incomes than did households in England (and elsewhere in Europe). The colonists also had greater purchasing power than did their English counterparts over all of the income ranks except at the top one percent."[29]

Thanks to its extraordinary natural endowments, and the handy doctrine of "Manifest Destiny,"[30] the United States was fated to keep on prospering. What is now the "lower forty-eight"[31] is a place of more navigable rivers and waterways, and more arable land than any other country, as well as numerous deep-water harbors, abundant oil, minerals, and other natural resources, a temperate climate, vast oceans protecting its borders to the east and west, with weaker and less fortunate neighbors to its north and south.[32] We'd probably have to go all the way back to Egypt around 7,000 B.C. to find a society with levels of equality and natural abundance comparable to those of the United States in its infancy.

No one is entirely sure why the Egyptians gave up their nomadic lifestyle for farming. Agriculture got off to a shaky start, but the fertile land of the Nile Delta gradually yielded up its riches. Population density increased, while the ownership of land and the accumulation of surpluses gave rise to divisions of labor and disparities of wealth. Economic, political, and social hierarchies developed to the point where, about 4,500 years later, the Pharaoh Khufu built himself a mausoleum, the Great Pyramid of Giza.[33] It was a pretty good imitation of the shape of Egyptian society under his rule.

As Sitaraman notes, James Madison and Alexander Hamilton could see an industrial age coming. They worried that it would destroy the equality of agrarian America. They were right to worry about inequality, though a little late. It was already a 5,000-year-old problem. And industrialization wasn't the cause—just the accelerant. In America, the journey to social and political complexity and uneven wealth was super-fast. What took a few thousand years in the Nile

Delta, took less than a century in the United States. With dazzling speed, revolutions in transport, energy, and communications whisked America from the land of Jefferson's "yeoman farmer"[34] to the splendor and savage inequality of the Gilded Age[35]—before tipping it into the Great Depression.

Yet, equality came roaring back after the Depression. By the 1960s, a thoroughly industrialized America was again the bastion of middle-class prosperity. What did this have to do with the Constitution?

Although the Progressive Era and the New Deal owe something to the genius of the middle-class constitution, they owe more to the political genius of two patricians, Theodore and Franklin Roosevelt, who either worked around it or amended it in order to bring about social and political change. And the Constitution had nothing at all to do with the victory bonus of World War II, which did so much to rebalance the distribution of America's abundance. The Gini coefficient (a measure of income inequality, in which a lower number indicates greater equality) began to fall in 1930.[36] It reached its lowest level ever in 1968.[37]

But the post-war boom didn't last long. Although it didn't become obvious until the 1970s, the boom started to fade in 1965, with the onset of the "Great Inflation."[38] As Federal Reserve Bank Senior Economist Michael Bryan puts it: "Over the nearly two decades it lasted, the global monetary system established during World War II was abandoned, there were four economic recessions, two severe energy shortages, and the unprecedented peacetime implementation of wage and price controls." It was, according to one prominent economist, "the greatest failure of American macroeconomic policy in the postwar period."[39] The collapse of the monetary regime, known as the Bretton Woods system, began in 1971 (with a little help from Richard Nixon).[40] The 1970s also saw the U.S. become a net importer of oil for the first time.[41] By the middle of the decade, real wages for most American workers leveled off, and, for some, began to fall.[42]

From the 1980s, progressive deregulation of financial markets, and an enormous shift in investment from manufacturing to increasingly exotic forms of financial speculation, led first to the Dotcom bust,[43] then to the Global Financial Crisis of 2007 to 2009.[44] The same period saw the fall of the Soviet Union, the rise of China, and those two very expensive Bush wars (in Afghanistan and Iraq).

The Constitution was no match for all this. It couldn't prevent the slide into a new Gilded Age—or maybe it's a new "Age of the Pharaohs." Today the now famous "one percent" holds thirty-three to forty-two percent of the national wealth and earns eighteen to twenty-three percent of national income, depending on whose estimates you believe.[45] Sitaraman doesn't have a satisfactory explanation for how this happened. That's because there isn't an explanation that has anything to do with the Constitution.

It doesn't matter how well you write a constitution; it won't protect against inequality. Vilfredo Pareto discovered that inequality is an iron law that tends to follow an 80:20 distribution. In 1906, after analyzing land-ownership data in Italy, he found that twenty percent of the people owned eighty percent of the land.[46] He was soon able to show that this ratio held for many things, including many natural systems. He believed that it applied to income and wealth "through any human society, in any age, or country."[47] Today, the U.S. has a more extreme distribution of wealth. In fact, it's the "Pareto principle" on steroids. This means that its political system now actively favors the rich.

Sitaraman recognizes this. He is the latest in a long line of Western political thinkers, beginning with Plato, to note that power follows wealth and that great disparities of wealth lead to political upheaval. This applies no matter what system of government you choose. Inequality finds its way into all of them. Of course, some systems are better than others, and Winston Churchill was right when he said: "Many forms of Government have been tried, and will be tried in this world of sin and woe. No one pretends that democracy is perfect or all-wise. Indeed, it has been said that democracy is the worst form of Government except for all those other forms that have been tried from time to time..."[48]

Plato disagreed. He was no fan of democracy. He

believed that it always leads to tyranny.[49] In *The Republic*, he wrote: "And democracy comes into power when the poor are the victors, killing some and exiling some…"[50] He had little faith in the common man, favoring rule by "philosopher kings."[51] Through the ages, critics of democracy have often echoed Plato's fear that the poor will oppress the rich. Generally, it's the other way around.

Plato's other criticism was that the people lack the expertise to govern. This is a more telling argument, though not for the reason he gave. He thought that human behavior flows from desire, emotion, and knowledge and that ordinary people have too much desire, too much emotion, and too little knowledge.[52] Do rulers really have less desire and emotion than their subjects, or does power inflame their desires and emotions? As for the problem of knowledge, it's not that the people lack it, rather that they need to delegate to those who, supposedly, have it: politicians, bureaucrats, and judges. The Constitution struck a pretty good balance between the legislative, executive, and judicial branches of government. Yet, this didn't help much. Economic power always figures out where political power lies, then preys on it.

There's also the issue of complexity. Thomas Frey of the Da Vinci Institute calls complexity a "disease" that affects every system. He says: "the cost of managing the complexity increases at an exponential rate until the system finally collapses."[53] Steven Teles, an associate professor of political science at Johns Hopkins University, came up with a name for the political strain of the "complexity disease." He calls it "kludgeocracy."[54] In computer programming, a "kludge" is a quick and dirty patch.[55] Teles says that much of American public policy is just like a kludge, "clumsy but temporarily effective."[56] Too many kludges and the system crashes. In the meantime, he says: "The complexity that makes so much of American public policy vexing and wasteful for ordinary citizens and governments is also what makes it so easy for organized interests to profit from the state's largesse."[57]

In short, "we the people"[58] are obliged to delegate to feckless lawmakers the running of a system that's weighed down by complexity and fueled by the power of money. Where does the money come from?

During and after the Civil War, wealth began to migrate from real people to fictional people—corporations. In 1888, President Rutherford B. Hayes lamented that government for the people had been replaced by "government of the corporation, by the corporation, and for the corporation."[59] Increasingly favored by laws and tax breaks, these fictional people have also acquired constitutional rights—courtesy of the Supreme Court. They have rights under the First Amendment (free speech),[60] the Fourth Amendment (limiting search and seizure)[61] and, ironically, the Fourteenth Amendment, the purpose of which was to protect human rights—primarily the rights of African Americans who had won their freedom shortly before it was adopted.[62] Since the 2014 *Hobby Lobby Case*,[63] corporations can invoke their religious beliefs to get out of paying for insurance coverage for contraception under the Affordable Care Act. Even when you die, you won't escape the power of corporations—all the righteous ones, with their strong "religious beliefs," are going to be waiting for you in heaven.

Corporations may pretend to be religious, but today they make no pretense about their political power. Corporate lobbying is a national addiction. Appropriately, "Big Pharma" is the chief dispenser.[64] As Megan Wilson, writing in *The Hill*, puts it: "Drugmakers have poured close to $2.5 billion into lobbying and funding members of Congress over the past decade."[65] They're not the only ones. In 2016 alone, fifty corporations and industry groups shelled out more than $716 million to lobby the federal government and Congress.[66]

Money has always tainted politics. But we're now in an age where influence peddling is overt—no more smoke-filled backrooms. It's done in the daylight of the marbled lobbies from which it takes its new name.[67] So, next time you go to a polling station, be sure to take your checkbook.

The middle-class constitution still counts. In many ways, it's the reason America remains "a city upon a hill"—even though "the Hill" is teaming with lobbyists. It's a much steeper hill now. Too many people are sliding towards the bottom—including the middle class. It's a small consolation that no American President has yet dared to build a pyramid like the one at Giza. The nearest proxy is the Presidential Library. Franklin Roosevelt started the trend in 1941.[68] His library cost four hundred thousand dollars.[69] Obama is raising a billion dollars to build his.[70] Trump doesn't read, so he doesn't need a library. If he sticks around long enough, he'll probably build a Presidential Twitter Palace, with an adjoining golf course. It may well be as expensive as the Great Pyramid of Giza, which cost about the same in today's money as Apple's new headquarters in Cupertino—around five billion dollars.[71]

The United States—so richly endowed by nature and so free of historical baggage—started out as an unusually egalitarian republic. It founded its constitution on freedom and equality, framing it so as to prevent the concentration of political power. Yet, it still bent to the rule that politics follows money, succumbing to the age-old power law. Now the U.S. is a nation of shameless politicians, shameful inequality and shaming politics. How is it for "cities" that aren't on a hill?

---

[1] Ashley Collman, "Barack Obam-AIR! New Photos Show Former President Kite-Surfing and Horsing Around with Billionaire Buddy Richard Branson," *Daily Mail*, February 7, 2017,

http://www.dailymail.co.uk/news/article-4199624/New-photos-Barack-Obama-kite-surfing-Richard-Branson.html#ixzz4zJJjPrux.

[2] Jessica Purkiss and Jack Serle, "Obama's Covert Drone War in Numbers: Ten Times More Strikes than Bush," *The Bureau of Investigative Journalism*, January 17, 2017, https://www.thebureauinvestigates.com/stories/2017-01-17/obamas-covert-drone-war-in-numbers-ten-times-more-strikes-than-bush.

[3] "Sarah Palin 2012 Ad – 'Hopey Changey,'" YouTube video, 0:30, posted by "AndersonGOP," April 10, 2011, https://www.youtube.com/watch?v=BEgrrvywXhI.

[4] Linda Greenhouse, "Reversal of Fortune for Bill Clinton and Kenneth Starr," *New York Times*, September 1, 2016, https://www.nytimes.com/2016/09/01/opinion/the-president-the-prosecutor-and-the-wheel-of-fortune.html.

[5] Lisa Hagen, "Clinton Manager 'Reticent' to Comment on Report Clinton Floated Drone Strike against WikiLeaks," *Hill*, October 3, 2016, http://thehill.com/blogs/ballot-box/hillary-clinton-drone-strike-wikileaks-julian-assange.

[6] Alan Greenspan, *The Age of Turbulence: Adventures in a New World* (London: Penguin Books, 2008), Chapter 3.

[7] Wil S. Hylton, "Alan Greenspan Takes a Bath," *GQ*, March 2, 2005, https://www.gq.com/story/alan-greenspan-budget-federal-reserve; Justin Martin, *Greenspan: The Man Behind Money* (Cambridge, MA: Perseus Publishing, 2001), Chapter 1.

[8] Fred Branfman, "America Keeps Honoring One of Its Worst Mass Murderers: Henry Kissinger," *Alternet*, April 16, 2013, https://www.alternet.org/news-amp-politics/america-keeps-honoring-one-its-worst-mass-murderers-henry-kissinger.

[9] "Compiled by DuPre Jones," *New York Times*, October 28, 1973, http://www.nytimes.com/1973/10/28/archives/the-sayings-of-secretary-henry-language-negotiation-humility-the.html.

[10] Kissinger won the award jointly with Le Duc Tho for their work on the Paris Peace Accords that effectively ended the Vietnam War. See: "Henry Kissinger – Facts," *Nobelprize.org*, 2018, https://www.nobelprize.org/nobel_prizes/peace/laureates/1973/kissinger-facts.html.

[11] Linda J. Bilmes, "Iraq and Afghanistan: The US $6 Trillion Bill for America's Longest War Is Unpaid," *Conversation*, May 25, 2017, https://theconversation.com/iraq-and-afghanistan-the-us-6-trillion-bill-for-americas-longest-war-is-unpaid-78241.

[12] Kimberly Amadeo, "U.S. Debt by President: By Dollar and Percent," *Balance*, November 2, 2017, https://www.thebalance.com/us-debt-by-president-by-dollar-and-percent-3306296.

[13] See above, Chapter 1, endnote 5 for "Gilded Age." The financial bubble was known as the "Subprime Crisis" or "Subprime Mortgage Crisis," see: Kimberly Amadeo, "Subprime Mortgage Crisis, Its Timeline and Effect," *Balance*, January 11, 2018, https://www.thebalance.com/subprime-mortgage-crisis-effect-and-timeline-3305745.

[14] President Dwight D. Eisenhower is believed to have coined the expression "military-industrial complex." He used it in his Farewell Address in January 17, 1961: Dwight D. Eisenhower, "Farewell Radio and Television Address to the American People," (Washington DC, January 17, 1961). Online by Gerhard Peters and John T. Woolley, *The American Presidency Project*, http://www.presidency.ucsb.edu/ws/?pid=12086.

[15] George W. Bush, "Address to a Joint Session of Congress and the American People," September 20, 2001, https://georgewbush-whitehouse.archives.gov/news/releases/2001/09/20010920-8.html. A few days earlier, Bush called it the "war on terrorism," but "war on terror" seems to be the more popular expression for the military actions that Bush initiated after the terrorist attacks of September 11, 2001.

[16] Physicians for Social Responsibility, *Body Count: Casualty Figures After 10 Years of the "War on Terror" Iraq, Afghanistan, Pakistan* (IPPNW, March 2015), https://www.ippnw.de/commonFiles/pdfs/Frieden/Body_Count_first_in ternational_edition_2015_final.pdf.

[17] George W. Bush, "Portraits of Courage: A Commander in Chief's Tribute to America's Warriors," *Bush Centre,* n.d. http://www.bushcenter.org/exhibits-and-events/exhibits/2017/portraits-of-courage-exhibit.html.

[18] Kane Farabaugh, "Former President Bush Honors Veterans with Portraits of Courage," *VOA*, March 4, 2017,

https://www.voanews.com/a/president-george-bush-portraits-of-courage/3748579.html.

[19] Luke Harding, "What We Know About Russia's Interference in the US Election," *Guardian*, December 17, 2016, https://www.theguardian.com/us-news/2016/dec/16/qa-russian-hackers-vladimir-putin-donald-trump-us-presidential-election.

[20] Substituted for "approbation."

[21] Substituted for "soteriology of national unity."

[22] Chuck Anesi, *Fascism: The Ultimate Definition*, October 2008, http://www.anesi.com/Fascism-TheUltimateDefinition.htm.

[23] John F. Kennedy, "Address of President-Elect John F. Kennedy Delivered to a Joint Convention of the General Court of the Commonwealth of Massachusetts," (The State House, Boston, January 9, 1961). Also known as the "'City Upon a Hill' speech": John F. Kennedy Presidential Library and Museum, https://www.jfklibrary.org/Asset-Viewer/ohJztSnpV06qFJUT9etUZQ.aspx. The phrase comes from Matthew 5:14—part of the parable of *Salt and Light* from Christ's *Sermon on the Mount*.

[24] Ronald Reagan, "Election Eve Address 'Vision for America'" (November 3, 1980). Online by Gerhard Peters and John T. Woolley, *The American Presidency Project*, http://www.presidency.ucsb.edu/ws/?pid=85199.

[25] Aram Bakshian Jr., "The Wrong Cure for a Real Crisis," *Washington Times*, June 14, 2017, https://www.washingtontimes.com/news/2017/jun/14/book-review-the-crisis-of-the-middle-class-constit/.

[26] Ganesh Sitaraman, *The Crisis of the Middle Clas-Constitution: Why Economic Inequality Threatens our Republic* (New York: Knopf, 2017).

[27] Rebecca J. Rosen, "Can the Country Survive Without a Strong Middle Class?" *Atlantic*, March 21, 2017, https://www.theatlantic.com/business/archive/2017/03/middle-class-constitution/519909/.

[28] Peter H. Lindert and Jeffrey G. Williamson, "American Incomes 1774 – 1860," National Bureau of Economic Research, Working Paper No. 18396 (September 2012), http://www.nber.org/papers/w18396.

[29] Lindert and Williamson, "American Incomes 1774–1860."

[30] Manifest Destiny is defined in *Dictionary.com* as "the belief or doctrine, held chiefly in the middle and latter part of the 19th century, that it was the destiny of the U.S. to expand its territory over the whole of North America and to extend and enhance its political, social, and economic influences," http://www.dictionary.com.

[31] The 48 contiguous states (that is, excluding Alaska and Hawaii).

[32] See: Peter Zeihan, *The Accidental Super Power: The Next Generation of American Preeminence and the Coming Global Disorder* (New York: Hachette Book Group, 2014), Chapters 2-4, for a good discussion of America's endowments.

[33] Joshua J. Mark, "Great Pyramid of Giza," *Ancient History Encyclopedia*, December 19, 2016, https://www.ancient.eu/Great_Pyramid_of_Giza/.

[34] Richard Hofstadter, "The Myth Of The Happy Yeoman," *American Heritage* 7, No. 3 (April 1956), https://www.americanheritage.com/content/myth-happy-yeoman.

[35] See above, Chapter 1, endnote 5.

[36] A widely used measure of income inequality named for Italian statistician Corrado Gini, who came up with the idea in 1912. The coefficient measures income distribution on a scale from zero (where income is equally distributed among all members of a society) to one (where a single person receives all the income). See: "Economic Inequality in USA," *Chartbook of Economic Inequality*, https://www.chartbookofeconomicinequality.com/inequality-by-country/usa/ (see green line in table).

[37] Salvatore Babones, "U.S. Income Distribution: Just How Unequal," *Inequality.org*, February 14, 2012, https://inequality.org/research/unequal-americas-income-distribution/.

[38] Michael Bryan, "The Great Inflation 1965-1982," *Federal Reserve History*, https://www.federalreservehistory.org/essays/great_inflation.

[39] Bryan, "The Great Inflation," quoting Jeremy J. Siegel, *Stocks for the Long Run: A Guide to Selecting Markets for Long-Term Growth* (New York, McGraw-Hill, 2nd ed., 1994).

[40] "Nixon and the End of the Bretton Woods System, 1971-1973," Office of the Historian, Department of State, United States of America, n.d., https://history.state.gov/milestones/1969-1976/nixon-shock.

[41] "U.S. Net Imports of Crude Oil and Petroleum Products," U.S. Energy Information Administration, Petroleum & Other Liquids, n.d., https://www.eia.gov/dnav/pet/hist/LeafHandler.ashx?n=pet&s=mttntus2&f=a. "Crude Oil Prices – 70 Year Historical Trend," *Macrotrends,* n.d., http://www.macrotrends.net/1369/crude-oil-price-history-chart.

[42] Drew DeSilver, "For Most Workers, Real Wages Have Barely Budged for Decades," *Pew Research Center,* October 9, 2014, http://www.pewresearch.org/fact-tank/2014/10/09/for-most-workers-real-wages-have-barely-budged-for-decades/; Lawrence Mishel, Elise Gould, and Josh Bivens, "Wage Stagnation in Nine Charts," *Economic Policy Institute,* January 6, 2015, http://www.epi.org/publication/charting-wage-stagnation/.

[43] Colin Gordon, "Wolves of Wall Street: Financialization and American Inequality," *Dissent,* April 17, 2014, https://www.dissentmagazine.org/online_articles/wolves-of-wall-street-financialization-and-american-inequality.

"Dotcom Bubble," *Investopedia,* https://www.investopedia.com/terms/d/dotcom-bubble.asp.

[44] "Crash Course: The Origins of the financial crisis," *Economist,* September 7, 2013, https://www.economist.com/news/schoolsbrief/21584534-effects-financial-crisis-are-still-being-felt-five-years-article.

[45] Bourree Lam, "How Much Wealth and Income Does America's 1 Percent Really Have?" *Atlantic,* March 12, 2016, https://www.theatlantic.com/business/archive/2016/03/brookings-1-percent/473478/.

[46] "Understanding the Pareto Principle (The 80/20 Rule)," *Better Explained,* https://betterexplained.com/articles/understanding-the-pareto-principle-the-8020-rule/.

[47] Beniot Mandelbrot and Richard L Hudson, *The (Mis)behavior of Markets: A Fractal View of Risk, Ruin, and Reward* (New York: Basic Books, 2004).

[48] From a speech in the House of Commons, November 11, 1947, and quoted in Winston Churchill and Richard Langworth, Ed., *Churchill by*

Himself: The Definitive Collection of Quotations (New York: PublicAffairs, 2008), 574.

[49] Plato, *The Republic of Plato,* translated into English with Introduction, Analysis, Marginal Analysis, and Index, by B. Jowett, M.A. The Third Edition revised and corrected throughout (Oxford: Clarendon Press, 1888), Book VIII, e-book, http://oll.libertyfund.org/titles/598.

[50] Plato, *The Republic*, Book VIII, 557.

[51] Plato, *The Republic*, Book V: "Until philosophers are kings, or the kings and princes of this world have the spirit and power of philosophy, and political greatness and wisdom meet in one, and those commoner natures who pursue either to the exclusion of the other are compelled to stand aside, cities will never have rest from their evils, —nor the human race, as I believe, —and then only will this our State have a possibility of life and behold the light of day."

[52] Although there is a quote attributed to Plato: "Human behavior flows from three main sources: desire, emotion, and knowledge," there is no proof that Plato ever expressed this opinion quite so succinctly. See: Dave Yount, "Statements that Plato Never Made!" n.d., http://www.mesacc.edu/~davpy35701/text/plato-things-not-said.html. The quote probably arose from a summary of Plato's theory of human behavior. And, as one-line summaries go, it's not bad. For a more comprehensive discussion, see: Anne Askew, "The Origins of Behaviour in the Philosophy of Plato," (Ph.D. dissertation, University of Adelaide, Australia, April 1975), https://digital.library.adelaide.edu.au/dspace/bitstream/2440/20614/1/09pha835.pdf.

[53] Thomas Frey, "The Complexity Disease," *Futurist Speaker*, April 14, 2008, http://www.futuristspeaker.com/business-trends/the-complexity-disease/. Thomas Frey is Executive Director and Senior Futurist at the DaVinci Institute.

[54] Steven M. Teles, "Kludgeocracy in America," *National Affairs*, No. 17 (Fall, 2013), http://www.nationalaffairs.com/publications/detail/kludgeocracy-in-america. Steven M. Teles is an associate professor of political science at Johns Hopkins University.

[55] Teles, "Kludgeocracy in America."

[56] Teles, "Kludgeocracy in America."

[57] Teles, "Kludgeocracy in America."

[58] From the opening phrase of the Preamble to the United States Constitution.

[59] Katie Bacon, "The Dark Side of the Gilded Age," *Atlantic*, June 2007, https://www.theatlantic.com/magazine/archive/2007/06/the-dark-side-of-the-gilded-age/306012/. The article is about Jack Beatty's book *Age of Betrayal: The Triumph of Money in America, 1865-1900* (Knopf, 2008). The quote from President Hayes comes from Mr. Beatty.

[60] Ciara Torres-Spelliscy, "The History of Corporate Personhood," *Brennan Center for Justice at New York University School of Law* (blog), April 7, 2014, https://www.brennancenter.org/blog/hobby-lobby-argument. For a comprehensive analysis of corporate First Amendment rights, see: John C. Coates, IV, "Corporate Speech and the First Amendment: History, Data, and Implications," *Constitutional Commentary* 30, No. 2 (Summer 2015), available at: https://papers.ssrn.com/sol3/papers.cfm?abstract_id=2566785.

[61] Torres-Spellicsy, "Corporate Personhood."

[62] Torres-Spellicsy, "Corporate Personhood."

[63] Burwell v. Hobby Lobby (previously Sebelius v. Hobby Lobby Stores), 573 U.S. (2014).

[64] The Centre for Responsive Politics, "Lobbying Spending Database Opensecrets," *Opensecrets.Org*, n.d., https://www.opensecrets.org/lobby/top.php?indexType=i.

[65] Chris McGreal, "How Big Pharma's Money – And Its Politicians – Feed the US Opioid Crisis," *Guardian*, October 19, 2017, https://www.theguardian.com/us-news/2017/oct/19/big-pharma-money-lobbying-us-opioid-crisis.

[66] Megan R. Wilson, "Lobbying's Top 50: Who's Spending Big," *Hill*, February 7, 2017, http://thehill.com/business-a-lobbying/business-a-lobbying/318177-lobbyings-top-50-whos-spending-big.

[67] The verb "lobby" is defined in the *Online Etymological Dictionary* as "seek to influence legislation" (originally by frequenting the lobby of a legislature to solicit members), 1862, American English, from lobby (n) in the political sense, https://www.etymonline.com/search?q=lobby+percent28vpercent29.

[68] Dan McGinn, "$1 billion for Obama's Library? Stop this Presidential Trend," *Chicago Tribune*, May 9, 2016, http://www.chicagotribune.com/news/opinion/commentary/ct-obama-presidential-library-chicago-perspec-0510-jm-20160509-story.html.

[69] McGinn, "$1 billion for Obama's Library?"

[70] McGinn, "$1 billion for Obama's Library?"

[71] Natalie Wolchover, "How Much Would It Cost to Build the Great Pyramid Today?" *Live Science*, February 22, 2012, https://www.livescience.com/18589-cost-build-great-pyramid-today.html; Don Reisinger, "Apple's New 'Spaceship' Headquarters Cost this Much, Study Says," *Fortune*, October 6, 2017, http://fortune.com/2017/10/06/apple-park-build-cost/.

Chapter 3

ABOUT MONEY:

In Snafu We Trust

Snickers are the world's best-selling candy bars, with global sales of more than three and a half billion dollars in 2012.[1] Mars has been making them since 1930.[2] The original "Snickers" was the Mars family's favorite horse.[3] Yet, that didn't put anyone off—because who knew? In the United States, a Snickers bar will set you back anywhere from around sixty cents to a dollar.

Imagine this:

Mars figure out a way to make Snickers bars that don't melt or spoil. Impressed by this, Amazon buys Mars. Later, Amazon becomes the biggest global-super-corporation. Soon after, there's a worldwide financial crisis much bigger than the one in 2008. Hyperinflation wipes out the value of all currencies. Amazon's boss, Jeff Bezos, does a deal with governments around the world to abolish their currencies and use Snickers as the global currency. In a matter of weeks, all prices are recalibrated in Snickers (or Snicks, as everyone starts calling them). For five Snicks, you can buy a Big Mac, large fries, and medium Coke anywhere in the world.

Snicks may seem like a strange currency until you consider a few of the things that have been used for money in the past, like bottle caps, smoked mackerel, pigs' teeth, potato mashers and woodpecker scalps.[4] Sadly, the list includes human beings.[5]

So, what is money?

You can use anything as money if it's at least as durable as paper. Snickers will do fine. It's not so much about the "thing" you use. It's more about the deal between the people who use it. In our scenario, for Snicks to be money, everybody has to agree on just three things. First, they'll accept Snicks as a means of payment. Under the Amazon deal, their governments did this for them by agreeing that Snicks would be legal tender. The laws of every country now say that you can use Snicks to pay debts, including taxes. Second, a Snick would be the "unit of account" to measure value. No problem—all prices are now in Snicks. Everybody knows what a Snick buys. Third, Snicks would be a "store of value," which just means that Snicks will last and that every

Snick is worth the same as every other Snick. Again, no problem—the new wrapper is tamper-proof, hard to counterfeit, and twenty times more durable than an iPhone. Pretty quickly, people stop using actual Snickers, except as snacks. They use credit cards or debit cards, or they pay electronically.

In the days before Snicks, only about six percent of the money was in banknotes and coins.[6] The rest was electronic—mostly digital ledgers kept by banks. Sweden, the first European country to issue banknotes (in 1661), was well on the way to becoming cashless.[7] Today there are no bank vaults full of Snicks. People don't walk around with their pockets or handbags full of them. Even in prisons, they use debit cards shaped like little Snickers bars.

So, money isn't so much a "thing" as it is an electronic system for making payments that works if everybody agrees on a few basic details. But it's a system that someone has to run.

Printed on the new Snickers wrapper are the words: "In Amazon we trust." That's because Amazon now does the job that central banks used to do: it runs the system. The hardest part of the job is controlling the supply of money. For example, if there's too much money, its value goes down relative to the things you can buy with it. So, prices go up. Get the balance wrong and people lose faith in money. In recent times, the most infamous example of this was in

Germany after World War I. Having borrowed heavily to finance the war, Germany was hit with a crippling reparations bill when it lost. In an attempt to pay its debts, it made a series of huge increases to its money supply. The result was catastrophic. In 1919, a loaf of bread cost twenty-five Pfennigs. At the height of hyperinflation in November 1923, the price was eighty billion Marks.[8]

Before Snicks, central banks needed commercial banks to make the payment system work. After Snicks, it's exactly the same. Commercial banks keep the electronic ledgers (bank accounts). They "move" Snicks around, though all that really moves are electrical impulses powering the software in computers that process payments by crediting and debiting those electronic ledgers.

That's not all the commercial banks do. They take deposits from customers who have money but aren't using it (depositors) and lend to customers who need money but don't have it (borrowers). They pay interest to their depositors and charge higher interest to their borrowers. But they don't "match" loans against deposits. Usually, the demand for loans is much higher than total deposits. And, banks need to hold some of their deposits as a reserve against depositors asking for their money back. So, new money has to be "created" in order to satisfy the demand for new loans. Governments allow commercial banks to do this.

When a bank credits a borrower's account with the

amount of a new loan, this is money that didn't "exist" before. In a growing economy, there's typically strong demand for loans, so new money has to be created—the money supply grows. When borrowers repay loans or banks write off bad loans, money is "canceled"—the money supply contracts. It's not so different from Snickers when they were just candy bars. From Halloween to the Christmas Holidays, demand is high, so they make more Snickers bars, which are sold and then eaten. After New Year's, demand falls back, so they make fewer Snickers bars. Then demand picks up again ahead of Easter, so again they make more. It's similar with money. When people want new loans, banks make new money. When those loans are repaid, or written off, that money goes out of existence.

If money is an electronic payment system that works by creating and canceling debt, how can money be debt when it's what we use to repay debt? That's because we repay debt with debt. We use someone else's debt to pay off our debt. Instead of using our own IOUs, we use Snicks, which are Amazon's IOUs. Before Snicks, we used government IOUs— either banknotes or digital dollars. What would've happened if you'd gone to the U.S. government with a hundred-dollar bill and asked them to honor it? What does it mean to "honor" an IOU that's in the form of a banknote?

From 1958 to 1971, if you held dollars outside the United States, you could've demanded gold in exchange for your hundred-dollar bill, because the U.S. dollar was pegged to gold.[9] Thirty-five dollars was worth one ounce of gold. For a hundred dollars, you could have asked for 2.857 ounces of gold. In practice, almost nobody did this. Generally, everyone accepted that a hundred bucks would keep buying what it usually bought. In practice, that's what the U.S. government was promising—that everyone would accept the banknote in exchange for goods or services worth a hundred bucks, or to repay a loan of a hundred bucks. The promise wasn't only about the hundred-dollar bill; it was just as much about the whole dollar currency system. After 1973, the dollar was no longer pegged to gold, or to anything else. Its value was allowed to float. The U.S. government obliged itself to keep the currency functioning without reference to anything tangible.

So, money is debt, and debt is simply an obligation you measure using numbers to indicate value. It doesn't have to be backed by anything. The promise alone is enough. A currency that isn't backed by anything except a promise is a bit like Snickers without the candy bar inside. If Amazon took out the candy bar and replaced it with compressed air, it would look the same. If you really wanted a candy bar, you'd have to buy one using 'air-Snicks,' and the price of the candy might go up or down by reference to 'air-Snicks.' The 'air-Snicks' would remain valuable because Amazon would keep the system working just as it did before. But Amazon hasn't replaced the candy bars with compressed air. If you have a hundred Snicks in the bank, you can demand a hundred Snickers bars, and that's what they'll give you. You can then trade them for whatever a hundred Snicks usually buys, or you can eat them—then you'd have to burn off 26,600 calories.[10] Why would you bother with that? You trust Amazon to keep the Snicks currency system working. People still like to eat Snickers. It costs a Snick to eat a candy bar. And, with every bar they eat, the money supply is reduced by one Snick. Amazon never makes more candy bars than people want to eat. Why would they? Most Snicks are electronic—more than 999,999 out of every million. Snicks don't need candy bars to make them work as money. Amazon's promise is enough.

When we think of money as debt, it makes sense that commercial banks are given the role of creating it. Money starts out as accounting entries in electronic ledgers and, because the banks keep the ledgers, the demand for money— loan applications—starts in the banking system. The banking system responds to loan applications by creating new money. The central bank ultimately controls how much money the commercial banks create, as well as how fast the money supply grows. It does this mainly by controlling the rate of interest, which is the main valve in this flow. That's because interest is the "price" borrowers pay banks to create new money.

We can now refine our definition of money. It is the name we give IOUs backed by a government (or an institution we trust, like Amazon) that circulate in an electronic payment system. Banks sit at the center of the system, creating new IOUs for a price (interest) and canceling old ones. The number of new IOUs they create is regulated by a central bank (for Snicks, it's Amazon). Okay, it's still a simplification, but it's good enough for us to see that money is an abstraction for measuring debt obligations and for regulating the price of debt. How did money get to be this way?

As David Graeber explains in his 2011 book *Debt: The First 5,000 Years*, money has always been debt and it has always been largely abstract.[11] Graeber is a professor of anthropology at the London School of Economics. He doesn't start with the conventional wisdom about money; he starts with ancient history.

A guy walks into a bar in Babylon in 3,000 B.C. His name is Akkad and he sells chickens for a living. Akkad takes a seat at the bar next to his drinking buddy, Qatna. Akkad orders a drink and asks the bartender to put it on his tab. That's literally what the bartender does. He chalks a number on a clay tablet beneath the numbers already there. Later, Akkad sells Qatna a chicken, but Qatna has no coins to pay for it. So, he turns to the bartender and asks him to take an amount equal to the price of the chicken off Akkad's tab and put it on his tab.

This isn't Graeber's example, but he uses others like it to show that, even when cultures used commodities like metal coins as money, a much bigger system of circulating debts (IOUs) always operated in the background.

When the bartender reduces Akkad's tab by the price of the chicken and increases Qatna's tab by the same amount, he is acting like a bank. He's making a new loan to Qatna by increasing his tab. And he's reducing Akkad's existing loan by taking the same amount off Akkad's tab. In other words, Qatna "pays" Akkad for the chicken using the "bank of the bartender." Multiply this kind of three-way deal all across Babylon and you have a debt system of money that's not so different from our own. Meanwhile, in downtown Babylon, there are moneylenders conjuring up "new money" by making loans without regard to the number of coins the king has in circulation. They know that there are usually more loans (IOUs) than there are coins. They don't care because they can trade the IOUs. Most people in the city are happy to accept IOUs instead of coins—everyone can "spend" them as though they were coins.

Systems of circulating IOUs have been around for as long as human societies have existed. As Graeber puts it: "The reasons why anthropologists haven't been able to come up with a simple, compelling story for the origins of money is because there's no reason to believe there could be one.

Money was no more ever 'invented' than music or mathematics or jewelry. What we call 'money' isn't a 'thing' at all; it's a way of comparing things mathematically, as proportions: of saying one of X is equivalent to six of Y. As such it is probably as old as human thought."[12]

Let's get back to the price of money—interest.

Leave a hundred Snicks in a drawer for a year and nothing happens. Deposit a hundred Snicks in a bank and, a year later, you have a 105 Snicks. The bank pays to "rent" your Snicks. The rent (five Snicks) is interest—from the Latin verb *intereo*, which means, "to be lost."[13] The longer you "lose" the use of your Snicks, the more interest the bank pays you. Essentially, interest is the "time value" of the money you lend the bank (or anyone else).

From ancient times, making money from lending money—the idea that a debt necessarily grows with time—has been considered immoral, even though interest is as old as moneylending and moneylending is as old as money itself. Early in the Christian era, the essence of the moral objection to lending money for profit was that charging interest to those in need of money put self-interest above altruism. This put love of self above love of God. As finance writer Yaron Brook explains: "Christian morality, the morality of divinely mandated altruism, expounds the virtue of self-sacrifice on behalf of the poor and the weak; it condemns self-interested actions, such as profiting—especially profiting from a seemingly exploitative and unproductive activity such as usury."[14]

Thomas of Chobham (circa 1160 to circa 1235)[15] was, perhaps, the first Christian theologian to talk about interest as the time value of money. He wrote: "The usurer sells nothing to the borrower that belongs to him. He sells only time, which belongs to God. He can therefore not make a profit from selling someone else's property."[16]

By the 18th century, although God still owned time, he was considered to be renting it out to mankind. In return, mankind had to use it productively. In 1776, in the *Wealth of Nations*, Adam Smith wrote: "As something can everywhere be made by the use of money, something ought everywhere to be paid for the use of it."[17] Yet, Smith warned that moneylending needed to be regulated because speculative bubbles inflate when it's too easy to make money from lending money. He saw regulation as a practical necessity, as well as an ethical one. It was a job for government. God dropped out of the equation.

For debt to expand with time, so must productivity. This is the flipside of Smith's maxim. If you pay for the use of money, you must make something with it. Ultimately, that something is goods or services.[18] It follows, then, that interest-bearing debt is, as Graeber puts it: "the promise of future productivity."[19] Borrowed money has to be used to expand productivity; otherwise, it doesn't generate enough to repay the loan with interest.

In the 19th and 20th centuries, the last vestiges of the Christian moral objection to interest were usury laws. These laws allowed moneylending but prohibited excessive rates of interest. By then, the world's monetary systems ran on interest. In the early 1920s, the war debt that destroyed the value of Germany's currency had a cascade effect, damaging the currencies of the major powers, including the United States, which was the main lender nation.[20]

Ironically, it took another war to stabilize money. After World War II, the U.S. took charge. It aligned the currencies of most developed countries with the dollar, except those of the Communist Bloc.[21] This was the Bretton Woods system. Although the dollar was linked to gold, the linkage was flexible, and it allowed the U.S. and other member governments to borrow in excess of their gold reserves.[22] For a time, the system worked well enough. But, it depended on increases in productivity, leading to an escalated rivalry between seller nations (exporters) and buyer nations (importers). Although this kind of rivalry was nothing new, the Pax Americana[23] created ideal conditions for the resurgent economies of Europe and Japan to sell goods into the vibrant U.S. market. This competition, coupled with heavy U.S. military spending and foreign aid, weakened the dollar, leading to a series of dollar devaluations. The Bretton Woods system collapsed in 1973, ushering in a system of floating international exchange rates.[24]

Meanwhile, U.S. manufacturers responded to competition by reining in wages at home and moving production abroad. In the eighties, President Reagan began the liberation of domestic credit markets from Depression-era controls. U.S. household debt started to grow to fill the widening gap between the rising supply of "stuff" and the falling value of wages. When the Subprime Mortgage Crisis[25] hit in 2008, household debt was so large that trillions of dollars worth should have been canceled. It was a claim on the future productivity of American households that couldn't be satisfied. But there was no cancellation.

As Graeber puts it: "In the wake of the subprime collapse, the U.S. government was forced to decide who really gets to make money out of nothing: the financiers, or ordinary citizens. The results were predictable. Financiers 'were bailed out with taxpayer money.'"[26] No one is entirely sure how much the bailout cost. As Senator Elizabeth Warren noted: "...the biggest money for the biggest banks was never voted on by Congress. Instead, between 2007 and 2009, the Fed provided over $13 trillion in emergency lending to just a handful of large financial institutions."[27]

The cost of that bailout is now part of an eleven-digit number—the U.S. national debt, which is a gigantic pledge on the future productivity of Americans, now living and yet to be born.

At the end of 2016, the U.S. owed its foreign creditors around eighteen trillion dollars.[28] If you have the greatest military force in history and you owe the world eighteen trillion dollars, then you own the world. All around the world "central bank reserves are now held in the form of U.S. Government IOUs that can be run up without limit. In effect, America has been buying up Europe, Asia, and other regions with paper credit—U.S. Treasury IOUs that it has informed the world it has little intention of ever paying off."[29] This is how Professor Michael Hudson put it when he launched the second edition of his book *Super Imperialism* in 2002.[30] In the preface of the book, he went on to say: "To the extent that these Treasury IOUs are being built into the world's monetary base they will not have to be repaid, but are to be rolled over indefinitely. This feature is the essence of America's free financial ride, a tax imposed at the entire globe's expense."[31] Hudson may not be right that the U.S. never has to repay its national debt. If it were to cut its military spending and give up its role as global cop, the rest of the world might not keep funding its deficits.

At the end of 2016, the average U.S. household owed its creditors $132,500.[32] If you're an average American, and you owe the bank $132,500, then the bank owns you. Almost two centuries ago, the United States formally abolished debtors' prisons—or did it? Graeber notes that people are still routinely jailed for failing to pay their debts. Quoting a report by the Minneapolis-Saint Paul *Star Tribune*, he writes: "In Minnesota, the use of arrest warrants against debtors has jumped 60 percent over the past four years, with 845 cases in 2009... In Illinois and southwest Indiana, some judges jail debtors for missing court-ordered debt payments. In extreme cases, people stay in jail until they raise a minimum payment. In January [2010], a judge sentenced a Kenney, Ill., man 'to indefinite incarceration' until he came up with $300 toward a lumber yard debt."[33]

Throughout history, debt and force have gone hand-in-hand. Debtors who couldn't pay suffered imprisonment, torture, slavery, and even death.[34] It was different for their rulers. They had armies and they wrote the laws, so they could borrow as much as they dared—sometimes "forgetting" to repay. In the end though, debt is a trap for the powerful as well as the weak. Ordinary folk don't have the power to refuse to pay. Their rulers can refuse to pay because they have the power make others pay. Yet, if you're a ruler and you're in debt, you dare not lose power because then you too will have to pay.

America could break the deadlock between power and debt by paying down its national debt. Until recently, that's what conservative U.S. politicians advocated. But this would mean raising taxes. And who would pay the taxes—average Americans drowning in debt? No—large corporations and the rich would have to pay. They don't want to pay. And, they have the political power to refuse to pay, as the recent Trump tax cuts demonstrate.[35] So, the U.S. has to retain its military power. It has to use that power to make others pay—to keep foreigners buying its IOUs. One day, the rest of the world may get tired of paying, or a new superpower may take the place of the U.S., as the U.S. once took the place of Great Britain. As for average Americans, if jobs and wages continue to stagnate, they too will keep borrowing... until Repo Man comes.[36]

The idea of money as debt is brilliant, though it's easy to forget that this makes money a promise about future productivity, not present value. You can spend the promise today and defer the productivity for as long as you can keep borrowing. America has made a lot of dollar promises. It keeps making them, rolling them over, and then making bigger promises. Sooner or later, something has to give. In the meantime, please don't let that put you off Snickers.

---

[1] "Top 10 Best Selling Candy Bars Brands in the World," *Trending Top Most*, n.d., http://www.trendingtopmost.com/worlds-popular-list-top-10/2017-2018-2019-2020-2021/product/best-selling-candy-bars-brands-world-india-market-usa-famous-expensive-cheapest-reviews/; E.J. Schultz, "Snickers Surging to Top of Global Candy Race," *AdAge*, September 20, 2012, http://adage.com/article/news/snickers-surging-top-global-candy-race/237349/.

[2] Haley Willard, "10 Things You Didn't Know About Snickers," *Daily Meal*, November 4, 2014, https://www.thedailymeal.com/10-things-you-didnt-know-about-snickers

[3] Willard, "Snickers."

[4] David Graeber, *Debt: The First 5,000 Years,* rev. ed. (Melville House Publishing, 2014), 60. See also: Talia Avakian, "The 10 Strangest Things that Have Been Used as Money Around the World," *Business Insider*, April 20, 2016, https://www.businessinsider.com.au/alternative-forms-of-currency-2016-4?r=US&IR=T#/#rai-stones-1; "12 Unusual Objects Used as Money," *Elite Readers*, n.d., https://www.elitereaders.com/12-unusual-objects-used-money/.

[5] Graeber, *Debt*, 171 and 172.

[6] Jeff Desjardins, "All of the World's Money and Markets in One Visualization," *The Money Project*, December 17, 2015, http://money.visualcapitalist.com/all-of-the-worlds-money-and-markets-in-one-visualization/?link=mktw; Mitchell Hartman, "How Much Money Is there in the World?" *Marketplace*, October 30, 2017, https://www.marketplace.org/2017/10/30/world/how-much-money-there-world.

[7] Jon Henley, "Sweden Leads the Race to Become Cashless Society," *Guardian*, June 5, 2016, https://www.theguardian.com/business/2016/jun/04/sweden-cashless-society-cards-phone-apps-leading-europe.

[8] Joel Anderson, "A Look at German Inflation: A National Coin Week Exhibit, 1914-1924," n.d., http://www.joelscoins.com/exhibger2.htm; see also: C.N. Trueman, "Hyperinflation and Weimar Germany," *History Learning Site*, May 22, 2015, http://www.historylearningsite.co.uk/modern-world-history-1918-to-1980/weimar-germany/hyperinflation-and-weimar-germany/ (Although the prices of bread quoted in these two sources don't match exactly, it's the scale of the increase that's important.)

[9] Sandra Kollen Ghizoni, "Nixon Ends Convertibility of US Dollars to Gold and Announces Wage/Price Controls, August 1971," *Federal Reserve History*, November 22, 2013, https://www.federalreservehistory.org/essays/gold_convertibility_ends.

[10] Sabrina Stapleton, "How Many Calories Are in a Snickers Bar?" *Livestrong.com*, October 3, 2017,

https://www.livestrong.com/article/302359-how-many-calories-are-in-a-snickers-bar/.

[11] This is central to the thesis of Graeber, *Debt*.

[12] Graeber, *Debt*, 52.

[13] Thomas H. Greco Jr., *Money: Understanding and Creating Alternatives to Legal Tender* (White River Junction, VT: Chelsea Green Publishing, 2001), 166 quoting from Sydney Homer, *A History of Interest Rates* (New Brunswick, NJ: Rutgers University Press, 1963).

[14] Yaron Brook, "The Morality of Moneylending: A Short History," *Objective Standard*, January 22, 2014, https://www.theobjectivestandard.com/issues/2007-fall/morality-of-moneylending/.

[15] Thomas of Chobham, c.11680c.1235, *The History of Economic Thought*, http://www.hetwebsite.net/het/profiles/chobham.htm.

[16] Quoted in Jeremy Rifkin, *The European Dream* (Cambridge, UK: Polity Press, 2004), 105.

[17] Adam Smith, *The Wealth of Nations*, 194.

[18] Banks and financiers are the exception. As intermediaries and lenders, they make nothing out of money except money. Historically, that's why banks and financiers were often considered parasitic even after Christianity accepted moneylending as a practical necessity.

[19] David Graeber, "A Practical Utopian's Guide to the Coming Collapse," *Baffler*, No. 22 (April 2013): "What is debt, after all, but the promise of future productivity?" https://thebaffler.com/salvos/a-practical-utopians-guide-to-the-coming-collapse.

[20] Liaquat Ahamed, *Lords of Finance: The Bankers Who Broke the World* (London: Windmill Books, 2009); see: Part Two "After the Deluge 1919-1923," especially Chapter 9 "Barbarous Relic."

[21] For a definition of "Communist Bloc," see: *Encyclopedia.com*, http://www.encyclopedia.com/history/encyclopedias-almanacs-transcripts-and-maps/communist-bloc.

[22] Paul Stevens, "Bretton Woods: 1944-1971," *Foundation for Economic Education*, May 1, 1973, https://fee.org/articles/bretton-woods-1944-1971/.

[23] For a definition see: *Merriam-Webster Dictionary*, s.v. "Pax Americana," https://www.merriam-webster.com.

[24] "Nixon and the End of the Bretton Woods System."

[25] See: Amadeo, "Subprime Mortgage Crisis."

[26] Graeber, *Debt*, 381.

[27] Pam Martens and Russ Martens, "Warren: Citigroup, Morgan Stanley, Merrill Lynch Received $6 Trillion Backdoor Bailout from Fed," *Wall Street on Parade*, March 4, 2015, (quoting Senator Warren), http://wallstreetonparade.com/2015/03/warren-citigroup-morgan-stanley-merrill-lynch-received-6-trillion-backdoor-bailout-from-fed/.

[28] "Gross External Debt Position: By Sector 1/ as of December 31, 2016," Department of the Treasury, June 30, 2016, http://ticdata.treasury.gov/Publish/deb2a2016q4.html.

[29] Michael Hudson, "How America Will Get Europe to Finance its 2002-03 Oil War with Iraq," *Michel Hudson: On Finance, Real Estate and the Powers of Neoliberalism*, November 25, 2002, http://michael-hudson.com/2003/03/press-release-super-imperialism/. This was a press release in relation to the launch of: Michael Hudson, *Super Imperialism: The Economic Strategy of American Empire* (Pluto Press, 2nd edition, 2003); the 1st edition of this book was published in 1972.

[30] Hudson, "How America."

[31] Hudson, *Super Imperialism*, Preface, 12.

[32] Suzanne Woolley, "Do You Have More Debt than the Average American?" *Bloomberg*, December 15, 2016, https://www.bloomberg.com/news/articles/2016-12-15/average-credit-card-debt-16k-total-debt-133k-where-do-you-fit-in.

[33] Graeber, *Debt*, 434-435, quoting from Chris Serres and Glenn Howatt, "In Jail for Being in Debt," *Star Tribune* (Minneapolis–St. Paul), March17, 2011, www.startribune.com/local/95692619.html. See: "In for a Penny: The Rise of America's New Debtors' Prisons," American Civil Liberties Union, October 2010, www.aclu.org/files/assets/InForAPenny_web.pdf.

[34] Graeber, *Debt*, especially Chapter 4 "Cruelty and Redemption."

[35] Heather Long, "How an Unequal Tax Cut Grew More Unequal," *Washington Post*, December 1, 2017,

https://www.washingtonpost.com/business/economy/as-tax-bill-evolved-benefits-for-corporations-and-the-wealthy-grew/2017/12/01/17f1478e-d6c0-11e7-b62d-d9345ced896d_story.html?utm_term=.ba62a1163a90.

[36] *Repo Man* is a 1984 movie written and directed by Alex Cox. See: Vincent Canby, "Screen: 'Repo Man,' Cars and California," *New York Times*, July 6, 1984, http://www.nytimes.com/movie/review?res=9D07E2DD153BF935A35754C0A962948260.

Chapter 4

ABOUT TAXES:

A Certain Snafu

In 1972, Carl Gerstacker, Chairman of the Dow Chemical Company, told the world his secret wish: "I have long dreamed to buy an island owned by no nation... and of establishing the World Headquarters of the Dow Company on the truly neutral ground of such an island, beholden to no nation or society."[1] Gerstacker was thinking about taxes.

Most countries tax their corporations only on the profits they make at home. The United States has a deficit to finance and a massive army to feed, so it taxes its corporations on their worldwide profits.[2] This is surely what led Gerstacker to dream of "Dow Island." But he was mistaken. Dow didn't need to buy an island to save on U.S. taxes.

There are at least thirty countries that make it easy to

move foreign profits around and shelter them from the IRS.[3] They're called tax havens, with an estimated fifty percent of the world's cross-border assets and liabilities passing through them—somewhere between twenty-one and thirty-two trillion dollars (as of 2010).[4] Many of them are exotic islands like the one Gerstacker imagined. In places like Bermuda, the British Virgin Islands, and the Cayman Islands, tiny companies own assets that big transnational corporations use around the world. One of the ways these "Treasure Island" companies make money is by charging for the use of those assets. Yet, if you look in the Yellow Pages in any of the Treasure Islands, you won't find their names. Nor will you find any factories, offices or staff if you visit because the companies are little more than anonymous "post boxes." They are indirectly controlled by the transnational corporations from which they siphon off profits. Their only purpose is to shelter those profits from the taxes imposed by the U.S. and other countries in the "real world."

Many Treasure Islands are on international blacklists, so they need "pirate" countries to ship the treasure to them. Some of the pirates, like Luxembourg, Ireland, Switzerland, and Singapore, are small countries with laws designed to make it easy to ship treasure while skimming off some of it on its way through. Then, there are countries like The Netherlands and the United Kingdom. They're not pirates; they're former colonial powers with long histories of tolerating pirates, when it suits their elites.

It's not just about foreign profits. Some corporations smuggle some of their U.S. profits offshore. From 2001 to 2006, Microsoft shifted the rights to software code and other assets, developed largely in the U.S., to subsidiaries in Bermuda, Ireland, Singapore, and Puerto Rico.[5] About half the profits from U.S. sales washed ashore in Puerto Rico because a subsidiary there charged Microsoft in the U.S. a license fee for using the technology it acquired from… Microsoft in the U.S. The license fee was a tax-deductible expense in the U.S. and income in Puerto Rico, where the government is so broke that Microsoft was able to muscle a tax rate of just two percent.[6]

Even inside the U.S., large corporations have always been able to get away with paying less than the statutory rate of tax thanks to a bewildering array of tax breaks. Then there's "corporate welfare." Between 2008 and 2014, the fifty largest corporations in the U.S. received an average of twenty-seven dollars in federal loans, loan guarantees, and bailouts for every dollar they paid in federal taxes.[7] Think of this as a tax rebate—much larger than the tax actually paid.

If you were to ask them, big corporations would tell you that they're willing to pay a reasonable rate of tax. What's a reasonable rate? According to a 2017 report by the Institute on Taxation and Economic Policy: "two hundred and fifty-eight Fortune 500 companies were consistently profitable in each of the eight years between 2008 and 2015… Eighteen of the corporations, including General Electric, International Paper, Priceline.com, and PG&E, paid no federal income tax at all over the eight-year period. A fifth of the corporations (48) paid an effective tax rate of less than ten percent over that period."[8] The average rate was 21.2 percent—a little over half the statutory rate.[9] When tax dodges enable corporations to pick their own rate, it's easy for them to lose track of what's reasonable. Tax dodging is a game with a dynamic like the old Tom and Jerry cartoons—the chase just keeps escalating.

And sometimes Jerry goes a little too far. In 2012, Reuters reported that Starbucks had paid virtually no tax in the United Kingdom since setting up there in 1998. It had racked up sales of $4.8 billion from its 735 outlets, but it was filtering its profits to Switzerland. When customers in the U.K. learned about this, there was a public outcry that quickly led to a boycott. So, Starbucks switched their tax lawyers to decaf, and "volunteered" to pay £20 million to the U.K. taxman.[10]

At a hearing of the Senate Permanent Subcommittee on Investigations in May 2013, Apple's CEO, Tim Cook, assured the Senators that Apple still regarded itself as an American company, even though its overseas sales outstripped its domestic sales.[11] Cook and two other Apple executives appeared before the Subcommittee to answer for sheltering billions of dollars of overseas income from U.S. corporate tax.[12]

Apple booked all its sales in Europe through two subsidiaries in Ireland. But, under Irish law, these subsidiaries weren't resident there for tax purposes. So, they didn't have to pay corporate tax there.[13] In fact, they weren't resident anywhere in the world—and they weren't taxed anywhere. This kind of income now has a name. It's called "stateless income."[14] Forget about Treasure Islands, this is Fantasy Island.[15]

In his opening remarks, Cook told the Senators: "We don't depend on tax gimmicks."[16] He might even have believed this. There's a strange paradox about tax dodging. Typically, corporations like Apple hire a bunch of lawyers and accountants—brainy nerds who seem like they gave up chess because it was too easy. These nerds comb through the tax laws of dozens of countries. They prepare structure papers and flowcharts that look like the wiring diagrams for the Space Shuttle. Then they write documents that move the ownership of billions of dollars of shares, assets, and rights, with barely a ripple in the real world. To the geeks at Apple, this kind of dematerialized manipulation probably looks familiar. It's a bit like writing software code. Yet, take one of the tax nerds down to street level and ask him to stop a teenager at random and give her a broad outline of the "tax problem," and the "tax solution," and the teenager would probably say: "That bullshit actually works? As if, dude!" That's pretty much what Senator Levin said, only politely.

It's impossible to fix U.S. corporate tax without addressing the issue of tax on offshore profits. "The 50 largest American companies made about $4 trillion in profit from 2008 to 2014, according to SEC filings, and kept about a quarter of that amount outside the country."[17] Collectively, American corporate "citizens" had more than two trillion dollars sitting offshore in 2014.[18] Before the Trump tax cuts, the figure had risen to over three trillion dollars.[19]

During his opening address to the Senators, Cook smugly quoted his hero, President Kennedy: "To whom much is given, much will be required."[20] Later, when it became clear that Apple would keep deferring U.S. tax on its foreign stash, Senator Levin asked Cook if he agreed with President Kennedy's April 1961 message to Congress. Levin then read a passage in which Kennedy criticized American corporations for avoiding U.S. tax on foreign earnings with gimmicks much like those used by Apple.[21] Cook tried to pretend he didn't get the irony. After an awkward pause, he deflected the question, then went on to make his position clear. Apple is American—in America, not abroad—so keep your hands off our foreign income. It's not as though Apple has anything against the U.S. in particular. It plays hardball everywhere it operates. For the sake of 4,000 jobs, the Irish government allowed Apple to push it around on tax.[22] Ireland needs the kind of jobs that Apple provides—it's still recovering from the Global Financial Crisis. Among governments across the world, corporate tax is a competitive sport with a perverse scorecard, where winner takes least.

Before the Trump tax cuts, if Apple had brought home its foreign hoard of $246 billion, it would have had to pay federal corporate tax on it (then thirty-five percent).[23] Cook didn't want to pay it. Now, thanks to Trump and the Republican Party, he no longer has to pay anywhere near as much. As well as benefitting from a forty percent cut in corporate tax,[24] Apple gets to repatriate its foreign cash in return for paying even lower rates of tax (eight to fifteen and a half percent)—with payment spread over eight years.[25] That's a great deal for Apple. Not so much for the Federal Treasury.

But how big a problem is corporate tax dodging? After all, corporate tax represents only about nine percent of the total tax receipts of the federal government.[26] Isn't this small change, comparatively speaking? It is now, but it wasn't always like this. In the Eisenhower era, when corporate profits were lower and, for most American companies, domestic sales were higher than foreign sales, corporate tax was about a third of total tax receipts.[27] Today more American companies are global. For many, like Apple, Google, Microsoft, and Starbucks, their businesses (and profits) are growing faster abroad than at home. And this changes the way they think about "home."

Cook told the Senators that he couldn't imagine Apple ever leaving the U.S., but other American CEOs have done more than just imagine this. Burger King and Johnson Controls "migrated" by merging themselves into smaller foreign companies in low-tax countries, which ended up "owning" them.[28] This is called inversion. Pfizer and Walgreen started their own inversions, but bowed to pressure to stay in the U.S.[29] The beauty of inversion is that nothing really changes, except on paper. When the U.S. is no longer your tax home, it's even easier to shift taxable profits around the world to keep them away from the IRS, no matter where those profits are earned. A better name for inversions would be "perversions."

Like American corporations, ordinary Americans pay tax on their worldwide earnings. For most of them, this isn't an issue. The bigger issue is tax on domestic income and gains. When the Sixteenth Amendment introduced a federal tax on income in 1913, only the richest one percent of Americans had to pay it.[30] It was a modest tax. The highest rate was only seven percent.[31] Nonetheless, it was designed to "soak the rich." The Depressions and Panics of the Gilded Age[32] had left Americans feeling that income from capital was effortless, even decadent. On the other hand, they thought that income from labor was virtuous and shouldn't be taxed (or not as much). They made a choice that was political and social—many considered it a moral choice.

Then came World War I. It was expensive, so, to pay for it, Congress broadened the tax base and hiked the rates. Taxes kept growing to finance the steady extension of government services, but more than anything else, to pay for wars and for America's role as guarantor of the world order after 1945— the Pax Americana. In his farewell address in January 1961, President Eisenhower alerted America to its financial burden as leader of the free world. He said: "Our military organization today bears little relation to that known by any of my predecessors in peacetime, or indeed by the fighting men of World War II or Korea... We have been compelled to create a permanent armaments industry of vast proportions... We annually spend on military security more than the net income of all United States corporations."[33]

Today, American households pay eighty-one percent of federal taxes.[34] Tax rates are progressive, reflecting a diluted version of the same ethos that the rich should pay more. And the rich do pay more. They pay a sizable chunk of the nation's tax bill. But this chunk represents a shrinking proportion of their growing wealth.[35] The average tax rate of the top one percent, which began falling in 1979, fell again under Trump's Tax Cuts and Jobs Act.[36] As David Cay Johnston puts it in his book *Perfectly Legal*, the deck is stacked against wage earners: "Congress lets business owners, investors and landlords play by one set of rules, which are filled with opportunities to hide income, fabricate deductions and reduce taxes. Congress requires wage earners to operate under another, much harsher set of rules in which every dollar of income from a job, a savings account or a stock dividend is reported to the government."[37]

The ways the rich dodge taxes are just as creative as those used by big corporations. The result is much the same. Johnston sums it up: "When taxes are examined overall—including state and local income, sales and property taxes—America has something close to a flat tax. The top fifth of Americans pays just a penny more out of a dollar in taxes overall than the poorest fifth..."[38]

In November 2017, Trump said: "We're also going to eliminate tax breaks and complex loopholes taken advantage of by the wealthy."[39] Was he right—is that what his Tax Cuts and Jobs Act does? Not even close. As Annie Lowrey, writing in *The Atlantic*, noted: "The Tax Policy Center has found that the biggest benefits would go to families in the top 5 percent as of 2019, with the smallest benefits going to those in the lowest income quartile. By 2027, families in the lowest two income quartiles would be receiving, on average, no benefit at all, with the biggest gains accruing to families in the top 0.1 percent of the income distribution. Moreover, the richest-of-the-rich families would exclusively benefit from initiatives like the reduction in or an elimination of the estate tax, which would let individuals like Trump pass millions and millions of dollars more to their heirs."[40] In other words, to whom much is given, much more will be given.

Why is this happening? Is it because taxes in the U.S. are too high?

Among the world's thirty-five richest countries, the total tax burden of the U.S. ranks thirty-second.[41] Danes pay the highest taxes.[42] Justice Oliver Wendell Holmes Jr. said: "Taxes are what we pay for a civilized society."[43] The Danes agree: they're willing to pay for their civilized society. Dodging tax isn't the national sport that it is for wealthy Americans.

Justice Holmes believed that, by paying taxes, we each commit part of our life to our civilization. He didn't say how much of it we should have to commit. He believed that, before the law, every life has equal value. So, for one man to have to spend half his life working to pay his taxes, while another spends almost no time at all, would have struck Holmes as an unequal commitment and, for that reason, uncivilized. Taxes are vital for a civilized society, and because of that, they are a burden that is certain. Today, it is equally certain that there are some who are allowed by law to avoid their fair share of that burden.

In order to make profits, American corporations rely on Pax Americana abroad and civil society at home. Yet, they don't want to pay for them. Increasingly, corporations born in the USA see themselves as part of a stateless alternative society whose citizens are corporate executives and global stockholders. They have their own name for the price of civilization in the countries in which they do business. They refer to the taxes they have to pay as "leakage." In countries like the U.S. and the U.K., they plug the leaks using technical dodges. In countries like Ireland and Puerto Rico, they use bullying and job handouts. In shady Treasure Islands and pirate countries, it's just chicanery dressed up as law.

The "one percent" is also an alternative society—a virtual fifty-first state comprising communities across the country that are "gated," sometimes literally. They have their own schools, their own health care, and their own law enforcement. The United States was born out of a tax revolt; so was the state of the one percent—their revolt was just slower and stealthier.

In the U.S., the post-war boom ended with the sixties, but the memory lingered. So, it was a shock to Americans when, in 1979, President Carter told them: "We are at a turning point in our history. There are two paths to choose. One is a path I've warned about tonight, the path that leads to fragmentation and self-interest. Down that road lies a mistaken idea of freedom, the right to grasp for ourselves some advantage over others. That path would be one of constant conflict between narrow interests ending in chaos and immobility. It is a certain route to failure."[44] Carter said the other path involved sacrifice for the good of society. He wasn't talking specifically about taxes. He was talking generally about the "price" of American civil society. At the time, Americans were hurting from high inflation and high gas prices following the Second Oil Shock.[45] Later that year, when Ronald Reagan assured them they didn't have to make a hard choice, they were happy to listen. By 1984, it was "morning in America again."[46] Reagan said that taxes were like a dam that stopped wealth from trickling down to everyone. He prescribed tax cuts for the corporations that created jobs and for the rich who invested capital.

For a time, employment, tax receipts, and stock prices rose and inflation fell. These things were largely the result of a massive build-up in defense spending financed by debt. George H.W. Bush had earlier called this "voodoo economics";[47] yet, he, and every President since, has had to live with the delusion that the federal government can take less in taxes from corporations and the rich, while everyone somehow gets rich. This voodoo was strong enough to turn the pursuit of riches into an all-American virtue, so that Presidents Clinton and George W. Bush had to keep it alive for ordinary Americans by giving them easy access to credit. 'W' was a true believer. He did more than just keep it alive; he nurtured it with lavish military spending and equally lavish government borrowing. Both Clinton and 'W' pursued a policy of "let them eat credit."[48] Americans were encouraged to borrow money, buy a house, flip it—then "rinse and repeat." The idea was that, if everyone got into the game of capital gain, those below wouldn't notice that the biggest gains were going to those at the top.

Even President Obama, who had to clean up after the Sub-Prime Mortgage Crisis, gradually allowed speculative credit to rise from the dead. He didn't buy into the voodoo, but he had to let it loose again. Now that he's out of office, it's clear that he did buy into the central idea that it's glorious to be rich. In February 2017, he and Michelle signed a lucrative book deal with Penguin Random House.[49] How long will it be before they too go out and hire tax lawyers?

Until Trump's Tax Cuts and Jobs Act, the federal tax code was about 2,600 pages. "It's like 2½ times the length of Stephen King's *It*—except you replace 'scary clown' with 'accounting methods.'[50] That's how Andrew Grossman, legislative counsel for the congressional Joint Committee on Taxation described it in 2014. In April 2017, T.R. Reid, author of *A Fine Mess*, told an interviewer: "Every 32 years, we need to repeal the existing code and rewrite it from scratch. That's because the accumulation of new rules and provisions over the years finally reaches a point, every 32 years, where the thing is so complex it's incomprehensible."[51] The Tax Cuts and Jobs Act added another 429 pages to the "fine mess."[52]

Before Trump, there was a broadly shared view about tax reform. As Reid notes, it even has its own acronym:

BBLR, which stands for "Broaden the Base to Lower Rates." Basically, it means that you cut out all the tax breaks so that more revenue is taxed and the system is simpler, therefore harder to game. Then you can lower the tax rates while still taking in the same in tax revenue (or even more). Special interests would lose out, but almost all taxpayers would be better off—so would the Treasury. Trump's tax law isn't the rewrite Reid had in mind. It lowers the rates without broadening the base. It adds complication, while reducing the resources of the IRS. Worst of all, it doesn't help the Federal Treasury. Over the next decade, the U.S. will have to borrow almost a trillion and a half dollars to cover the widening gap between federal spending and federal tax revenue.[53]

Trump understands the connection between civilized society and taxes well enough to keep his own tax records secret. There was never a chance that he would betray his self-interest or the interests of Corporate America and the one percent. He is the antithesis of Justice Holmes. For Trump, taxes are the price other people pay for the kind of civilized society he doesn't think he needs. But he's dead wrong. And his mindset is dangerous for a man with two armies to feed— the U.S. Military and the legions of the disappointed.

Civilized society fragments when those who can most afford to pay believe they can safely dodge their fair share of the tax burden, while those who do pay their fair share become less able to pay. Sure, the U.S. can keep borrowing from foreigners to fund its growing budget deficits—and the next corporate bailout, and the next military conflict, and the next natural disaster, and the effects of climate change, and all the other stuff it has to fund. As powerful as it is though, even the U.S. needs to foster the belief that, one day, it might actually pay its debts to the rest of the world. Sooner or later, there will be a limit to its borrowings. In 2010, when he was Chairman of the Joint Chiefs of Staff, Admiral Michael Mullen said: "The most significant threat to our national security is our debt."[54] At his 2017 confirmation hearing for Defense Secretary, General James Mattis agreed[55] (his boss doesn't) that trillion and a half hike in the deficit shows that he could care less.[56]

When the time comes for the U.S. to rein in its borrowings, the ninety-nine percent will have to pay more in taxes if Corporate America and the one percent won't. Sooner or later, the ninety-nine percent will flag. There's a name for this too: it's called tax exhaustion. That's the off-ramp America is headed for.

---

[1] Khalil Hamdani and Lorraine Ruffing, *United Nations Centre on Transnational Corporations: Corporate Conduct and the Public Interest* (Abingdon, Oxon: Routledge, 2015), 42, quoting Carl Gerstacker.

[2] Norton Francis et al., *The Tax Policy Centre's Briefing Book: A Citizens' Guide to the Fascinating (Though Often Complex) Elements*

of the Federal Tax System (Tax Policy Center, 2016), "How Does the Current System of International Taxation Work?" http://www.taxpolicycenter.org/briefing-book/how-does-current-system-international-taxation-work.

[3] Javier Garcia-Bernardo et al., "Uncovering Offshore Financial Centers: Conduits and Sinks in the Global Corporate Ownership Network," *Scientific Reports* 7, Article No. 6246 (2017), http://www.nature.com/articles/s41598-017-06322-9.

[4] Garcia-Bernard, "Uncovering Offshore Financial Centers."

[5] Matt Day, "How Microsoft Moves Profits Offshore to Cut Its Tax Bill," *Seattle Times*, December 16, 2015, updating a report originally published on December 12, 2015, https://www.seattletimes.com/business/microsoft/how-microsoft-parks-profits-offshore-to-pare-its-tax-bill/.

[6] Day, "Microsoft."

[7] "Broken at the Top: How America's Dysfunctional Tax System Costs Billions in Corporate Tax Dodging," Oxfam Media Briefing, Oxfam America, April 2016, https://www.oxfamamerica.org/static/media/files/Broken_at_the_Top_4.14.2016.pdf.

[8] Matthew Gardner, Robert S. McIntryre and Richard Phillips, "The 35 Percent Corporate Tax Myth: Corporate Tax Avoidance by Fortune 500 Companies, 2008 to 2015," Institute on Taxation and Economic Policy, March 2017, https://itep.org/wp-content/uploads/35percentfullreport.pdf.

[9] Gardner, "35 Percent Corporate Tax Myth."

[10] Tom Bergin, "Special Report: How Starbucks Avoids UK taxes," *Reuters*, October 15, 2015, https://www.reuters.com/article/us-britain-starbucks-tax/special-report-how-starbucks-avoids-uk-taxes-idUSBRE89E0EX20121015.

[11] "Non-U.S. Share of Apple's Revenue from 1st Quarter 2006 to 4th Quarter 2017," *Statista – The Statistics Portal*, n.d., https://www.statista.com/statistics/263435/non-us-share-of-apples-revenue/.

[12] "Apple CEO Tim Cook Testifies at Senate Hearing," YouTube video, 37:11, posted by "PBS NewsHour," May 21, 2013, https://www.youtube.com/watch?v=Lx6YINOfjaQ; "Apple CEO Tim

Cook at Senate Hearings (part 2)," YouTube video, 21:52, posted by "PBS NewsHour," May 21, 2013, https://www.youtube.com/watch?v=hRmLm6tYNhQ.

[13] "State Aid: Ireland Gave Illegal Tax Benefits to Apple Worth Up to €13 Billion," European Commission Press Release, August 30, 2016, http://europa.eu/rapid/press-release_IP-16-2923_en.htm.

[14] Edward D. Kleinbard, "Stateless Income," *Florida Tax Review* 11, No. 9 (2011), 701-6, https://www.sbs.ox.ac.uk/sites/default/files/Business_Taxation/Docs/W P1208.pdf.

[15] After the EU clamped down on Ireland on the basis that Apple's tax status there amounted to Ireland providing Apple with illegal state aid, Apple shifted its base to Jersey. See: Jesse Drucker and Simon Bowers, "After a Tax Crackdown, Apple Found a New Shelter for its Profits," *New York Times*, November 6, 2017, https://www.nytimes.com/2017/11/06/world/apple-taxes-jersey.html.

[16] PBS NewsHour, "Apple CEO Tim Cook Testifies."

[17] Alexia Fernández Campbell, "The Cost of Corporate Tax Avoidance," *Atlantic*, April 14, 2016, reporting on Oxfam, "Broken at the Top," https://www.theatlantic.com/business/archive/2016/04/corporate-tax-avoidance/478293/.

[18] David Alexander and Eric Beech, Ed., "Big U.S. Firms hold $2.1 Trillion Overseas to avoid taxes: Study," *Reuters*, October 6, 2015, https://www.reuters.com/article/us-usa-tax-offshore/big-u-s-firms-hold-2-1-trillion-overseas-to-avoid-taxes-study-idUSKCN0S008U20151006.

[19] Lynnley Browning, Laura Davison and Matthew Townsend, "Apple Among Giants Due for Foreign Tax Bill Under House Plan," *Bloomberg*, November 3, 2017, https://www.bloomberg.com/news/articles/2017-11-02/house-bill-would-tax-offshore-corporate-profit-at-up-to-12.

[20] PBS NewsHour, "Apple CEO Tim Cook Testifies."

[21] PBS NewsHour, "Apple CEO Tim Cook (part 2)." Senator Levin read this passage: "The undesirability of continuing deferral is underscored where deferral has served as a shelter for tax escape through the unjustifiable use of tax havens such as Switzerland. Recently more and more enterprises organized abroad by American

firms have arranged their corporate structures—aided by artificial arrangements between parent and subsidiary regarding intercompany pricing, the transfer of patent licensing rights, the shifting of management fees, and similar practices which maximize the accumulation of profits in the tax haven—so as to exploit the multiplicity of foreign tax systems and international agreements in order to reduce sharply or eliminate completely their tax liabilities both at home and abroad," John F. Kennedy, "Special Message to the Congress on Taxation" (Congress, Washington DC, April 20, 1961). Online by Gerhard Peters and John T. Woolley, *The American Presidency Project*. http://www.presidency.ucsb.edu/ws/?pid=8074.

[22] Julia Fioretti and Tom Bergin, "EU Says Ireland Swapped Apple Tax Deal for Jobs," *Reuters*, September 30, 2014, https://www.reuters.com/article/us-apple-ireland-tax/eu-says-ireland-swapped-apple-tax-deal-for-jobs-idUSKCN0HP0QT20140930.

[23] This is up from $180 billion in 2016: Browning, Davison and Townsend, "Apple Among Giants," also see: Oxfam, "Broken at the Top," 18 (table).

[24] CBO, the Reconciliation Recommendations of the Senate Committee on Finance.

[25] CBO, the Reconciliation Recommendations of the Senate Committee on Finance. See also: Browning, Davison and Townsend, "Apple Among Giants."

[26] Francis et al., *The Tax Policy Centre's Briefing Book;* see "What Are the Sources of Revenue for the Federal Government?"

[27] "Federal Tax Revenue by Source, 1934-2018," *Tax Foundation,* November 21, 2013, https://taxfoundation.org/federal-tax-revenue-source-1934-2018/.

[28] "Whopper of a Tax Dodge: How Burger King's Inversion Could Shortchange America," *Americans for Tax Fairness*, December 2014, https://americansfortaxfairness.org/files/Whopper-Tax-Dodge.pdf; Leslie Picker, "Tyco Merger Will Shift Johnson Controls' Tax Liability Overseas," *New York Times,* January 25, 2016, https://www.nytimes.com/2016/01/26/business/dealbook/johnson-controls-to-combine-with-tyco-in-tax-inversion-deal.html.

[29] Caroline Humer and Ransdell Pierson, "Obama's Inversion Curbs Kill Pfizer's $160 Billion Allergan Deal," *Reuters*, April 5, 2016, https://www.reuters.com/article/us-allergan-m-a-pfizer/obamas-

inversion-curbs-kill-pfizers-160-billion-allergan-deal-idUSKCN0X21NV; Paul Ziobro and Michael Calia, "Walgreen Board Wasn't Comfortable With 'Inversion,'" *Wall Street Journal*, August 6, 2014, https://www.wsj.com/articles/walgreen-to-buy-remaining-stake-in-alliance-boots-1407321248.

[30] T.R. Reid, *A Fine Mess: A Global Quest for a Simpler, Fairer, and More Efficient Tax System* (London: Penguin Press, 2017), 46.

[31] Reid, *A Fine Mess*, 46.

[32] See above, Chapter 1, endnote 5.

[33] Eisenhower, "Farewell Radio and Television Address."

[34] Income tax is 47percent and payroll tax is 34 percent = 81percent: "Policy Basics: Where Do Federal Tax Revenues Come From?" *Center on Budget and Policy Priorities*, September 5, 2017, https://www.cbpp.org/research/federal-tax/policy-basics-where-do-federal-tax-revenues-come-from.

[35] "Income Inequality in the United States," *Inequality.org*, n.d., https://inequality.org/facts/income-inequality/.

[36] Congressional Budget Office, *Trends in the Distribution of Household Income Between 1979 and 2007* (October, 2011), https://www.cbo.gov/publication/42729; Heather Long, "The Senate Just Passed a Massive Tax Bill. Here's What Is in It," *Washington Post*, November 30, 2017, https://www.washingtonpost.com/news/wonk/wp/2017/11/30/what-is-in-the-senates-massive-tax-bill-and-what-could-change/?utm_term=.00fa85a0b714.

[37] David Cay Johnston, *Perfectly Legal: The Covert Campaign to Rig Our Tax System to Benefit the Super Rich – and Cheat Everybody Else* (London: Penguin Group, 2003), 10.

[38] Johnston, *Perfectly Legal*, 317.

[39] Donald Trump, "Remarks by President Trump on Tax Reform," (St. Charles Convention Center, St. Charles, Missouri, November 30, 2017) available at The White House, Office of the Press Secretary, https://www.whitehouse.gov/the-press-office/2017/11/30/remarks-president-trump-tax-reform.

[40] Annie Lowrey, "The 7 Myths of the GOP Tax Bill," *Atlantic*, December 1, 2017,

https://www.theatlantic.com/business/archive/2017/12/the-7-myths-of-the-gop-tax-bill/547322/.

[41] Ian Salisbury, "This Chart Shows How Much Americans Pay in Taxes vs. the Rest of the World," *Money*, July 19, 2017, http://time.com/money/4862673/us-tax-burden-vs-oecd-countries/.

[42] Salisbury, "This Chart."

[43] Compania General De Tabacos De Filipinas v. Collector of Internal Revenue, 275 U.S. 87, 100 (Justice Oliver Wendell Holmes Jr. in dissent) (1927). This quote is inscribed above the entrance to the building of the Internal Revenue Service in Washington DC.

[44] Jimmy Carter, "Address to the Nation on Energy and National Goals: The 'Malaise Speech,'" (Oval Office, Washington DC, July 15, 1979). Online by Gerhard Peters and John T. Woolley, *The American Presidency Project*, http://www.presidency.ucsb.edu/ws/?pid=32596.

[45] See generally Philip K. Verleger, Jr., "The U.S. Petroleum Crisis of 1979," *Brookings Papers on Economic Growth* 2 (1979), https://www.brookings.edu/bpea-articles/the-u-s-petroleum-crisis-of-1979/.

[46] Michael Beschloss, "The Ad That Helped Reagan Sell Good Times to an Uncertain Nation," *New York Times*, May 7, 2016, https://www.nytimes.com/2016/05/08/business/the-ad-that-helped-reagan-sell-good-times-to-an-uncertain-nation.html. See also "Ronald Reagan TV Ad: 'It's Morning in America Again,'" YouTube video, 0:59, posted by Andre Morgado, November 12, 2006, https://www.youtube.com/watch?v=EU-IBF8nwSY.

[47] *The Free Dictionary by Farlex*, s.v. "voodoo economics," https://www.thefreedictionary.com/Voodoo+economics.

[48] It is the name of Chapter 1 of Raghuram G. Rajan, *Fault Lines: How the Hidden Fractures Still Threaten the World Economy* (Princeton, NJ: Princeton University Press, 2010). See also: "Let Them Eat Credit," Schott's Vocab: A Miscellany of Modern Words and Phrases (blog), *New York Times*, July 6, 2010, https://schott.blogs.nytimes.com/2010/07/06/let-them-eat-credit/.

[49] Mark Abadi, "The Obamas Are Getting a Record-Setting Book Deal Worth at Least $60 Million," *Business Insider*, February 28, 2017, http://www.businessinsider.com/obama-book-deal-2017-2; Alexandra Alter, "Obamas Make Book Deal with Penguin Random House," *New*

York Times, February 28, 2017,
https://www.nytimes.com/2017/02/28/business/media/obama-book-deal-penguin-random-house.html.

[50] Andrew L. Grossman, "Is the Tax Code Really 70,000 Pages Long? No, Not Even Close," *Slate*, April 2014, http://www.slate.com/articles/news_and_politics/politics/2014/04/how-long-is-the-tax-code-it-is-far-shorter-than-70,000-pages.html.

[51] Interview with T.R. Reid the author of *A Fine Mess* by Chris Schluep, "Now Is the Perfect Time to Think About Taxes – T.R. Reid on A Fine Mess," *Omnivoracious, The Amazon Book Review*, April 18, 2007, https://www.amazonbookreview.com/post/8b29d081-3613-4a87-a44e-892be6670456/now-is-the-perfect-time-to-think-about-taxes-t-r-reid-on-a-fine-mess.

[52] Long, "The Senate."

[53] CBO, the Reconciliation Recommendations of the Senate Committee on Finance, 2.

[54] CNN Wire Staff, "Mullen: Debt Is Top National Security Threat," *CNN*, August 27, 2010, http://edition.cnn.com/2010/US/08/27/debt.security.mullen/index.html.

[55] "Gen. Mattis Agrees That The National Debt Is Our Biggest National Security Threat," User created clip of Defense Secretary Confirmation Hearing, *C-Span*, January 12, 2017, https://www.c-span.org/video/?c4645271/gen-mattis-agrees-debt-biggest-security-threat.

[56] The exact estimate by the CBO is $1,414 billion: CBO, the Reconciliation Recommendations of the Senate Committee on Finance. See also: Patel and Parlapiano, "The Senate's Official Scorekeeper."

Chapter 5

ABOUT WORK:

Snafu's Lost Garden

SCENE: Garden of Eden – late afternoon:

Eve: "How did it go?"

Adam: "Got Him down to a fifteen-hour week—no health plan though."

Eve: "What about the apples?"

Adam: "Sorry, honey, no deal."

Eve: "I'm tired of nuts and leaves and berries. I want apples."

Adam: "How do you know you'll even like them?"

Eve: "Adam, I have something here I'd like you to try…"

"So the Lord God banished them from the Garden of Eden, and he sent Adam out to cultivate the ground from which he had been made." (Genesis 3:23)[1]

A dam and Eve might be mythological proxies for our African ancestors, who gave up hunting and gathering in the Rift Valley about 60,000 years ago, wandered into the Fertile Crescent, and later, tried their hand at farming.[2] We know that farming began as an arduous and precarious experiment, so it's plausible that they were worse off as farmers long enough for them to eulogize their "good life" as foragers—perhaps remembering it as something like the Garden of Eden.[3]

In 1966, anthropologist Marshall Sahlins put forward an interesting thesis about ancient foragers. He drew on studies of contemporary hunter-gatherers that showed they needed to "work" only three to five hours a day. Like ancient foragers, they had few needs and they could satisfy them quite easily. This led him to propose that our nomadic ancestors were the "original affluent society."[4] He was alluding to John Kenneth Galbraith's 1958 book *The Affluent Society*.[5] Sahlins took Galbraith's critique of the "scarcity principle" of economic theory[6] and projected it back in time. The Eden of our ancestors might seem like a place of scarcity, but they knew all they had to do was move around to get whatever they needed. As Sahlins put it: "We are inclined to think of hunters and gatherers as poor because they don't have anything; perhaps better to think of them for that reason as free. Their extremely limited material possessions relieve them of all cares with regard to daily necessities and permit them to enjoy life."[7]

For Adam Smith, Thomas Malthus, and David Ricardo, the founders of modern economics, the "economic problem" was scarcity. They were preoccupied with how to organize society's limited resources to produce the goods necessary to meet its needs. This led them to see production as urgent and imperative. By the time Galbraith wrote his book, countries like America had largely solved the problem of scarcity. Their new problem was how best to distribute their abundance. Yet, the old idea of the urgency of production lingered, partly because production was now as much about satisfying wants as it was about satisfying needs. In his book, Galbraith argued that economists (and industrialized society generally) had lost sight of the purpose of production.

There are two ideas at the heart of the scarcity principle. First, there's no practical difference between human needs and human wants. Second, needs and wants, taken together, have no limit. This means that society never has enough resources to satisfy them. This drives production, seeming to justify it as an end in itself. Galbraith and Sahlins regarded these ideas as heresy—for different reasons.

Sahlins believed that ancient foragers had no wants

beyond their needs, no fear of scarcity, and therefore no interest in production. If they'd been told of the scarcity principle, they would have been mystified, much as the aborigines of central Australia are incredulous when "whitefellas" die of thirst in the Outback.[8] They see water sources everywhere. You have to know where to look, but to them it's obvious. They see abundance where we see scarcity.

Galbraith rejected scarcity for almost the opposite reason. He thought we had produced our way out of it. The post-war boom in America was near its height when he wrote his book. In the U.S., there was mass affluence on a scale never seen before. So, Galbraith thought the scarcity principle had outlived its usefulness. As he looked at the abundance around him, he concluded that manufacturing had become an obsession, leading to over-production fueled by advertising— the endless stimulation of artificial wants, disguised as needs, or peddled as status markers. Galbraith's ideas about the relentless march of production and consumption weren't new. In the late 19th century, Andrew Carnegie made an epigram of the new consumerism when he said: "Capitalism is about turning luxuries into necessities."[9] In 1899, economist and sociologist Thorstein Veblen highlighted the symbolic aspect of consuming when he coined the expression "conspicuous consumption."[10] *The Affluent Society* became a bestseller.[11] As the U.S. went through the turbulent sixties, the book got people thinking about the values underlying their wants, and the question of why we work.

Almost thirty years earlier, John Maynard Keynes had mused about work. In his 1930 essay, "Economic Possibilities for our Grandchildren, "[12] Keynes predicted that productivity would increase sufficiently by 2030 to enable us to work only fifteen hours a week for a living wage.[13] He was right about enough to make his prediction intriguing. In their book *How Much is Enough?*, Robert and Edward Skidelsky summarize the part of his prediction that related to income: "Growth of real income per capita has been much as Keynes expected. The coincidence is in fact a bit of a fluke. Keynes assumed no major wars and no population growth in the countries covered. In fact there was another world war, and population has grown by about one-third. But he underestimated productivity growth. The two mistakes canceled each other out, with the result that per capita incomes indeed rose fourfold in the seventy years from 1930, up to Keynes's lower bound."[14]

Although he was right about the coming abundance, Keynes was wrong about the decline in working hours. He published his essay not long after the start of the Great Depression when the "shorter hours movement" in the United States was at its height. This movement had succeeded in reducing the workweek from about sixty-nine hours in 1830 to less than fifty hours, with the biggest reductions coming during World War I and early in the Great Depression.[15] As

Professor Robert Whaples[16] puts it: "The movement for shorter hours as a depression-fighting work-sharing measure built such a seemingly irresistible momentum that by 1933 observers were predicting that the '30-hour week was within a month of becoming federal law.'"[17] It was not to be. President Franklin Roosevelt, concerned that a thirty-hour week might go from an emergency measure to a permanent policy, brokered a series of deals. In return for relaxing industrial competition, big business fell into line with a program of minimum wages, flexible regulation of hours, guaranteed unionization, collective bargaining, and overtime rates for work in excess of forty hours a week. At the time, this was just enough to buy off workers' demands for shorter hours.[18]

Then came World War II. Industrial production surged—so did working hours. Although working hours fell back after the War, attitudes to work changed. Perhaps for the first time since Eden, workers opted for work over leisure for a reason other than need. While Americans eagerly embraced post-war abundance, the scarcity of the Great Depression left a curious legacy. They remembered the idleness, but not that it was forced on them. They remembered the hardship of the War but forgot that this too was forced. Instead, they romanticized the "War Effort" as the virtuous path to the new abundance. From this perspective, work takes on "many of the earmarks of a modern religion, and increased leisure is a prime candidate for the modern heresy."[19] The Employment Act of 1946 institutionalized the "modern religion," making the federal government responsible for ensuring full employment, as well as high production. Shorter hours became a negative economic indicator.[20]

The first wave of Baby Boomers, who came of age in the sixties, had no memory of anything but abundance. For them, their parents' religion of work made little sense, especially in that its only purpose seemed to be ever-greater consumption. It's hard to tell how much of Galbraith's thesis they bought into, but they certainly liked the fact that some old dude in a suit hated consumerism as much they did. But, before the first wave of Boomers reached thirty, their "sell-by date" as hippies, the distribution of abundance began to skew. When the seventies came, they had little choice but to enter the "house of work."

When the Employment Act of 1946 passed, few predicted the tension its twin objectives of full employment and high productivity would create—certainly not Keynes (who died that year). In 1930, Keynes thought capitalism would fade away when the accumulation of wealth no longer served its social purpose of delivering the "good life" for everyone. But, at the height of World War II, somebody else saw that full employment tied to high production wasn't a marriage made in heaven. That person was Michał Kalecki, a Polish economist who published a short article, "Political

Aspects of Full Employment," in 1943.[21] In *Buying Time*, Wolfgang Streeck summarizes Kalecki's thinking, that "… permanent full employment brought the danger that workers would become over-demanding once they had forgotten the insecurity and deprivation associated with unemployment. At that point, discipline might break down at the workplace as well as in the political arena. This was why, in Kalecki's view, capital should have an interest in lasting structural unemployment, serving to warn employees of what they might face if their demands became excessive."[22]

Kalecki proposed a theory of "political business cycles" that went like this: "In the slump, either under the pressure of the masses, or even without it, public investment financed by borrowing will be undertaken to prevent large scale unemployment. But if attempts are made to apply this method in order to maintain the high level of employment reached in the subsequent boom, strong opposition by 'business leaders' is likely to be encountered."[23] Big business and the rich would then use their influence to pressure the government to cut the budget deficit. This would, in turn, lead to another slump. Then the government would borrow again in order to spend its way out of it.

Although Kalecki was more of a realist than Keynes, like Keynes, he was an optimist. He thought that democracy would find a way out of these cycles. He said: "'Full employment capitalism' will have, of course, to develop new social and political institutions which will reflect the increased power of the working class. If capitalism can adjust itself to full employment a fundamental reform will have been incorporated in it. If not, it will show itself an outmoded system which must be scrapped."[24] He didn't say what the new social and political institutions might be. He may have been anticipating something like the partnership between business, the state, and labor that emerged in West Germany after the War. The State took a stake in industry, workers took a stake in management, and industry came to see labor more as an asset than a cost.

Kalecki also had a darker vision. But he thought it unlikely. For almost thirty years, the cycles played out in the U.S. much as Kalecki foretold, through six recessions and corresponding fluctuations in rates of employment.[25] Then, in the early seventies, something unexpected happened. Arab oil embargos aggravated an inflationary spiral that had begun in 1965.[26] The result was a prolonged slump. It began in 1973 and produced a new phenomenon called stagflation—a combination of rising prices, rising unemployment and low growth.[27] In 1971, President Nixon had tried to quell inflation by devaluing the dollar, a step that led to the abandonment in 1973 of the post-war Bretton Woods system under which the dollar was pegged to gold at a fixed price, and other currencies were pegged to the dollar.[28] Nixon had also implemented price and wage controls (a first in peacetime).[29]

By allowing the dollar to float against other currencies, Nixon achieved his immediate goal of reducing its value, thereby making U.S. exports cheaper and effectively lowering the value of U.S. government debt. But neither he nor Presidents Ford or Carter succeeded in arresting the slump. Early in the Reagan Administration, unemployment hit 10.8 percent.[30]

According to Kalecki's theory, the government should step in with public investments and subsidies to bring down unemployment and stimulate consumption. This was also the theory Keynes proposed in 1936 in *The General Theory of Employment, Interest, and Money*.[31] Reagan did something different. He pumped up military spending, cut taxes for corporations and the rich, weakened labor, and shrank welfare.

This is where Kalecki's darker vision first comes into play. He wrote: "The [capitalists'] dislike of Government spending, whether on public investment or consumption, is overcome by concentrating Government expenditure on armaments."[32] This, he said, "starts from the overcoming of unemployment, develops into an armament economy of scarcity, and ends inevitably in war."[33] Originally, Kalecki thought that this could only apply under a fascist regime. Twenty years later, he reconsidered: "In my [1943] article the policy of securing full employment by military spending was linked with total fascism. It appears, however, that a fascist coup is by no means necessary for armaments to play an important role in countering mass unemployment."[34] Kalecki believed that the first stages of an arms build-up remove the economic friction between full production and full employment. For a while, capitalists and the state have a common interest in both. Had Kalecki lived long enough, he'd probably have thought that a government in the thrall of its military–industrial complex, like the Reagan Administration, would be enough to bring his dark vision out of the shadows.[35] But Reagan avoided a major war.

In the bipolar world of the Cold War, competitive military escalation was all but inevitable. During the arms race[36] that followed World War II, and lasted until the collapse of the Soviet Union in 1991,[37] it wasn't only the capitalists who put armaments ahead of workers. In the Soviet Union, the military and industry were even more tightly fused because there was no private sector, although the Soviets were careful to maintain the illusion of full employment, as the old communist workers' joke goes: "They pretend to pay us, we pretend to work."[38]

By the end of Reagan's second term, warming up the Cold War had the collateral benefit of bringing unemployment down to 5.3 percent.[39] But, when Reagan's voodoo economics[40] stalled, the first President Bush was forced to raise taxes, though he vetoed a congressional plan to ease unemployment.[41] In 1992, Bush lost to Clinton, who rode a fall in energy prices, and the rise of information technology, back towards abundance. Although Clinton spent much of the windfall paying down the deficit, he managed to revive the "animal spirits"[42] of capitalism—and unemployment fell again.

One of the ways Clinton stimulated the economy was by allowing financial deregulation, begun under Reagan, to gather pace. He allowed Depression-era banking regulations to be rolled back. Before long, the U.S. economy experienced something called "financialization"[43]—where making money from finance and speculation becomes easier than making money from making "stuff." Keynes and Kalecki didn't touch on this in their essays. They never imagined that workers would be drawn into a debt spiral—along with the rest of the economy. But, through the 1990s and beyond, that's what happened.

In June 2001, the hot money that had poured into tech stocks took fright, and the Dotcom bubble popped. Then came 9/11. Recession followed and President George W. Bush, reprising the Reagan playbook, cut taxes. This time there *was* war—against Afghanistan, then Iraq. When the credit juggernaut crashed in 2008 and the Global Financial Crisis hit, 'W' bailed out banks and some big corporations, but not workers or small businesses. Then, Obama and Congress borrowed and spent, as Kalecki and Keynes would have expected, in an attempt to revive the economy and lower unemployment.

The expansion of credit begun in the nineties had enabled workers to cushion the effects of lower wages. But, as credit got out of hand, American households ran up huge debts to buy bigger TVs, bigger cars, and bigger houses. As Galbraith had warned, escalating and competitive wants took on the urgency once reserved for satisfying needs—and loose credit amplified this.

Despite all the changes since the seventies, two things have remained remarkably constant. The first is real wages (wages adjusted for inflation). After almost doubling from the end of World War II to 1973, real wages for most American workers have flattened or even fallen. Since then, median family income has declined despite an increase in two-earner families.[44] The second constant is working hours. They've hovered around forty hours a week, even though productivity has powered ahead.

Benjamin M. Friedman sums up this period in a 2015 article: "Until the 1970s, Keynes was right on both fronts: per capita output grew at the upper end of the range he predicted, most families' incomes grew even faster (inequality was mostly narrowing during that period), and the workweek continued to decline. But with widening inequality from the early 1970s on, the growth of most families' incomes became far slower than he had predicted, and the workweek stopped declining. The latter combination has persisted ever since."[45] Friedman is not quite right about working hours. In fact, the workweek hasn't declined appreciably since the end of World War II. It's been around forty hours a week for the past seventy years.[46]

In the wake of the Global Financial Crisis, when wages, jobs, and credit all dived at once, American workers wondered what hit them. Slowly, they began to realize that special interests had quietly captured both political parties. Through more than forty years of good economic times and bad, their wages and benefits had been kept low, unions had been neutralized, welfare spending had been rationed, and they'd been fed a growing diet of credit. They directed their wrath not so much at the employers and capitalists who'd engineered this but more at the politicians who'd allowed it to happen. For those same forty years, other forces had also been working against their interests in ways that angered them too.

The growth of international trade in the post-War era exposed American manufacturers and service providers to more intense foreign competition, so when the post-War boom ended, they responded by "offshoring" manufacturing jobs to low-wage countries. Then, with advances in information technology, this expanded to include service jobs—and not just low-paid jobs. At home, immigrants, many of them illegal, were always readily available to do unskilled work. This was work that many Americans might not have wished to do. Even so, it became less available to them. And the presence of a large immigrant workforce weakened unions and kept wage demands modest.

Most important of all was the accelerating pace of technological unemployment. "This means unemployment due to our discovery of means of economizing the use of labour outrunning the pace at which we can find new uses for labour."[47] That's how Keynes defined it in his 1930 essay. He dismissed it as "a temporary phase of maladjustment"[48] that would be corrected with shorter working hours as soon as the coming abundance allowed. Here again, Keynes was too optimistic. As Freidman notes, since the Industrial Revolution, Western economies have been pretty good at creating new jobs to replace those that became obsolete. Yet he thinks this may not continue for much longer. He sees it as increasingly likely that laborsaving technologies, like driverless trucks, robots, and voice recognition systems, will outrun the supply of new jobs in America.[49]

By 2016, all of this meant that there was some logic to electing a businessman to try to fix things. Donald Trump was elected President to make America run like a successful corporation—and to bring back well-paid jobs. It's not something he can do. Trump is unable to grasp that the jobs American employers sent abroad aren't coming back. He refuses to accept that technological unemployment is, by far, the biggest problem—a problem he can only fix if he spends money on education and training. And he has employed enough immigrants himself to know that most of them fill jobs that Americans don't want. Rolling back global trade and kicking out immigrants isn't going to help.

Trump says he wants to build new infrastructure. That's a great idea: renewing public infrastructure would create needed jobs. If they were still around, Keynes and Kalecki would approve. Having cut taxes for corporations and the rich, Trump would need to finance new infrastructure with government debt.[50] But he has less room to do this because he financed his tax giveaways with debt. Lately, he seems to prefer spending on defense to spending on infrastructure. So, once again, Kalecki's darker vision looms.

Trump nurtures an idea of himself as the messianic leader of a nationalistic "corporatist state"—much as Benito Mussolini did. The two men are similar—except that one concocted an almost academically pedantic ideology[51]—the other can't spell ideology.

In 1930, Keynes saw the good life on the horizon—material sufficiency, knowledge and wisdom, and the leisure to enjoy them. As this utopia approached, work and capital would slow down in unison. In 1943, Kalecki thought labor would keep up its struggle with capital—neither would be strong enough to win—so, unless there was war, they'd be forced to compromise. In 1958, Galbraith thought we'd detoured past the good life, with production driving consumption in escalating cycles of creating and satisfying new wants. In the 1970s, the "affluent society" began to give way to the "affluent minority." Through it all, the "armaments economy" that Kalecki feared continued to grow, aligning the state with capital and marginalizing labor.

Keynes might have been right about the working week after all. In 2030, it might be fifteen hours—not because workers are enjoying the good life by then, but because they're not. He might have been wrong instead about technological unemployment. It might not be a "temporary maladjustment." Instead, jobs might be temporary—and scarce.

---

[1] Genesis – New Living Translation

[2] The "Out of Africa" migration was probably 60,000 to 80,000 years ago. See: Michael Gross, "The Complicated Origins Of Our Species," *Current Biology* 24, No. 8 (April 2014), available at *Science Direct*, http://www.sciencedirect.com/science/article/pii/S096098221400390X. Recent evidence suggests that periodic migrations may have been occurring as long ago as 200,000 years; see Hannah Devlin, "Oldest Known Human Fossil outside of Africa Discovered in Israel," *Guardian*, January 26, 2018, https://www.theguardian.com/science/2018/jan/25/oldest-known-human-fossil-outside-africa-discovered-in-israel. Agriculture began much later, probably about 10,000 years ago: Farnaz Broushaki et al., "Early Neolithic Genomes from the Eastern Fertile Crescent," *Science* 10.1126/science.aaf7943 (2016), http://science.sciencemag.org/content/early/2016/07/13/science.aaf7943.full.

[3] See: Dora Jane Hamblin, "Has the Garden of Eden Been Located at Last?" *Smithsonian Magazine* 18, No. 2 (May 1987).

[4] Marshall Sahlins, *Stone Age Economics* (Aldine Atherton, Inc., 1972), Chapter 1 "The Original Affluent Society."

[5] Galbraith, *The Affluent Society.*

[6] "Scarcity Principle," *Investopedia,* https://www.investopedia.com/terms/s/scarcity-principle.asp.

[7] Sahlins, *Stone Age Economics*, 14 including a quote from Martin Gusinde, *The Yamana: The Life and Thought of the Water Nomads of Cape Horn* (New Haven, Conn: Human Relations Area Files, 1961), 1.

[8] This is an expression mainly used by Australian aboriginals. It means any non-aboriginals, regardless of gender. Aboriginals sometimes call themselves "blackfellas." Neither term is meant to be disparaging. J. Stensrude, *A Dictionary of Ozian Terminology,* n.d. – "Ozian" is slang for "Australian" (from "Oz," slang for "Australia") http://www.stensrude.com/Oz.html#whitefella.

[9] Although widely quoted and attributed to Carnegie, it is hard to find the source of this quote. Carnegie did write something similar in his June 1889 article "Wealth" (more commonly called "The Gospel of Wealth") originally published in the *North American Review*: "What were the luxuries have become the necessities of life." See: Andrew Carnegie, "The Gospel of Wealth," Carnegie Corporation of New York, 2017, https://www.carnegie.org/media/filer_public/0a/e1/0ae166c5-fca3-4adf-82a7-74c0534cd8de/gospel_of_wealth_2017.pdf.

[10] Thorstein Veblen, *The Theory of the Leisure Class: An Economic Study in the Evolution of Institutions* (1899, Project Gutenberg, 2008), Chapter 4 "Conspicuous Consumption," http://www.gutenberg.org/ebooks/833.

[11] Holcomb B. Noble and Douglas Martin, "John Kenneth Galbraith, 97, Dies; Economist Held a Mirror to Society," *New York Times*, April 30, 2016, http://www.nytimes.com/2006/04/30/obituaries/30galbraith.html.

[12] Keynes, "Economic Possibilities."

[13] "Three-hour shifts or a fifteen-hour week may put off the problem for a great while. For three hours a day is quite enough to satisfy the old Adam in most of us!": Keynes, "Economic Possibilities."

[14] Robert Skidelsky and Edward Skidelsky, *How Much is Enough? Money and the Good Life* (New York: Other Press, 2012), 19.

[15] Robert Whaples, "Hours of Work in U.S. History," *EH.net*, n.d., https://eh.net/encyclopedia/hours-of-work-in-u-s-history/.

[16] Robert Whaples PhD is a professor of economics at Wake Forest University at Winston-Salem, North Carolina.

[17] Robert Whaples, "The Shortening of the American Work Week: An Economic and Historical Analysis of its Context, Causes, and Consequences,"(Ph.D. dissertation, University of Pennsylvania, 1990), 76 quoting Benjamin Kline Hunnicutt, *Work Without End: Abandoning Shorter Hours for the Right to Work* (Philadelphia, PA: Temple University Press, 1988).

[18] Whaples, "The Shortening of the American Work Week," 77-80.

[19] Whaples, "The Shortening of the American Work Week," 80 quoting from Benjamin Klein Hunnicutt, "The New Deal and the End of Shorter Hours," (paper presented at the Social Science History Association meetings, 1988).

[20] Whaples, "The Shortening of the American Work Week," 82.

[21] Michał Kalecki, "Political Aspects of Full Employment," *Political Quarterly* 14, No. 4 (October 1943), 322-31.

[22] Wolfgang Streeck, Patrick Camiller, trans. and David Fernbach, trans., *Buying Time: The Delayed Crisis of Democratic Capitalism,* (London: Verso, 2ed, 2017), 46.

[23] Kalecki, "Political Aspects," 329.

[24] Kalecki, "Political Aspects," 331.

[25] (1) February to October 1945, (2) November 1948 to October 1949, (3) July 1953 to May 1954, (4) August 1957 to April 1958, (5) April 1960 to February 1961, and (6) December 1969 to November 1970: "List of recessions in the United States," *Wikipedia* https://en.wikipedia.org/wiki/List_of_recessions_in_the_United_States.

[26] Allan H. Meltzer, "Origins of the Great Inflation," *Federal Reserve Bank of St. Louis Review* 87, No. 2, part 2 (March/April 2005): 145-75, https://files.stlouisfed.org/files/htdocs/publications/review/05/03/part2/Meltzer.pdf.

[27] Alan S. Blinder and Jeremy B. Rudd, "The Supply-Shock Explanation of the Great Stagflation Revisited," National Bureau of Economic Research, Working Paper 14563 (December 2008), http://www.nber.org/papers/w14563.pdf.

At a seminar called by Gerald Ford in 1974, Professor Paul Samuelson is said to have coined the expression "stagflation" to describe "a period of rising unemployment and inflation." However, Iain Macleod, a British Conservative Party politician, who became Chancellor of the Exchequer in 1970, had used it in his writing in 1965: *Merriam-Webster Dictionary*, s.v. "stagflation," https://www.merriam-webster.com.

[28] Paul Stevens, "Bretton Woods: 1944-1971," *Foundation for Economic Education*, May 1, 1973, https://fee.org/articles/bretton-woods-1944-1971/.

[29] Stevens, "Bretton Woods."

[30] David B. Sicilia, "A Brief History of U.S. Unemployment," *Washington Post*, n.d., http://www.washingtonpost.com/wp-srv/special/business/us-unemployment-rate-history/.

[31] John Maynard Keynes, *The General Theory of Employment, Interest and Money* (New York: Harcourt, Brace and Company, 1936). According to Joan Robinson, Kalecki had anticipated Keynes' theory, but abandoned his own manuscript when he read Keynes' book: Joan Robinson, "Michal Kalecki: A Neglected Prophet," *New York Review of Books* 23, No. 3 (March 1976), http://www.nybooks.com/articles/1976/03/04/michal-kalecki-a-neglected-prophet/.

[32] Kalecki, "Political Aspects," 327.

[33] Kalecki, " Political Aspects," 327.

[34] Michał Kalecki, Jerzy Osiatyński, Ed., and Chester Adam Kisiel, trans., *Collected Works of Michal Kalecki: Volume I Capitalism: Business Cycles and Full Employment* (Oxford: Clarendon Press, 1990), 573-4 quoting Michał Kalecki, *Szkice o Funkcjonowaniu Wspolczesnego Kapitalizmu* (Warszawa: Panstwowe Wydawnictwo Nauk, 1962), 7-8.

[35] Kalecki died in 1970.

[36] John Swift, "The Soviet-American Arms Race," *History Review* Issue 63 (March 2009), http://www.historytoday.com/john-swift/soviet-american-arms-race.

[37] On December 25, 1991, Mikhail Gorbachev resigned, marking the official end of the Soviet Union: Michael Dobbs, "Gorbachev Resignation Ends Soviet Era," *Washington Post,* December 26, 1991, https://www.washingtonpost.com/archive/politics/1991/12/26/gorbachev-resignation-ends-soviet-era/00444c16-0fe3-4b35-96df-e514956ee354/?utm_term=.2209167221d0.

[38] "They Pretend to Pay Us, We Pretend to Work," *Economist*, August 26, 1999, http://www.economist.com/node/234594. It is sometimes expressed: "We pretend to work and they pretend to pay us"; see, for example, Yoani Sanchez, "As They Used to Say in the USSR: We Pretend to Work and They Pretend to Pay Us," *Huffington Post*, n.d., https://www.huffingtonpost.com/yoani-sanchez/as-they-used-to-say-in-th_b_564573.html.

[39] Sicilia, "A brief history."

[40] *The Free Dictionary by Farlex*, s.v. "voodoo economics," https://www.thefreedictionary.com/Voodoo+economics.

[41] David E. Rosenbaum, "The 1992 Campaign: Candidates' Records; Bush and Congress: Rising Feud Produced a Legislative Deadlock," *New York Times*, August 9, 1992, http://www.nytimes.com/1992/08/09/us/1992-campaign-candidates-records-bush-congress-rising-feud-produced-legislative.html?pagewanted=all.

[42] John Maynard Keynes coined this expression: "Animal Spirits," *Investopedia*, https://www.investopedia.com/terms/a/animal-spirits.asp.

[43] "Financialization," *Investopedia*, https://www.investopedia.com/terms/f/financialization.asp.

[44] Benjamin M. Friedman, "Work and Consumption in an Era of Unbalanced Technological Advance," *Journal of Evolutionary Economics* 27, No. 2 (2017), first published online by Springer-Verlag on November 9, 2015.

[45] Friedman, "Work and Consumption," 230.

[46] Whaples, "Historical Working Hours."

[47] Keynes, "Economic Possibilities."

[48] Keynes, "Economic Possibilities."

[49] Friedman, "Work and Consumption," 232.

[50] *Tax Cuts and Jobs Act* 2017, https://www.congress.gov/bill/115th-congress/house-bill/1/text; Heather Long, "The Senate Just Passed a Massive Tax Bill. Here's What Is in It," *Washington Post*, November 30, 2017, https://www.washingtonpost.com/news/wonk/wp/2017/11/30/what-is-in-the-senates-massive-tax-bill-and-what-could-change/?utm_term=.00fa85a0b714.

[51] See: Benito Mussolini and Giovanni Gentile, "The Doctrine of Fascism" (1932), available at World Future Fund, http://www.worldfuturefund.org/wffmaster/Reading/Germany/mussolini.htm.

Chapter 6

ABOUT MARKETS:

The Invisible Snafu

In July 1790, a mildly eccentric bachelor of modest means died in Edinburgh at the age of sixty-seven after a long illness. Obituaries in the local newspapers were short. They contained few personal details beyond the curious anecdote that, as a child, he'd once been kidnapped by gypsies.[1] Yet, he died a prominent academic, a philosopher of the Scottish Enlightenment, and the author of two important books, one of them a bestseller.[2] His books were long, and just once in each of them, he used a fairly common literary metaphor. We know this because his second book, the bestseller, went on to become a classic in its field. Like the Bible, it's often quoted though seldom read. And the metaphor he used? Well, it became a legend.

The man was Adam Smith, the bestseller was *An Inquiry into the Nature and Causes of the Wealth of Nations*, his field was Political Philosophy (but sometime after his death, it became Economics), and the metaphor was—"an invisible hand."[3]

No one paid much attention to Smith's use of the "invisible hand" metaphor until 172 years later, when the passage from the *Wealth of Nations* that contained it was quoted in another bestseller. This was a textbook called *Economics*, by Paul Samuelson, then a young professor at MIT.[4] First published in 1948, it too became a classic, and it made Samuelson a millionaire. Over the next sixty years, it went through nineteen editions, sold more than four million copies, and was translated into forty-one languages.[5] It may be the most influential Economics textbook of all time, and it did much to elevate Smith's metaphor to its mystical status in the mid-20th century and beyond.

It wasn't just Samuelson's textbook. When the ideas of John Maynard Keynes lost traction with the onset of stagflation in the 1970s, the metaphor soon became a mantra for his detractors. Keynes, whose theories dominated economic thought after World War II, believed that government regulation and investment had important roles to play in smoothing business cycles. But, when government spending in the U.S and the U.K. produced the "impossible" combination of low growth, high unemployment, and high inflation (stagflation),[6] Keynes's time was up. Into his place stepped Milton Friedman, a professor of economics at the University of Chicago. Friedman vehemently opposed government meddling in markets. "If you put the federal government in charge of the Sahara Desert, in five years there'd be a shortage of sand."[7] Friedman's pro-market-anti-government message resonated with Margaret Thatcher, who became U.K. Prime Minister in 1979, and Ronald Reagan, who became President in 1981. They cut or outsourced government services, privatized state assets, slashed regulations, smashed unions, and cut taxes on corporations and the rich, all in the name of setting markets free.

Today, "invisible hand" is liturgical shorthand for the central article of faith of a secular religion that doesn't have a name, because its priesthood consists of factional groups of economists who go by various names: "Austrian School," "Chicago School," "Laissez Faire," "Neoclassical," "Neoliberal," "Free Market," and "Market Fundamentalist." In order to make things simple, let's call them "the Invisibles." The Invisibles disagree among themselves about some things, but they all agree that an invisible hand guides markets. Their main dogma is simple—if markets are allowed to be free, they will regulate themselves and achieve equilibrium.

What's a market anyway?

A market is a system for making commercial exchanges. It's a catchall name for everything that goes into buying and selling, or lending and borrowing. It includes the things people do, the systems they use, the procedures they follow, and the data they create in making the exchanges. The exchanges can be about goods, services, securities, rights—or pretty much anything of value. They almost always involve money. But a market may involve exchanging anything of value for anything else of value. Of course, "market" can refer to a place where exchanges are made, but often there is no market "place." While some exchanges are made face-to-face, many more are made electronically or by phone, by fax, or by means of legal documents. For economists, it's not so important where exchanges are made. For them, the stock market, for example, is not the building at 11, Wall Street in Manhattan. It's the collective activity of trading stocks, bonds, and other securities. The people at 11, Wall Street do this using computers and fast telecom connections. There are other people and other computers in other buildings across the United States and across the world, and they're on the other side of billions of trades. The term "stock market" describes all of them, all the trades they make, and all the data they produce.

There are all kinds of markets for all kinds of things. Whenever you buy a tee shirt using your credit card, you make trades in two markets—a retail clothing market and a consumer credit market. You buy the tee shirt from a store that is itself a market. It's also part of a constellation of citywide, statewide, nationwide, and worldwide retail clothing markets. You pay for the tee shirt with a card that involves you, the store, your bank, and a credit-card company—all making trades in a local consumer credit market. That market is part of a network of consumer credit markets that span the country and the world.

The tee shirt is the finished product of trades in many markets. It started out as raw cotton at a farm in Mississippi. Before the cotton was even harvested, a trader at an investment bank in New York bought it on the commodities futures market. Later, he sold it on the wholesale cotton market to a mill in Indonesia. To pay for the cotton, the mill borrowed from a syndicate of banks in the international trade finance market. It exchanged Indonesian rupiah for U.S. dollars on the foreign exchange market. Then it hired a Scandinavian company in the international shipping market to ship the cotton. At the same time, it bought insurance in the London insurance market to cover the risk that the cotton would be lost or damaged while in transit. When the cotton reached Indonesia, the mill wove it into fabric using German machinery it bought in the international machine-tools market. It hired its workers in the local labor market and bought water and electricity in regional utilities markets. Later, the Indonesian mill shipped cotton fabric to a clothing workshop in Bangladesh. The Bangladeshi workshop bought Chinese dyes in the wholesale chemicals market. Then, it dyed the yarn and made it into a tee shirt. And so on… until the tee shirt reached the store you bought it from.

Making, delivering and selling your tee shirt may have involved anywhere from twenty to fifty different markets across the world. When you're done with it, you might sell it in a secondhand clothing market, though it's more likely to end up in a landfill as part of the vast market for waste. Every year, Americans buy an average of sixty-four items of clothing,[8] and they throw away about eighty-one pounds of clothing they've accumulated over a longer period.[9]

How do you make markets free?

According to the Invisibles, you just stop governments from interfering with them. Even if government intentions are good, their regulations never are. So, they should leave markets to regulate themselves. Smith was not the first thinker to extol the virtues of markets and to decry government interference. But Samuelson's textbook put Smith in the right place at the right time to play the role of Moses for the Invisibles. In the latter part of the 20th century, the Invisibles needed a prophet to overshadow Keynes.

Smith died a year into the French Revolution—a year into the period of 125 years that started with that revolution and ended with the start of World War I in 1914. Some historians call this period the "Long Nineteenth Century."[10] It was part of the opening phase of the most transformative period in human history. And, of all the changes that happened during the Long Nineteenth Century, the most profound were the economic changes that took place in Europe, especially in Britain. Barry Buzan and George Lawson, academics at the London School of Economics, capture the scale of the changes: "Whereas in 1700, Asian powers produced 61.7% of the world's GDP, and Europe and its offshoots only 31.3%; by 1913, Europeans held 68.3% of global GDP and Asia only 24.5%. In 1890, Britain alone was responsible for 20% of the world's industrial output and, by 1900, it produced a quarter of the world's fuel energy output."[11] So, an economic theory was needed to explain all of this.

In the *Wealth of Nations*, Smith anticipated some aspects of this transformation. He lived through the early part of the Industrial Revolution, which began in Britain around 1750.[12] His key insight was that the true source of a nation's wealth lay in making work more productive by promoting the division of labor and the use of machinery and capital. He thought that, in an ideal competitive economy, both parties should benefit from every exchange. And, given the freedom to choose, market participants would only make the exchanges they got the most benefit from. Smith assumed that, if there were no barriers to competition, the mechanism of exchange would lead to an allocation of land, labor, and capital—the "factors of production" (as they would later be called)—in proportion to their productive contributions. His ideas about free and rational exchanges in competitive markets anticipated the "*liberté*" and "*égalité*" of the coming French Revolution, and the triumph of reason over religion.[13]

Here was a man ahead of his time. Not only did he foresee the centrality of markets but he also wrote their first commandments: thou shalt be free, thou shalt be competitive. As markets require mutual benefits, parties should pursue self-interest and maximize their gains. This was not only rational, it was good for markets, and what was good for markets was good for society. For the Invisibles, this made Smith the father of their dualistic creed of the free, self-regulating market and the new "economic man" (*homo economicus*)—a rational, selfish specimen whose purpose was to maximize his gains.

But there were a couple of tiny problems with Smith's reimagined role as "market Moses."

Smith had no general theory of markets beyond his belief that they were vital to the economy and required freedom and competition. He didn't say that markets regulate themselves. Even the passage in the *Wealth of Nations* that contains the invisible hand metaphor proved a little inconvenient for the Invisibles. It's embedded in an argument against mercantilism, which was the dominant school of European economic thought in Smith's time. According to mercantilism, the wealth of a nation is best improved by making few imports and many exports as a means of increasing its stock of gold. The metaphor appears as part of Smith's demolition of mercantilism. The context is that of an entrepreneur who trades in domestic industry instead of export: "By preferring the support of domestic to that of foreign industry, he intends only his own security; and by directing that industry in such a manner as its produce may be of the greatest value, he intends only his own gain; and he is in this, as in many other cases, led by an invisible hand to promote an end which was no part of his intention. Nor is it always the worse for the society that it was no part of it."[14]

All Smith said was that sometimes the pursuit of narrow self-interest in market transactions can benefit society in unintended ways. It's a long way from there to the self-regulating free market of the Invisibles. Never mind, they said, Smith was definitely a free-market guy, so he's our guru.

The second problem for the Invisibles was Smith's first book, *The Theory of Moral Sentiments*, published seven years earlier in 1759. It should be read in conjunction with the *Wealth of Nations*. Together they run to over 1,400 pages, so maybe the Invisibles balked at this.[15] The main idea of *Moral Sentiments* is, perhaps, best summarized in this passage: "And hence it is, that to feel much for others and little for ourselves, that to restrain our selfish, and to indulge our benevolent affections, constitutes the perfection of human nature; and can alone produce among mankind that harmony of sentiments and passions in which consists their whole grace and propriety."[16]

There goes "economic man." Sure, Smith believed that there are times when we need to be self-interested, but he was clear that selfishness should not be our guiding principle. P.J. O'Rourke, who did take the time to read both books, summarizes Smith's philosophy this way: "Smith set out to discern how systems of morality, economics, and government arise and how, by comprehending the way these systems work, people could better their ethical, material, and political conditions."[17] The biblical Moses recognized that you can wander around for a long time with reams of scripture, but if you really want to focus the minds of your followers, you need to go up a mountain and come back down with just a few simple rules. So, the Invisibles followed his lead. They ignored Smith's first book entirely, chose a few passages from the *Wealth of Nations*, carved them on a stone tablet marked "invisible hand," and anointed Smith as their lawgiver. Amen.

The Long Nineteenth Century brought changes beyond anything Smith could have foreseen. In the "dark satanic mills"[18] of the Industrial Revolution, the uses of capital and the division of labor unfolded in ways he'd never imagined. For Smith and his immediate successors, Thomas Malthus and David Ricardo, production was about ending scarcity. According to Smith: "Consumption is the sole end and purpose of all production; and the interest of the producer ought to be attended to, only so far as it may be necessary for promoting that of the consumer."[19]

Before long, production left scarcity behind. Coal and steam gave way to petroleum and electricity. The telegraph gave way to the telephone. And there were advances in steel, machine tools, chemicals, and munitions. "By the end of the 19th century, four states (Britain, France, Germany, and the United States) provided two-thirds of the world's industrial production. And one of these powers, Britain, became the first global superpower, counting a quarter of the world's inhabitants as its subjects, while claiming a similar proportion of its territory."[20] For these countries, this was the golden age of "capitalism," "a word and a phenomenon neither used by, nor known to, Adam Smith."[21] Capitalism changed the goal of production from the elimination of scarcity to the accumulation of surpluses. New needs had to be found—new scarcities created—new markets opened up. Helpfully, these countries ruled much of the world. They ran their colonies as part of a global market system, though they weren't too keen on competition. Meanwhile, America bought or fought its way to fifty states, almost destroyed itself in the Civil War—a conflict over the infamous market for human beings—but recovered strongly after 1865, when the war ended. By the end of the Long Nineteenth Century, the U.S. was poised to take over Britain's role as the global superpower.

The other imperative for producers was to hold down the costs of production. Labor was the highest cost. Smith made two implicit assumptions about labor. First, the exchange of work for wages would be made in a free market. Second, labor would receive its proportionate share of the fruits of production.[22] Both these assumptions turned out to be wrong. The division of labor multiplied production but it commoditized work. Many skilled artisans were replaced by unskilled factory workers whose output was not a product but a series of repetitive tasks that could be performed by a child—and frequently were. Labor became no different from any other commodity in the production process and, like any other commodity, it had to be cheap so that the rational, self-interested producer could maximize his gains. Nor was there a level playing field in the labor market (until the advent of labor unions) because labor was abundant. With the Industrial Revolution came a demographic transition that saw accelerating rates of population growth across the newly industrialized states. The population of Europe increased from about 125 million in 1750 to over 500 million in 1914.[23] In the same period, the United States grew from less than four million to almost a hundred million.[24] The commercialization of agriculture dislocated farm workers. "Those forced off the land usually moved to cities, which expanded quickly as a result: between 1800 and 1900, London grew from just over one million to 6.5 million inhabitants, the population of Berlin rose by 1000% and that of New York by 500%."[25]

The rapid transition to an industrialized market economy was like a force of nature. It was almost as though an accelerated version of Charles Darwin's new theory of evolution in the *Origin of Species* (1859) and the *Descent of Man* (1871) had been applied to the economy.[26] Unlike Smith and the other moral philosophers of his generation, "the liberal economists of the nineteenth century took for granted the existence of an economic sphere which was controlled by natural laws and, therefore, free of the jurisdiction of the state."[27] These economists were the first Invisibles. They believed fervently in these natural laws, with the result that, "never before in human history had the idea prevailed that human destiny depends on economic laws detached from any moral and ethical consideration."[28] The Invisibles were right. These economic laws were, in fact, a "force of nature"— human nature—in its most venal aspect.

At first, there was little political opposition to the idea of the economy as a force of nature. Ordinary people didn't immediately look to governments for help. The state was not a significant economic player. No one held it responsible for the industrialized market economy, nor for the recessions, unemployment, and poverty that were its byproducts. But, as the ranks of the "tired," "poor," and "huddled masses"[29] grew, movements for greater democracy and social welfare began to emerge and gather momentum, led mainly by organized labor. [30]

The Long Nineteenth Century might not have been so transformative had it not been for the balance of power that kept Europe at peace for an unusually long time. In 1914, that balance of power fell apart. By then, the duties of government had begun to include responsibility for the well-being of citizens and for the management of business cycles. With World War I, the role of government began to expand. For the next thirty-one years, war was the main event, leading governments to ramp up their stewardship of the economy. This 20th century transition was "captured in Roosevelt's definition of the New Deal: 'plain English for a changed concept of the duty and responsibility of government toward economic life.'"[31]

With the end of World War II came a boom that lasted just long enough to fund President Johnson's "Great Society"—the most comprehensive reform agenda since the "New Deal," and one that seemed to promise a historic compromise between capital and labor.[32] For a time, it looked as though full production, full employment, and a social safety net could coexist. But the boom ended with the 1960s, and the economic theories of John Maynard Keynes that underpinned the Great Society got caught in the crossfire.

This gave Milton Friedman an opening to revive the old-time religion of the free market. He had no theory for the resurrection of the invisible hand other than the supposed impossibility of a government-planned economy. It was more of a political conviction, shared by many at the time, that government had become too big too fast, interfered too much with personal freedom, and should leave the economy to the markets—as "nature" intended. Friedman was single-minded about this. As Paul Krugman explains: "In the decades ahead, this single-mindedness would become Friedman's trademark. Again and again, he called for market solutions to problems—education, health care, the illegal drug trade—that almost everyone else thought required extensive government intervention. Some of his ideas have received widespread acceptance, like replacing rigid rules on pollution with a system of pollution permits that companies are free to buy and sell. Some, like school vouchers, are broadly supported by the conservative movement but haven't gotten far politically. And some of his proposals, like eliminating licensing procedures for doctors and abolishing the Food and Drug Administration, are considered outlandish even by most conservatives."[33] In the eighties, Thatcher and Reagan rode into battle as Friedman's crusaders, trampling the remnants of the Keynesian "heresy."

On the whole, the return to market fundamentalism has been a resounding failure. For example, liberating financial markets almost blew up the world in 2008. Even Friedman's devoted acolyte, Alan Greenspan, had to admit that "those of us who have looked to the self-interest of lending institutions to protect shareholders' equity, myself included, are in a state of shocked disbelief."[34] For a time, governments even had to dust off the Keynesian bible on how to borrow and spend your way out of a slump. In the U.K. they had to nationalize several big banks.[35]

There's a reason Freidman and the other Invisibles failed to offer a convincing theory of the invisible hand—there just isn't one. In his 1944 book *The Great Transformation*, Karl Polanyi, a Hungarian-American economist, historian, and anthropologist, demolished the idea that markets are natural, somehow existing outside society.[36] He showed that markets are man-made—deeply embedded within society, governed by its laws and customs, subject to its political preferences, and moderated by its cultural norms.

When Friedman's born-again Invisibles talked about deregulating markets to make them free, what they really meant was reregulating them to make them free for those with the political power to ensure that their rational self-interest prevailed over everyone else's. Once again, the financial markets provide an example. At the time of writing, the Federal Funds Rate, the overnight lending rate between creditworthy banks, is 1.25 percent.[37] But, if you want a hundred-dollar payday loan, this is how the Consumer Federation of America describes the deal: "The average loan term is about two weeks. Loans typically cost 400% annual interest (APR)[38] or more. The finance charge ranges from $15 to $30 to borrow $100. For two-week loans, these finance charges result in interest rates from 390 to 780% APR. Shorter term loans have even higher APRs."[39] Not so long ago, only the mafia charged that kind of interest because usury was a crime. The invisible hand of nature didn't change this. It was the visible hand of the finance lobby.

Smith himself was well aware of the dirty hands that distort markets. "People of the same trade seldom meet together, even for merriment and diversion, but the conversation ends in a conspiracy against the public, or in some contrivance to raise prices."[40] He wrote this in a passage in the *Wealth of Nations* that the Invisibles didn't include in their stone tablet.

Friedman had a completely different approach to competition. He thought that, rather than foster markets with enough producers to keep each other honest, anti-trust laws should instead promote market efficiency. As long as producers kept prices low, it didn't matter how few of them there were—cartels and monopolies should be allowed. Was he right?

Let's say the last tee shirt you bought was from Walmart. It was certainly cheap. But the lady at the checkout worked part-time. She made ten bucks an hour and had no health insurance.[41] The trucker who shipped it from the port is probably bankrupt now.[42] The business community that was thriving when the store first opened is a shadow of what it used to be.[43] Among suppliers to Walmart there's a saying: "There's only one thing worse than not doing business with Walmart, and that's doing business with Walmart."[44] Meanwhile, in Bangladesh, the kid who sewed your tee shirt is working in a different factory now. She's making sixty-eight bucks a month.[45] Toxic dyes pollute her drinking water. As she toils more than seventy hours a week in hot, cramped conditions, she worries that the shoddy factory she works in might collapse or burn down.[46] Yes, that's market efficiency—and, no, that's not what Smith had in mind.

Under the Friedman doctrine, cartels and monopolies were tolerated. The result was as Smith would have expected. "In 2016, The Economist published three cover stories on America's monopoly problem. The magazine reported that two-thirds of all corporate sectors have become more concentrated since the 1990s, that corporations are far more profitable now than at any time since the 1920s, and that an inordinate amount of profit goes to a very few immense investment funds, such as BlackRock and State Street. In April, the White House Council of Economic Advisers came to much the same conclusion, and called for a 'robust reaction to market power abuses.'"[47] Instead of a 'robust reaction,' there's been robust political support.

Concentrations of market power drive inequality, which

is now greater than at any time since the 1960s—perhaps, since 1928.[48] This is not just the result of a perverse notion of competition, or the pretense that lopsided markets are somehow efficient. The Invisibles have managed to deify the economy itself—to put it above social concerns such as inequality.

In *The Great Transformation*, Polanyi, looking back at the theology of the 19th-century Invisibles, warned against the "economistic fallacy"—the idea that markets are not only separate from society, but that society should serve the needs of markets. Fred Block and Margaret Somers summarize Polanyi's thesis in their 2014 book *The Power of Market Fundamentalism*: "His view is that Western societies are as much shaped by culture as are tribal societies; it is just that the content of our cultural beliefs now reflect the core ideas of Western liberalism—belief in the sovereignty of the self-interested, materially-motivated individual, and the sacred status we effectively attribute to a rapidly developing economy. Just like any tribal individual who finds it difficult to think outside of the framework provided by his or her own culture, we are ourselves prisoners of modernity's culture of the market's natural inviolability. The consequence is that we understand ourselves and our social relationships in ways that are radically incomplete."[49]

This goes some way towards explaining why today's Invisibles cling to their warped creed. They too are prisoners of the market culture that never really died despite the "Reformation" that Keynes and others led. Some of today's Invisibles understand the weakness of their dogma. They are the pious hypocrites, captured by special interests, who preach the sermons that suit those interests. Others enjoy wielding the power our culture bestows on economists. Although Samuelson wasn't a true Invisible, he once said: "I don't care who writes a nation's laws—or crafts its advanced treaties—if I can write its economics textbooks."[50] He was joking, but only a little. Like the diehard Invisibles, he wanted his to be the hand that wrote the economic scriptures. But most Invisibles are neither hypocritical nor messianic— just faithful disciples, schooled in the teachings of their "church," and unwilling to look beyond them.

Polanyi recognized back in 1944, that the "economistic fallacy" had already permeated the West. Although he could not have foreseen the integration of the Soviet Bloc and China into global markets, nor how readily they would drink the Kool-Aid and embrace deregulation, privatization, and their own versions of market capitalism, he knew that no country could eradicate the fallacy single-handedly. He was also right that it couldn't be left to politicians. "Polanyi recognized that democratic institutions are inherently imperfect; voters will periodically elect people who promise things that are neither possible nor desirable."[51] Does that remind you of anyone? But he thought that the solution to this problem "is more democracy, not less."[52]

Recently, the new boss of another global religion felt the need to join the debate Polanyi started: "Each meaningful economic decision made in one part of the world has repercussions everywhere else; consequently, no government can act without regard for shared responsibility. Indeed, it is becoming increasingly difficult to find local solutions for enormous global problems which overwhelm local politics with difficulties to resolve. If we really want to achieve a healthy world economy, what is needed at this juncture of history is a more efficient way of interacting which, with due regard for the sovereignty of each nation, ensures the economic well-being of all countries, not just of a few." That was Pope Francis.[53]

It's time to see markets not as hovering on a cloud above society but as "embedded" in a global social system—a system that's complex, adaptive, unpredictable, and definitely not self-regulating—a system in which people are not tokens on a celestial Monopoly board but the essence and purpose of the system itself. The fundamentalism of the Invisibles is destructive. They have become "Inquisitors," taking the fire and sword of the market to education, health care, housing, aged-care, policing, prisons, and even armies. They have led us to commoditize, privatize, and trade practically everything for the profit of a tiny minority at the expense of society. This is not "natural." Nor is it just amoral and asocial—it is immoral and antisocial. It can only lead to an unholy Hobbesian "war of all against all."[54]

---

[1] John Rae, *Life of Adam Smith* (McMillan & Co, 1985), 372.

[2] The books were: (1) Adam Smith, *The Theory Of Moral Sentiments*, (Edinburgh: Alexander Kincaid and J. Bell, 1759) and (2) Adam Smith, *An Inquiry into the Nature and Causes of the Wealth of Nations* (London: W. Strahan and T. Cadell, 1776). *Wealth of Nations* was a "bestseller" before Smith died. The third of Smith's main books, *Essays on Philosophical Subjects*, was published five years after his death (in 1795). A collection of lectures and a collection of essays were also published posthumously.

[3] See: Gavin Kennedy, "Adam Smith and the Invisible Hand: From Metaphor to Myth (June 2007)," *Journal of the American Institute for Economic Research* 6, No 2 (May 2009): 239-63, https://econjwatch.org/file_download/252/2009-05-kennedy-watchpad.pdf?mimetype=pdf.

[4] Paul A. Samuelson, *Economics: An Introductory Analysis* (New York: McGraw Hill Book Company, 1948).

[5] Mark Skousen, "The Perseverance of Paul Samuelson's Economics," *Journal of Economic Perspectives* 11, No. 2 (Spring 1997): 137-152. From 1985 (12th edition) onwards the book has been co-authored by William Nordhaus. The latest edition is the 19th, published in 2008.

[6] At a seminar called by Gerald Ford in 1974, Professor Paul Samuelson is said to have coined the expression "stagflation" to describe "a period of rising unemployment and inflation." However, Iain Macleod, a British Conservative Party politician, who became Chancellor of the Exchequer in 1970, had used it in his writing in 1965: *Merriam-Webster Dictionary*, s.v. "stagflation," https://www.merriam-webster.com. The term generally includes slow growth as well as rising unemployment and high inflation.

[7] Although often attributed to Milton Friedman, he may not have said exactly this. He did write something similar in his Newsweek column on March 10, 1980 and, in 1983, *The Philadelphia Inquirer* printed

remarks from a magazine editor named William Rusher who ascribed to Friedman a saying that was very close. See: "A Shortage of Sand in the Sahara," *Quote Investigator*, https://quoteinvestigator.com/2014/12/09/sand/.

[8] Elizabeth L. Cline, *Overdressed: The Shockingly High Cost of Cheap Fashion* (New York: Penguin Group, 2013), 5.

[9] Eleanor Goldberg, "You're Probably Going To Throw Away 81 Pounds of Clothing This Year: And 95 Percent of It Could Be Reused or Recycled," *Huffington Post* (Australia), September 6, 2016, http://www.huffingtonpost.com.au/entry/youre-likely-going-to-throw-away-81-pounds-of-clothing-this-year_us_57572bc8e4b08f74f6c069d3.

[10] Barry Buzan and George Lawson, "The Global Transformation: The Nineteenth Century and the Making of Modern International Relations," *International Studies Quarterly* 57, No. 3 (October 2013): 620-634, available at LSE Research Online, http://eprints.lse.ac.uk/44894/.

[11] Buzan and Lawson, "The Global Transformation,"12.

[12] Robert. J. Gordon, "Is U.S. Economic Growth Over? Faltering Innovation Confronts the Six Headwinds," National Bureau of Economic Research, Working Paper No.18315 (August 2012), http://www.nber.org/papers/w18315.

[13] The motto of the French Revolution was "Liberté, Égalité, Fraternité," first proclaimed by Maximilien Robespierre in 1790: Maximilien Robespierre, *Oeuvres De Maximilien Robespierre*, (Presses Universitaires De France, 1950), vol. IV, 643.

[14] Smith, *Wealth of Nations*, Book IV, Chapter II, p. 456, paragraph 10.

[15] Smith, *Wealth of Nations*, 960 pages, and Smith, *Theory of Moral Sentiments*, 368 pages—a total of 1,428 pages.

[16] Smith, *Theory of Moral Sentiments*, Part I, Section I, Chapter V, 25, paragraph 5.

[17] P.J. O'Rourke, *On the Wealth of Nations: Books that Changed the World* (Atlantic Monthly Press, Grove/Atlantic, 2007), 28.

[18] William Blake, *Jerusalem*, a poem from the text of the preface Blake wrote for inclusion with *Milton, a Poem*, 1804, printed in 1808, second stanza: "And did the Countenance Divine, / Shine forth upon our

clouded hills? / And was Jerusalem builded here, / Among these dark Satanic Mills?"

[19] Smith, *Wealth of Nations*, Book IV, Chapter VIII, 660, para. 49.

[20] Buzan and Lawson, "The Global Transformation," 3, quoting Saskia Sassen, *Territory, Authority, Rights* (Princeton University Press, 2006), 74.

[21] Gavin Kennedy, "The Origins of the Word 'Capitalism,'" *Adam Smith's Lost Legacy Blog*, January 14, 2009, https://adamsmithslostlegacy.blogspot.com.au/2009/01/free-capitalist-13-january-here-carries.html.

[22] Deborah Boucoyannis, "Contrary to Popular and Academic Belief, Adam Smith Did Not Accept Inequality as a Necessary Trade-Off for a More Prosperous Economy," *British Politics and Policy* (blog), February 18, 2014, http://blogs.lse.ac.uk/politicsandpolicy/adam-smith-and-inequality/

[23] Michael R. Haines, " Population of Europe: The Demographic Transition and After," *Encyclopedia of European Social History*, http://www.encyclopedia.com/international/encyclopedias-almanacs-transcripts-and-maps/population-europe-demographic-transition-and-after.

[24] United States Census Bureau, "Population, Table 4 'Population: 1790 to 1990,'" n.d., https://www.census.gov/population/censusdata/table-4.pdf.

[25] Buzan and Lawson, "The Global Transformation," 18 quoting C.A. Bayly, *The Birth of the Modern World 1780-1914* (Oxford: Blackwell, 2004), 189.

[26] Charles Darwin, *On the Origin of Species* (John Murray, 1859); Charles Darwin, *The Descent of Man, and Selection in Relation to Sex* (John Murray, 1871).

[27] Claus Thomasberger, "Fictitious Ideas, Social Facts and the Double Movement: Polanyi's Framework in the Age of Neoliberalism" (Paper presented at the 13th International Karl Polanyi Conference, "The Enduring Legacy of Karl Polanyi," Concordia University, November 6-8, 2014), 8.

[28] Thomasberger, "Fictitious Ideas," 8.

[29] From Emma Lazarus's poem at the foot of the Statue of Liberty.

[30] See: Giulio M. Gallarotti, "The Advent of the Prosperous Society: The Rise of the Guardian State and Structural Changes in the World Economy," *Review of International Political Economy* 7, No. 1 (Spring, 2000): 1-52; also see Guilio Gallarotti, Profile: http://ggallarotti.faculty.wesleyan.edu.

[31] Gallarotti, "The Advent of the Prosperous Society," 9.

[32] "Evaluating the Success of the Great Society: Lyndon B. Johnson's Visionary Set of Legislation Turns 50," *Washington Post*, May 17, 2014, http://www.washingtonpost.com/wp-srv/special/national/great-society-at-50/.

[33] Paul Krugman, "Who was Milton Friedman?" *New York Review of Books* 54, No. 2 (February 2007) http://www.nybooks.com/articles/2007/02/15/who-was-milton-friedman/.

[34] Edmund L. Andrews, "Greenspan Concedes Error on Regulation," *New York Times*, October 23, 2008, quoting Greenspan, http://www.nytimes.com/2008/10/24/business/economy/24panel.html.

[35] Jane Croft and Kate Burgess, "UK Nationalizes Bradford & Bingley," *Financial Times*, September 29, 2008, https://www.ft.com/content/1e5b888c-8c06-11dd-8a4c-0000779fd18c; Andrew Porter, James Kirkup and Gordon Rayner, "Financial Crisis: HBOS and RBS 'to Be Nationalised' in £50 Billion State Intervention," *Telegraph*, October 12, 2008, http://www.telegraph.co.uk/finance/financialcrisis/3185120/Financial-crisis-HBOS-and-RBS-to-be-nationalised-in-50-billion-state-intervention.html; "The Nationalisation of Northern Rock," House of Commons Public Accounts Committee, June 1, 2009, https://publications.parliament.uk/pa/cm200809/cmselect/cmpubacc/394/394.pdf; "Bailing out Britain's Banks: A Timeline," *Telegraph*, January 19, 2009, http://www.telegraph.co.uk/finance/newsbysector/banksandfinance/4285063/Bail-out-Britains-banks-A-timeline.html.

[36] Karl Polanyi, *The Great Transformation: The Political and Economic Origins of Out Time* (Beacon Press, 1944).

[37] The rate on December 7, 2017: "Federal Funds Data," Federal Reserve Bank on New York, https://apps.newyorkfed.org/markets/autorates/fed%20funds.

[38] APR is the annualized percentage rate of interest: *Investopedia, https://www.investopedia.com/terms/a/apr.asp.*

[39] Consumer Federation of America, "How Payday Loans Work," PayDay Loan Consumer Information, Consumer Federation of America, n.d., http://www.paydayloaninfo.org/facts.

[40] Smith, *Wealth of Nations*, Book I, Chapter X, Part II, paragraph 27.

[41] Jackie Wattles, "Walmart Increasing Wages; Union Says It's All Show," *CNN Money*, January 20, 2016, http://money.cnn.com/2016/01/20/news/companies/walmart-pay-raise-wages/index.html; Hiroko Tabuchi, "Walmart to End Health Coverage for 30,000 Part-Time Workers," *New York Times*, October 7, 2014, https://www.nytimes.com/2014/10/08/business/30000-lose-health-care-coverage-at-walmart.html?_r=0.

[42] Brett Murphy, "Shell Games: How Trucking Companies that Cheat Drivers Dodge Penalties," *USA Today*, October 26, 2017, https://www.usatoday.com/pages/interactives/news/rigged-shell-games-how-trucking-companies-that-cheat-drivers-dodge-penalties/.

[43] Steven Barrison, "Opinion: Study Shows Walmart Kills Small Biz," *New York Daily News*, May 4, 2011, http://www.nydailynews.com/new-york/brooklyn/study-proves-walmart-super-stores-kill-local-small-businesses-article-1.140129.

[44] David Bosshart, *Cheap?: The Real Cost of Living in a Low Price, Low Wage World* (London: Kogan Page, 2006), 68.

[45] Simon Parry, "The True Cost of Your Cheap Clothes: Slave Wages for Bangladeshi Factory Workers," *Post Magazine*, June 11, 2016, http://www.scmp.com/magazines/post-magazine/article/1970431/true-cost-your-cheap-clothes-slave-wages-bangladesh-factory.

[46] Rachel Abrams and Maher Sattar, "Protests in Bangladesh Shake a Global Workshop for Apparel," *New York Times*, January 22, 2017, https://www.nytimes.com/2017/01/22/business/bangladesh-protest-apparel-clothing.html?_r=0; Mike Flanagan, "The Flanarant – Factory Safety Isn't the Biggest Risks to Bangladeshi Workers," *Just-style*, 13 July 2017, https://www.just-style.com/comment/the-flanarant-factory-safety-isnt-the-biggest-risk-to-bangladesh-workers_id131173.aspx

[47] Barry C. Lynn, "America's Monopolies Are Holding Back the Economy," *Atlantic*, February 22, 2017,

https://www.theatlantic.com/business/archive/2017/02/antimonopoly-big-business/514358/.

[48] Edward N. Wolff, "Household Wealth Trends in the United States, 1962 to 2016: Has Middle Class Wealth Recovered?" NBER Working Paper No. 24085 (November 2017); Christopher Ingraham, "The Richest 1 Percent Now Owns More of the Country's Wealth than at any Time in the Past 50 Years," *Washington Post*, December 6, 2017, https://www.washingtonpost.com/news/wonk/wp/2017/12/06/the-richest-1-percent-now-owns-more-of-the-countrys-wealth-than-at-any-time-in-the-past-50-years/?utm_term=.c55b70acb68f. Cf: Emmanuel Saez, "Striking it Richer: The Evolution of Top Incomes in the United States," *Pathways Magazine, Stanford Center for the Study of Poverty and Inequality*, (Winter 2008), 6-7, as updated on September 3, 2013, https://eml.berkeley.edu//~saez/saez-UStopincomes-2012.pdf; Drew DeSilver, "U.S. Income Inequality, on Rise for Decades, Is Now Highest since 1928," *Pew Research Center,* December 5, 2013, http://www.pewresearch.org/fact-tank/2013/12/05/u-s-income-inequality-on-rise-for-decades-is-now-highest-since-1928/.

[49] Fred Block and Margaret R. Somers, *The Power of Market Fundamentalism: Karl Polanyi's Critique* (Cambridge, MA: Harvard University Press, 2014), 30 (citations omitted), Kindle.

[50] Michael M. Weinstein, "Paul A. Samuelson, Economist, Dies at 94," *New York Times*, December 13, 2009, quoting Samuelson, http://www.nytimes.com/2009/12/14/business/economy/14samuelson.html?pagewanted=all.

[51] Block and Somers, *The Power of Market Fundamentalism*, 42.

[52] Block and Somers, *The Power of Market Fundamentalism,* 42.

[53] Heather Horn, "Pope Francis's Theory of Economics," *Atlantic*, November 26, 2013, quoting Pope Francis, https://www.theatlantic.com/business/archive/2013/11/pope-franciss-theory-of-economics/281865/.

[54] Thomas Hobbes, *Leviathan or The Matter, Forme and Power of a Common-Wealth Ecclesiastical and Civil*, 1651. Project Gutenberg 2009, XIII.9, https://www.gutenberg.org/ebooks/3207.

Chapter 7

ABOUT COMPANIES:

Snafu's Fictional Creature

Not long after Mary Shelley's protagonist, Victor Frankenstein, created his fictional creature,[1] the English parliament went one better. In a series of laws made between 1844 and 1862, it gave everyone the right to create their own fictional creatures.[2] They were called companies. Of course, companies had existed in England and elsewhere for a long time, but this was the first time the English government let people create them whenever they wanted by following a simple procedure and paying a modest fee.

Today there are between 100 million and 300 million companies in the world—nobody knows the exact number.[3] Although "the company" was a remarkable innovation, we seldom think of it that way, if we think of it at all. So, legally speaking, what is a company, and what makes it remarkable?

A company is a "legal fiction"—something that exists only because the law says it exists. Although virtual, it is a "legal person" that can make contracts, open bank accounts, own assets, employ people, and sue and be sued. Its "legal personality" is represented by the registration of its constitutional documents with a state authority that issues a certificate proving its existence. Being immaterial, it is helpless, so it needs people to run it and work for it. A lot of us biological types do just that—we work for a legal fiction, or we run one, or help run one.

Very broadly, there are two kinds of companies: public and private. The main difference is that public companies can be listed on a stock exchange so as to offer their shares to the public, but private companies can't. Stock exchanges in the World Federation of Exchanges have listed almost 45,000 companies.[4] In the United States, there are about 3,700 listed companies.[5] Private companies, and public companies that aren't listed, outnumber listed companies somewhere between 2,000 to one and 6,000 to one.[6] Yet, it's the listed public companies we hear most about.

In theory, companies can "live" forever. In practice, they don't. Companies in the S&P 500[7] usually "die" in their teens.[8] A company dies by going bankrupt, closing down, or being taken over or merged with another company. Since 2008, listed companies have been in demographic decline in the U.S. For the first time, their death rate is higher than their birth rate.[9]

The genius of the company is that the liability of its shareholders is limited to the amount they paid for their shares. If a company runs out of money, shareholders don't have to put in more—they just walk away. This "limited liability," coupled with the subdivision of investments into very small shares, enables people to participate in a large enterprise for a limited outlay. Although the investment is subdivided, the company itself is not—only the rights to its profits and surpluses, which it distributes as dividends. Shareholders don't own any part of the assets of the company. Their shares are assets entirely separate from the company itself. If the company is listed, they can sell their shares whenever they want. When they sell, the company lives on. Nothing changes—it just has different shareholders. Another advantage of the company is that shareholders don't have to worry about running its business. They leave this to directors, who hire executives and workers.

Today, these attributes of the company seem unremarkable, but it's only a slight exaggeration to say that the modern world was built on the back of this legal fiction. Without it, enterprises that are risky and capital-intensive, like international trade, shipbuilding, railroads, auto-making, banks, mines, and steel mills, would have been difficult to fund and manage. During the Industrial Revolution in

England, the government raised little in taxes, so development capital was private. At first, partnerships provided this capital, but before long it was companies. In 19th century America, federal and state governments also raised little in revenue, so private corporations undertook the large-scale production required for the Civil War and the rapid industrialization after it. Even though governments now have sizable economic footprints, companies still dominate economies across the world.

The company was the law's most useful invention. Although it evolved over centuries, its "light bulb" moment was its mid-19th-century "democratization" in England. Until then, limited liability had been a privilege that the king (and later, parliament) granted to only a few—and never to the common folk. In the U.S., the states controlled the registration of companies—they still do. Even as colonies before the Revolution, they granted charters to set up companies, but only to those who could afford them. It was not until 1875 that the legal framework for the truly "democratic" company was put in place. This was the New Jersey Incorporation Act, and it served as a model for other states.[10] In the U.S. and the U.K., modern corporate law is often referred to as "Anglo-American" because of its English roots and the similar lines of legal development in each country.[11]

By the late 19th century, early adopters among England's common folk had taken the innovation in an interesting direction. One of them was Aron Salomon. He'd been a successful leather merchant and wholesale boot manufacturer in London's Whitechapel district for more than thirty years when, in 1892, he set up a company and sold his business to it. Unable to repay a loan, Salomon's company went bankrupt less than two years after he set it up. The lender sued both the company and Salomon, arguing that, because the company was effectively a one-man company, it was nothing more than the *alter ego* of Salomon, who should be liable to pay its debts.

The case was referred to the House of Lords, England's ultimate appeal court at that time. The lower courts had struggled with the idea that a businessman could shelter from his debts simply by interposing a company between himself and his creditors. But Salomon won his appeal. As Lord Chancellor Halsbury put it: "Once a company is legally incorporated it must be treated like any other independent person."[12] It was not simply Salomon's "alias," even though he controlled its every action. It was a separate "legal person" and Salomon wasn't liable for its debts. Later, this separation would come to be known as the "corporate veil," dividing the company from its shareholders and directors.

Salomon's Case is what lawyers call a "leading case." In the common-law system, invented in England and used almost universally in the U.S., judges can "make law" through cases, like this one, by issuing rulings about the way legislation is to be understood. The significance of *Salomon's Case* is not so much that it legitimized the one-man company but that it was the genesis of companies as a fully formed species, even though the law that created them had given them so little "DNA." In fact, the Companies Act had given them only one gene—the profits gene—making them a species whose sole evolutionary purpose was to make money.

Fast-forward 110 years to another leading case—the 2016 *Philip Morris Case*[13]—in which Judge Kessler of the U.S. District Court (for the District of Columbia) held that Philip Morris and eight other tobacco companies had engaged in a massive fifty-year scheme to defraud the public in violation of a Federal Racketeering Act.[14] At the time, over half a million people a year were dying of smoking-related diseases in the U.S.[15] As Jeffrey Clements writes in his 2014 book *Corporations Are Not People*: "Judge Kessler concluded that 'overwhelming evidence' proved that the cigarette corporations 'conspired together' to fraudulently deny that cigarettes caused cancer, emphysema, and a long list of other fatal diseases; to manipulate levels of highly addictive nicotine to keep people smoking; to market addictive cigarettes to children so that the corporations would have 'replacement smokers' for those who quit or died."[16] The Judge quoted Bennett LeBow, a tobacco company CEO, who said: "If the tobacco companies really stopped marketing to children, the tobacco companies would be out of business in 25 to 30 years because they will not have enough customers to stay in business."[17]

Did LeBow and his colleagues think of themselves as racketeers, drug pushers, and killers? They surely didn't. Any more than Lee Iacocca and executives at the Ford Motor Company back in the 1970s saw themselves as personally responsible for the deaths or mutilation of nine hundred people when Ford Pintos burst into flames after rear-end collisions. They knew about the risk and did nothing to prevent it because they were in a rush to get the Pinto to market, and they were working to a tight budget.[18] These executives didn't think of themselves as immoral, or even unethical. It's almost impossible to convict a company executive for "corporate killing."[19] Courts and juries generally won't "lift the corporate veil."[20] And, of course, you can't jail a company.

Slowly, the corporate veil had evolved from a commercially useful fiction into a pathology. Corporate executives came to think of the veil not just as a legal shield but also a moral and ethical one. It allowed them to do bad things in the name of the company, without ever attributing their actions to themselves. These were things they'd never dream of doing as private citizens. In time, we all got used to companies doing things that private citizens would be jailed for doing. When the law failed to punish them, the idea that companies were somehow immune from punishment—immune from human morality—slowly became ingrained in our minds. Subliminally, we came to think of companies as an artificial species allowed to do things we weren't allowed to do—evil things, like making cars with exploding gas tanks or getting kids hooked on a fatal drug. Hannah Arendt called this "the banality of evil."[21] If evil is allowed to become commonplace, it no longer registers as evil. Our reactions to it are dulled. It becomes stale, clichéd—banal. For the company, and the morally detached executives behind its veil, decisions to obey or disobey the law easily defaulted to a cold economic calculus.

There are even some legal scholars who think this economic calculus is acceptable. As Daniel Heath notes in his 2014 book *Morality, Competition and the Firm*: "Unfortunately, there is a certain line of thinking—again strongly influenced by economics—which denies that corporations have any moral obligation to obey the law. Perhaps the most high-profile exponents of this view are Frank Easterbrook and Daniel Fischel, who argue that managers should adopt a purely instrumental orientation towards regulation, and comply with it only when it is in the firm's interest to do so. Any punishment the firm may incur as a result of breaking the law should be regarded as just another cost of doing business. According to Easterbrook and

Fischel, 'Managers do not have an ethical duty to obey economic regulatory laws just because the laws exist.'"[22] Easterbrook is now a judge on the U.S. 7th Circuit. Fischel is a prominent expert witness, an emeritus professor of law and business, and former Dean of the University of Chicago Law School.

The company has other flaws that reinforce its 'moral immunity.' The Law Lords in *Salomon's Case*, like the legislature, failed to notice that the company is technically an "orphan"—it doesn't "belong" to anyone. The shareholders own their shares, but they don't own the company itself. The directors manage it, but they don't own it either. The Law Lords can be forgiven for their oversight because this defect isn't noticeable in a one-man company. Salomon owned more than 99.9 percent of the shares in his company—his wife and children owned the rest—so effectively he did "own" it. The one-man company is still popular and, although it is legally separate from the one man, it tends to reflect his personality and his moral and ethical choices. By contrast, General Electric has more than 400,000 shareholders—Microsoft has more than 100,000. Their shares are traded frequently, so nobody really owns those companies.[23] Sure, the big shareholders have some influence but they don't shape its outlook or feel responsible for its actions. If they don't like what it's doing, they tend to sell their shares rather than try to change its behavior. Unlike the one-man company, big companies don't really have a "personality," except the stunted, money-grubbing one the law gave them.

The greater the number of shareholders, the less control any one of them has over the company. Those who do have control—the directors—typically don't own many shares. They don't think of themselves as owners either. They think of themselves as managers or agents. And this gives rise to something lawyers and economists call the "agency problem"—the tendency of directors to take care of their own interests ahead of those of the company. There's a related problem, which we could call an "identity disorder." Given that the company is legally distinct from both its shareholders and its directors, who does it really belong to?

The leading case on this is *Dodge v. Ford Motor Company*, a 1919 decision of the Michigan Supreme Court.[24] The Dodge brothers, who brought the case, owned almost as many shares in the Ford Motor Company as Henry Ford himself. But Henry Ford dominated the board of directors, and he certainly thought of the company as something different from its shareholders. He said: "My ambition is to employ still more men, to spread the benefits of this industrial system [the Ford Motor Company] to the greatest possible number, to help them build up their lives and their homes. To do this we are putting the greatest share of our profits back in the business."[25] Ford saw workers and customers as having a stake in the company, just as shareholders did. The Dodge brothers saw it differently. They wanted the company to keep paying them generous dividends, not plow back profits for the benefit of workers and customers. The Michigan Court agreed with them. It ruled that the shareholders had to be treated like owners, even though all they really owned was the right to a share of profits—even though the company had other stakeholders.

Dodge v. Ford remains controversial in legal circles, but it created two rules that still stand. The first is called the "shareholder primacy" rule. Essentially, this rule says that, despite the fact that the company is legally distinct from its shareholders, it must "live" for them. Lynn Stout, a professor of law & business at Cornell Law School, describes this rule as a "fable." She's probably right, but the Michigan legislation didn't give the judges much latitude.[26] The law told them that the sole purpose of a company is to make profits, so they had to ask themselves: "Who are the profits for?" Easy answer: they're for the shareholders. So, the shareholders win out over everybody else with a stake in the company. Yet, it's a simplistic rule. A company is so much more than the profits it makes. Henry Ford's holistic view is the better one. The company should also be answerable to its workers and its customers, as well as to society generally. But these other stakeholders weren't written into the Michigan law—they weren't written into any Anglo-American corporations law.

With the second rule, the Michigan Court tried to take some of the edge off the first rule. The second rule is called the "business judgment" rule. It has since been refined. In its present form, it says that a court won't question the decisions of the directors as long as they are made in good faith and with reasonable care, and as long as the directors believe they're acting in the best interests of the company, with reasonable grounds for their belief.[27] This means that the directors can take into account the interests of other stakeholders. They can reinvest the company's profits if they think it's good for the company.

So, why did the Michigan Court question Henry Ford's decision to reinvest profits? It was because he had an ulterior motive. He knew the Dodge brothers wanted to use their dividends to set up a rival auto company. By reinvesting profits instead of distributing them, the Court thought Henry Ford was trying to starve the Dodge brothers of capital, rather than trying to benefit the Ford Motor Company. If you drive a Dodge, you have the Michigan Court to thank for that.

The business judgment rule had an unintended consequence. It left the foxes—the directors—in charge of the hen house—the company and its money. In an effort to stop them eating too many eggs, someone came up with the bright idea that, if you give directors shares in the company, their interests will line up with those of the shareholders (the hobby farmers who collect the eggs). So, in many companies, the shareholders voted for this. Yet, the foxes only got fatter. By 2016, "CEOs in America's largest firms made an average of $15.6 million in compensation, or 271 times the annual average pay of the typical worker."[28] Back in 1965, during the post-war boom, the ratio was twenty to one.[29]

But the hobby farmers staged a comeback when America's most influential economist, Milton Friedman, molded the "shareholder primacy rule" into an economic doctrine. In a 1970 article in the *New York Times Magazine*, Friedman mangled the shareholder primacy rule to come up with the proposition that a company's money (not just its profits) actually "belongs" to the shareholders. Nothing should stand in the way of them receiving it.[30] This meant that the directors could only use the company's money to directly benefit the current shareholders. Friedman's arguments were legally absurd. Steve Denning, writing in *Forbes* in 2013, does a good job of demolishing them.[31] Denning also makes the telling point that "at the time, private sector firms were starting to feel the first pressures of global competition and executives were looking around for ways to increase their returns. The idea of focusing totally on making money, and forgetting about any concerns for employees, customers or society seemed like a promising avenue worth exploring, regardless of the argumentation."[32] The rule acquired a new handle, "maximizing shareholder value," with Jack Welch, CEO of General Electric, as its poster boy. "In

1980, the year before Welch became CEO, GE recorded revenues of roughly $26.8 billion; in 2000, the year before he left, they were nearly $130 billion. The company went from a market value of $14 billion to one of more than $410 billion at the time of his retirement, making it the most valuable and largest company in the world, up from America's tenth largest by market cap in 1981."[33]

Now that the foxes were forced to play nicely with the hobby farmers, they had to be careful how they exercised their business judgment. In the end, they agreed to share the eggs. But the hens soon began to suffer. As Richard Straub, an academic and former IBM executive, put it in a 2016 article: "Most large companies seem to have lost the taste for entrepreneurship, their CEOs preferring to focus on using technology to maximize profit from existing businesses... or not to invest at all. They are too often governed by the interests of shareholders who regard corporations as speculative investment opportunities rather than human communities for which true owners would feel ties of responsibility and commitment."[34]

From 1965 to 2009, the rate of return on assets of big American corporations fell by seventy-five percent.[35] If you don't feed the hens, they don't lay as many eggs. Even Jack Welch, fox number one, had to admit that something was wrong in the hen house. He had a change of heart about shareholder value. In March 2009, he told the *Financial*

Times: "On the face of it, shareholder value is the dumbest idea in the world. Shareholder value is a result, not a strategy... your main constituencies are your employees, your customers and your products... Short-term profits should be allied with an increase in the long-term value of a company."[36] Yet, the problem of where the interests of shareholders end, and where the company itself begins is one that persists to this day. There's still confusion of identity. It's a bit like Frankenstein. Is it the monster or is it the maker?

The Law Lords in *Salomon's Case* missed another of the company's "birth defects." Parliament had accidentally given the company unlimited "reproductive rights." By means of much the same procedure as Salomon used to create his one-man company, the company itself could create any number of "daughter" companies (subsidiaries). This enabled it to limit its own liability by setting up a subsidiary with less capital that could undertake a risky venture without exposing the "mother" to risk. When Lehman Brothers collapsed in September 2008, it had 209 subsidiaries in twenty-one countries.[37] There's nothing inherently wrong with allowing the company to reproduce. But corporate law has always played catch-up in dealing with corporate families (groups) because, initially, it gave no real thought to this possibility. Only recently did it turn its attention to another reproductive oddity—the "motherless" company. Sometimes called a "special purpose entity" or "SPE," this type of company was conceived so as to disguise the identity of the real mother. When Enron filed for bankruptcy in December 2001, it had around 3,000 SPEs, many of them born to hide Enron's trading losses from shareholders, bondholders, and regulators, by making it look as though Enron wasn't the mother of family companies that were losing money.[38]

At first, the law paid little attention to the rearing of offspring, failing to notice that the company had unusual "growth hormones." If a listed company survives infancy, it can gain weight rapidly, often by cannibalizing others, so that by adolescence it becomes "obese." A diet rich in money will do that. Corporate cannibalism goes by the acronym "M&A" (Mergers & Acquisitions).

Even before Salomon corporatized his business in 1892, John D. Rockefeller, Cornelius Vanderbilt, J.P. Morgan, Andrew Carnegie, and others in the U.S. had done the same thing—with considerably more success. These men, known as "Robber Barons," supersized their companies by colluding with rivals to stifle competition and corner markets. They helped usher in the Gilded Age,[39] a period of extraordinary inequality and corruption. By the late 1890s, a wave of M&A began, culminating in 1899 with 1,208 mergers.[40] Although Congress had passed the Sherman Antitrust Act in 1890,[41] it remained toothless until Theodore Roosevelt became President in 1901 on a "trust-busting" mandate.[42] In 1904, he broke up Morgan's railroad trust, Northern Securities Company.[43] Then, in 1911, under President Taft, Rockefeller's powerful Standard Oil Trust of New Jersey was dismembered, as was American Tobacco.[44] More antitrust laws followed.[45] Although government enforcement was uneven over subsequent years, one proposition seemed unassailable: competition means not allowing any corporation to grow so big that it dominates the market it sells in.

Enter Milton Friedman. In the 1970s, he came up with another piece of weird "logic." He persuaded politicians that it didn't matter how big corporations grew, or how concentrated their market power became, as long as they ran markets efficiently, keeping prices low. President Reagan and U.K. Prime Minister Thatcher readily agreed. It fit their "small government" philosophy and played well with big corporate campaign donors. In the U.S., recurring waves of M&A followed, peaking in 2015 with over five trillion dollars in deals.[46] Although M&A has declined slightly since then, the binge continues because merging with competitors has become the easiest way to boost returns in flat markets. Professor Stout describes big corporations as "an endangered species"[47] because they keep eating each other. The bloated beasts that remain can charge us whatever prices they like. Bilking your customers is a much easier way to make profits than slugging it out with your competitors. As a result, corporate profits are at all-time highs for the fattest corporations[48]—competition, on the other hand, is "anorexic."

In the Tech Age, a new strain of obesity developed. The sumo-sized leaders of this strain are the "Frightful Five." This is what *New York Times* journalist Farhad Manjoo calls Amazon, Apple, Facebook, Microsoft and Alphabet (Alphabet is Google's holding company). Manjoo is concerned that these oversized adolescents are making a mockery of competition. There's more to it. As Manjoo puts it: "There's rising worry, too, over their softer, noneconomic influence over culture and information—for instance, fears over how Facebook might affect democracies—as well as the implicit threat they pose to the jurisdictions of world governments."[49] This is the "banality of evil" with a brand-new Facebook page. When you pair the profit gene with a cartel approach to data, you don't get exploding gas tanks or cigarettes for kids—instead, democracy itself gets lit up. As Patrick Ruffini wrote in the *Washington Post* on November 3, 2017: "There was a sense in this past week's congressional hearings with executives from Facebook, Twitter and Google that Russia's meddling in the 2016 presidential campaign was a raging success."[50] These companies profited from Russia's meddling. They enabled it. Nobody held them accountable. Google's motto is: "Don't be evil." The tech giants like to think of themselves as geeks with good intentions. Yet, the banality of their blind pursuit of profit enables them to be easily manipulated. A data cartel is more powerful than any army. It can be used to bury truth and subvert democracy. Trading in data—disseminating it globally on an industrial scale—is an awesome responsibility. Good intentions are not nearly enough. The shiny road to hell is paved with good intentions.

When the modern corporation was designed, it could have been given its own Bill of Rights, but in the 19th century, who knew that a fiction would need rights? It was left to the Supreme Court, which took the path of least resistance. For the most part, the Court treated the company like a real person. It gave it rights under the First Amendment (free speech), the Fourth Amendment (limiting search and seizure) and, ironically, the Fourteenth Amendment, the purpose of which was to protect *human* rights.

In 2010, in *Citizens United v. Federal Election Commission*, the Supreme Court ruled that a law forbidding a corporation from spending money within sixty days of an election to support or attack candidates for federal office violated First Amendment free-speech rights.[51] As Clements puts it: "Citizens United's elimination of the last modest restraint on corporate power and the lock-up of government by a ruling elite—elimination of fair spending rules in elections—is likely to complete the transformation of our economy into one where only a few people, rather than most people, have a shot to prosper."[52] Americans are now effectively out-voted by fictional creatures that can't vote themselves. These creatures can buy votes, and every vote they buy is calculated to make them more money.

It's not just in the U.S. that corporations manipulate governments in the name of profit. This is a global phenomenon. More than 3,000 international treaties allow foreign corporations to sue governments outside their own court systems in an arbitration process called an "investor–state dispute settlement" (ISDS).[53] There's an ISDS procedure in the North American Free Trade Agreement (NAFTA). It's in the chapter designed to protect the rights of foreign investors in each of the member countries. In 1997, Ethyl Corporation, a U.S. company, sued Canada under this procedure for banning a toxic gasoline additive called MMT. When the case settled, a lawyer for Ethyl said: "It wouldn't matter if a substance was liquid plutonium destined for a child's breakfast cereal. If the [Canadian] government bans a product and a U.S.-based company loses profits, the company can claim damages under NAFTA."[54] Between 1990 and 2014, corporations sued at least 120 countries in more than 650 ISDS arbitrations.[55]

The legal history of the company is not the history of a bad idea. It's the history of a good idea, badly designed. As Kent Greenfield puts it in his 2006 book *The Failure of Corporate Law*: "By centralizing power in management, limiting the involvement of other stakeholders in corporate decision making, and imposing a requirement that the firm's management care about making money first and foremost, the law has created an entity that is guaranteed to throw off as many costs and risks onto others as it can."[56] The creature itself prevents lawmakers from fixing the design. Victor Frankenstein intervened when the monster he designed started killing people. His interventions were ineffectual. The monster had become too powerful. It told him: "You are my creator, but I am your master—obey!"[57] Poor design made money the master of the company. Money politics made the company the master of the law. Like Frankenstein, the law lost control of its creation. Nothing concentrates the power of money like the modern corporation. It's a much scarier monster than Frankenstein's.

---

[1] Mary Shelley, *Frankenstein; or, The Modern Prometheus* (Lackington, Hughes, Harding Mavor & Jones, 1818), Kindle edition.

[2] Joint Stock Companies Act 1844 (7& 8 Vict. C110) (UK), as amended, and Companies Act 1862 (25 & 26 Vict. C.89) (UK).

[3] "How Many Companies Exist in the World?" *Quora*, n.d., https://www.quora.com/How-many-companies-exist-in-the-world. The most interesting estimates are provided by Sudhaker Gaitonde (low end) and Mohit Prasad (high end). There doesn't appear to be much hard data on this subject.

[4] Siobhan Cleary et al., "The Role of Stock Exchanges in Fostering Economic Growth and Sustainable Development," Joint Report, World

Federation of Exchanges and United Nations Conference on Trade and Development (UNCTAD)(September 2017), http://unctad.org/en/PublicationsLibrary/WFE_UNCTAD_2017_en.pdf

[5] Schumpeter, "Why the Decline in the Number of Listed American Firms Matters," *Economist*, April 22, 2017, https://www.economist.com/news/business/21721153-company-founders-are-reluctant-go-public-and-takeovers-are-soaring-why-decline.

[6] Not all listed companies are listed on stock exchanges that are members of the World Federation of Exchanges (WFE), so let's assume that there are 50,000 listed companies (roughly 45,000 listed on WFE exchanges and 5,000 on other exchanges). Using the range 100 million to 300 million for all the companies in the world gives ratios of between 2,000:1 and 6,000:1. Admittedly, this data is rough, but it is some indication of the scale of the distribution of public listed companies to all companies.

[7] "The S&P 500 is a stock market index that tracks the 500 most widely held stocks on the New York Stock Exchange or NASDAQ. It seeks to represent the entire stock market by reflecting the risk and return of all large cap companies. S&P stands for Standard and Poor, which are the names of two financial companies that merged": Kimberly Amadeo, "The S&P 500 and How It Works," *Balance*, June 29, 2017, https://www.thebalance.com/what-is-the-sandp-500-3305888.

[8] Rishi Iyengar, "This Is How Long Your Business Will Last, According to Science," *Time*, April 2, 2015, http://time.com/3768559/company-mortality-rate-survival-study/.

[9] Yuval Rosenberg, "US Companies Are Dying Faster than Ever," *Business Insider,* August 6, 2015, http://www.businessinsider.com/us-companies-are-dying-faster- than-ever-2015-8?IR=T.

[10] L E Talbot, *Critical Company Law* (Abingdon, Oxon: Routledge-Cavendish, 2008), 11.

[11] Talbot, *Critical Company Law*, 5.

[12] *Aron Salomon (Pauper) v A. Salomon and Company, Limited*, by original appeal, and *A. Salomon and Company, Limited v Aron Salomon*, by cross appeal, [1897] AC 22 (*Salomon's Case*), from the judgment of Lord Halsbury L.C. on page 30.

[13] United States of America and others v. Philip Morris USA, Inc., and others, 9F. Supp. 2d 1 (D.D.C. 2006) Civil Action No. 99-2496 (GK).

[14] The Honorable Judge Gladys Kessler U.S. District Court for the District of Columbia, Opinion in the *Philip Morris Case*, 1477 and 1478, http://www.publichealthlawcenter.org/sites/default/files/resources/doj-final-opinion.pdf.

[15] Genevra Pittman, "Half a Million Die from Smoking Yearly in U.S.," *Reuters*, April 1, 2011, https://www.reuters.com/article/us-smoking-deaths/half-a-million-die-from-smoking-yearly-in-u-s-idUSTRE72U4E220110331.

[16] Jeffrey D. Clements, *Corporations Are Not People: Why They Have More Rights than You Do and What You Can Do About It* (Berrett-Koehler Publishers, 2012), 21.

[17] Kessler, *Philip Morris Case*, 974.

[18] William H. Shaw and Vincent E. Barry, *Moral Issues in Business* (Belmont, CA: Wadsworth, 8th ed, 2001), 83-86.

[19] The Ford Pinto deaths are a good example of this, see: Charles E. Dole, "Pinto Verdict Lets US Industry Off Hook," *Christian Science Monitor*, March 14, 1980, https://www.csmonitor.com/1980/0314/031435.html.

[20] "Lifting of the corporate veil means disregarding the corporate *personality* and looking behind to the real person [or persons] who are in the control of the company": "Lifting the Corporate Veil," *Law Teacher*, n.d., https://www.lawteacher.net/free-law-essays/business-law/article-on-lifting-of-the-law-essays.php.

[21] Hannah Arendt, *Eichmann in Jerusalem: A Report on the Banality of Evil* (London: Penguin Books, 2006), Kindle. The book expands on a series of articles Arendt wrote for the New Yorker magazine in 1963.

[22] Joseph Heath, *Morality, Competition, and the Firm: The Market Failures Approach to Business Ethics* (New York: Oxford University Press, 2014), 18.

[23] For GE: "As of January 31, 2017, there were approximately 440,000 shareowner accounts of record": "Securities and Exchange Commission Form 10-K, GE 2016 Annual Report," 26, *Securities and Exchange Commission*,

https://www.sec.gov/Archives/edgar/data/40545/00000405451700000l0
/ge10k2016.htm.

For Microsoft: "On July 31, 2017, there were 101,825 registered holders of record of our common stock": "Securities and Exchange Commission Form 10-K, Annual Report of Microsoft Corporation for the Fiscal Year Ended June 30, 2017," 27, *Securities and Exchange Commission,*
https://www.sec.gov/Archives/edgar/data/789019/000156459017014900/msft-
10k_20170630.htm#ITEM5_MARKET_FOR_REGISTRANTS.

Note: Many individuals who hold shares have them registered under the address of their broker, banker, or financial advisor, so some of them share the same registered address. As the estimate in the Form 10-K is taken from the registered addresses, it not a reliable estimate of the actual number of shareholders. The actual number is likely to be higher than the estimate in the Form 10-K.

[24] Dodge v. Ford Motor Company, 170 N.W. 668 (Mich. 1919).

[25] Dodge v. Ford Motor Company, 170 N.W. 668, 671 (Mich. 1919).

[26] The "Michigan legislation" was the State of Michigan, Pub.Acts1903, No. 232. For Stout's views on the rule and why it is, in her view, a "fable," see: Lynn A. Stout, "Why We Should Stop Teaching Dodge v. Ford," *Virginia Law & Business Review* 3, No. 1 (Spring 2008) available at Cornell Law Library, Scholarship@Cornell Law: A Digital Repository, Cornell Law Faculty Publications, http://scholarship.law.cornell.edu/cgi/viewcontent.cgi?article=1826&context=facpub.

[27] "Business Judgment Rule," *Wex, Legal Information Institute,* https://www.law.cornell.edu/wex/business_judgment_rule#.

[28] Lawrence Mishel and Jessica Schieder, "CEO Pay Remains High Relative to the Pay of Typical Workers and High-Wage Earners," *Economic Policy Institute,* July 20, 2017, http://www.epi.org/publication/ceo-pay-remains-high-relative-to-the-pay-of-typical-workers-and-high-wage-earners/.

[29] Mishel and Schieder, "CEO Pay."

[30] Milton Friedman, "A Friedman Doctrine – The Social Responsibility of Business is to Increase its Profits," *New York Times Magazine,*

September 13, 1970,
https://timesmachine.nytimes.com/timesmachine/1970/09/13/22353570
2.html?action=click&contentCollection=Archives&module=LedeAsset
&region=ArchiveBody&pgtype=article&pageNumber=379.

[31] Steve Denning, "The Origins of 'The World's Dumbest Idea': Milton Friedman," *Forbes*, June 26, 2013.

[32] Denning, "The Origins."

[33] "John F. Welch Jr. Chairman & CEO 1981-2001," Past Leaders, GE https://www.ge.com/about-us/leadership/profiles/john-f-welch-jr.

[34] Richard Straub, "The Promise of a Truly Entrepreneurial Society," *Harvard Business Review*, March 25, 2016, https://hbr.org/2016/03/the-promise-of-a-truly-entrepreneurial-society.

[35] Denning, "The Origins."

[36] Francesco Guerrera, "Welch Condemns Share Price Focus," *Financial Times*, March 12, 2009, https://www.ft.com/content/294ff1f2-0f27-11de-ba10-0000779fd2ac.

[37] Michael J. Fleming and Asani Sarkar, "The Failure Resolution of Lehman Brothers," *Federal Reserve Bank of New York Economic Policy Review* (December 2014): 175-206, https://www.newyorkfed.org/medialibrary/media/research/epr/2014/14 12flem.pdf.

[38] Ron Rimkus, "Financial Scandals, Scoundrels & Crises: Enron Corporation," *CFA Institute*, December 7, 2016, https://www.econcrises.org/2016/12/07/enron-corporation-2001/.

[39] See above, Chapter 1, endnote 5.

[40] Bernard Bailyn et al, *The Great Republic: A History of the American People* (Lexington, MA: D.C. Heath and Company, 1985), 528.

[41] Sherman Act, 26 Stat. 209, 15 U.S.C. §§ 1–7.

[42] A "trust," in this context, was an arrangement by which large shareholders of companies prominent in an industry exchanged their shares for "trust certificates." This allowed a secretive board of trustees to control a stable of companies that appeared to the world to be independent of one another – a kind of secret, de facto merger.

[43] Dwight Lowell Dumond, *America in Our Time 1896-1946* (New York: H. Holt and Company, 1947), 123 and 124.

[44] Dumond, *America*, 126.

[45] Dumond, *America*, 126.

[46] Bouree Lam, "2015: A Merger Bonanza," *Atlantic*, January 9, 2016, https://www.theatlantic.com/business/archive/2016/01/2015-mergers-acquisitions/423096/.

[47] Lynn Stout, "The Shareholder Value Myth," YouTube video, 3:38, posted by "Rotman School of Management," April 16, 2013, https://www.youtube.com/watch?v=ZzztBF9nprA.

[48] Justin Fox, "The Real Story Behind Those 'Record' Corporate Profits," *Harvard Business Review*, November 24, 2010, https://hbr.org/2010/11/the-real-story-behind-those-re.html.

[49] Farhad Manjoo, "State of the Art, Tech's Frightful Five: They've Got Us," *New York Times*, May 10, 2017, https://www.nytimes.com/2017/10/18/technology/frightful-five-start-ups.html?_r=0.

[50] Patrick Ruffini, "Why Russia's Facebook Ad Campaign Wasn't Such a Success," *Washington Post,* November 3, 2017, https://www.washingtonpost.com/outlook/why-russias-facebook-ad-campaign-wasnt-such-a-success/2017/11/03/b8efacca-bffa-11e7-8444-a0d4f04b89eb_story.html?utm_term=.464441b88c90. Although Ruffini concludes that Russia's campaign wasn't all that successful and that ugly social divisions were already there to be exploited, his discussion of the impact of social-media manipulation in elections is interesting, and it indicates some of the difficulties of dealing with it.

[51] Citizens United v. Federal Election Commission, 558 U.S. 310 (2010). For a summary of the case, see: "*Citizens United v. Federal Election Commission* (08-205)," *Cornell University Law School*, https://web.archive.org/web/20170124175326/https://www.law.cornell.edu/supct/cert/08-205.

[52] Clements, *Corporations*, 111.

[53] Rachel L. Wellhausen, "Recent Trends in Investor-State Dispute Settlement," *Journal of International Dispute Settlement* 7, No. 1 (March, 2016).

[54] Lydia Zuraw, "Critics Say Food Safety Standards Could Be Threatened by U.S./EU Trade Agreement," *Food Safety News*, May 16, 2014, http://www.foodsafetynews.com/2014/05/food-safety-standards-could-be-threatened-in-u-s-eu-trade-agreement/#.WitkGBRgr8M.

[55] Rachel Wellhausen, "Investors Have Controversial New Rights to Sue Countries. Here's why this Matters for the U.S.," *Washington Post*, November 30, 2015, https://www.washingtonpost.com/news/monkey-cage/wp/2015/11/30/investors-have-controversial-new-rights-to-sue-countries-heres-why-this-matters-for-the-u-s/?utm_term=.83b49a80c09a.

[56] Kent Greenfield, *The Failure of Corporate Law: Fundamental Flaws and Progressive Possibilities* (Chicago, IL: University of Chicago Press, 2006), 16.

[57] Shelley, *Frankenstein,* 159.

Chapter 8

ABOUT WAR:

Snafu's Paradoxical Trinity

In one of a series of Tweets directed at recent college graduates, Bill Gates wrote in May 2017: "If I could give each of you a graduation present, it would be this—the most inspiring book I've ever read."[1] He was referring to *The Better Angels of Our Nature: Why Violence Has Declined* by Steven Pinker.[2] Guess what? He could easily have given all those graduates a copy of the book. Instead, he did Jeff Bezos a favor. After his Tweet, many graduates bought the book themselves—it jumped to No.1 on Amazon.[3]

Pinker says that, relative to population, wars have been claiming progressively fewer casualties over time. This is enticing. We want to believe it. But his claim has sparked plenty of controversy. There are those who argue that his definitions, statistics, and methods are flawed.[4] Does anyone ever agree about that stuff? As the old saying goes: "It has been wittily remarked that there are three kinds of falsehood: the first is a fib, the second is a downright lie, and the third and most aggravated is statistics."[5] There's a more telling criticism though.

Picture a couple of young dinosaurs lounging around in a primordial forest just after dinner on a Saturday night about sixty-five million years ago:

Big Dinosaur:	"Man, don't you just love it here? We're lords of the Earth."
Small Dinosaur:	"I feel a little uneasy, dude. What if some bad shit happens?"
Big Dinosaur:	"Relax—it's been like this for 165 million years. What could possibly go wrong?"

Then the asteroid hits.

These days, we are the lords of the Earth. It's hard to date the start of our civilization. The first stone settlements appeared about 14,000 years ago in the region that is now Israel and Jordan.[6] Saying that human violence has declined over the last few hundred years, as Pinker does, is a bit like saying that, because it hasn't rained in Seattle this afternoon, there must be a drought.

We keep forgetting that the past is an unreliable guide to the future, even though Nassim Nicholas Taleb reminds us how easily we are "fooled by randomness."[7] Taleb and Pasquale Cirillio criticized *Better Angels* on this ground (and others).[8] Pinker responded by saying that his thesis isn't supposed to be predictive.[9] He wrote almost seven hundred pages about why there's a downward trend in war and conflict.[10] You have to think he expects it to continue—otherwise it's, well, not really a trend.

According to Pinker, wars in the 20th century caused the deaths of about one hundred million people, directly or indirectly.[11] That's a lot of people, but it could so easily have been more. What if Nikita Khrushchev hadn't blinked first during the Cuban Missile Crisis of 1962?[12] This could have triggered MAD (Mutually Assured Destruction). There goes the United States and there goes the Soviet Union—another three hundred million people gone. That would have screwed with Pinker's thesis—and probably with Pinker himself, who was eight years old at the time and living in Montreal.[13] The Russians might not have nuked Montreal, but it would surely have been destroyed in the resulting nuclear winter.

"The better angels of our nature" comes from Abraham Lincoln's First Inaugural Address.[14] It is the last phrase of his passionate plea for unity. While it makes for a catchy title, it's a mystery why Pinker, an avowed atheist,[15] not only stuck with the angels metaphor but built on it. War, he says, is a struggle between our five "inner demons"—sadism, revenge, dominance, violence in pursuit of a practical benefit, and violence in pursuit of an ideology—and our four "better angels"—self-control, empathy, morality, and reason.[16]

Wait a minute—why is reason an angel? Is it because morality flows from reason, as Immanuel Kant believed?[17] Maybe not, because Pinker lists "morality" and "reason" as separate angels. It's worth exploring the relationship between reason and morality in order to try to understand why Pinker thinks that reason is an angel. If it were an angel, then war and violence would always be contrary to reason—always irrational. Can that be right?

Let's go back to Kant for a minute, because he gave a lot of thought to the connection between reason and morality. Although it's kind of hard to understand him, Kant's argument seems to be that, because the highest "good" is a combination of moral virtue and happiness, we must believe we can attain both—otherwise, morality would direct us to an empty ideal. As moral virtue is not always rewarded with happiness in this world, we need to allow for the existence of God and an afterlife in which morality is rewarded with happiness. Reason can't disprove the existence of God, so there must be a god and a happy afterlife for the morally righteous. Ergo—morality flows from reason. But Kant didn't complete the loop. Sure, reason can't disprove the existence of God, yet neither can it prove that God does exist. Reason doesn't really have anything to say about God or morality. So, what puts reason on the side of the angels? Isn't reason just neutral? David Hume, whom Kant admired, thought so.[18] So did Herbert Simon, who wrote: "We see that reason is wholly instrumental. It cannot tell us where to go; at best it can tell us how to get there. It is a gun for hire that can be employed in the service of whatever goals we have, good or bad."[19] It sounds right that reason and morality have nothing to do with each other. So, Pinker is right to separate them. He's also right that war isn't moral. Even a "just war" isn't exactly moral—just not immoral. So, morality is an angel. But Pinker is wrong that war is always unreasonable. It's perfectly reasonable to fight a war of self-defense, for example. Reason is neither an angel nor a demon. It can hang with either crowd.

Let's take another of Pinker's angels—"empathy." It even sounds angelic. Pinker claims that there is "an expanding circle" of empathy in the world.[20] Modern communications technology is increasing cosmopolitanism, making us more empathetic. Jeremy Rifkin, in his book *The Empathetic Civilization*,[21] adds renewable energy as a cause of the spread of empathy. He takes 674 pages to reach much the same conclusion as Pinker. There are over 3,500 books on

Amazon with "empathy" in the title.[22] I'm guessing the authors of most of them are in favor of it—though not cognitive psychologist, Paul Bloom. He's *Against Empathy*—that's the title of his 2016 book.[23] He says that: "The more empathy you have, the more violent you are—the more ready and willing you are to cause pain."[24] According to Bloom, empathy leads us to focus on "people like us," making us less tolerant of those who are not like us.

Does the debate about empathy have something do with its meaning? Not so much. Although it's a relatively new word (around 160 years old),[25] there seems to be general agreement that it means: "the ability to share and understand the feelings of another."[26] Even if we substitute it with an older, less controversial word, like "compassion" (Bloom's preference), it is, at best, an angel's wing feather, not a complete angel.[27] It is nowhere near a match for any "demon." And it has no real impact on war because there are, at least, three things that give war a veneer of abstraction that compassion can't penetrate. Those things are distance, time, and large numbers.

The history of war is the history of killing with increasing effectiveness at increasing distances. Early in the 13th century, the mounted archers of Genghis Khan made great use of an emerging technology—the stirrup. It enabled them to balance in their saddles long enough to shoot their arrows. The stirrup allowed distance killing to be combined with the speed of light cavalry. This helped Khan, an illiterate Mongolian nomad, assemble one the largest empires in history.[28] According to Peter Drucker, the stirrup led directly to the "military-agricultural complex"—the medieval knight, defending at least fifty peasant families in return for their material support.[29]

In this age of the "military-industrial complex,"[30] there's the aptly named "SS-18 Satan," an intercontinental ballistic missile, with a range of 16,000 kilometers.[31] "Satan's" maximum payload is 20,000 kilotons of TNT equivalent[32]— that's more than 1,300 times the explosive yield of the bomb dropped on Hiroshima, which killed 70,000 people.[33] Conceivably, "Satan" could kill a hundred million people. By comparison, the armies of Genghis Khan probably killed around forty million people.[34]

Can we feel compassion for forty million people who died eight centuries ago? Can we feel anything for the hundred million people "Satan" might kill next year? Only vaguely, because the past is an abstraction—so is the future. As for large numbers like forty million or a hundred million, they are simply too hard for compassion to deal with. As Erich Maria Remarque wrote in his 1956 novel, *The Black Obelisk*: [35] "It's strange, I think, all of us have seen so many dead in the war and we know that over two million of us fell uselessly—why, then, are we so excited about a single man, when we have practically forgotten the two million already?

But probably the reason is that one dead man is death—and two million are only a statistic."[36]

Compassion, sympathy, empathy—the shades of meaning don't matter much. We're talking about a feeling that doesn't cope with abstractions—a feeling easily overwhelmed by numbers, by time, and by distance. Sure, it's on the side of the angels, but it's not nearly strong enough to be one.

We could examine Pinker's other "better angels" and "inner demons." It wouldn't help. Only in fantasies is war a contest between demons and angels.

Eventually, Pinker exhausts those religious metaphors and launches into a discussion of the role of strong centralized governments, international trade, and the empowerment of women as factors preventing wars. Comparatively, the United States scores well on all of these. Yet, pick any year since 1776—there's a more than ninety percent chance that the United States was engaged in a war.[37] It seems that the U.S. has never gone a decade without some kind of war.[38] If you count the "Banana Wars" in Central America,[39] the only time the U.S. has gone more than five years without a war was between 1935 and 1941—during the isolationist period of the Great Depression.[40]

It would be nice if war were going out of fashion. It isn't. It remains persistent and global. The 2016 Global Peace Index Report found that just ten countries could be considered completely free from conflict.[41] According to the 2017 Report, global peacefulness has declined by 2.14 percent since 2008, with more countries showing deterioration than those showing improvement.[42] The 2017 Report said: "The historic ten-year deterioration in peace has largely been driven by the intensifying conflicts in the MENA region.[43] Terrorism is also at an all-time high, battle deaths from conflict are at a 25-year high, and the number of refugees and displaced people are [sic] at a level not seen in sixty years."[44]

Sadly, Pinker is wrong. There is no general downward trend in conflict. He is also wrong about the causes of war. There is one paramount cause—politics. And there's no general downward trend in politics: except in a qualitative sense.

Carl von Clausewitz said it best. "War is not merely a political act, but also a real political instrument, a continuation of political commerce, a carrying out of the same by other means."[45] He thought of war as so closely connected with political activity as to be inseparable from it.[46] Sun Tze[47] and Niccolò Machiavelli,[48] the two other members of the unholy trinity of war thinkers, thought so too. Mao Zedong, no stranger to organized mass violence, put it epigrammatically: "Politics is war without bloodshed, while war is politics with bloodshed."[49]

Clausewitz offered a definition of war. Some think it outdated. But, Andreas Herberg-Rothe defends the definition convincingly.[50] Quoting from it, he writes: "As a total phenomenon its dominant tendencies always make war a paradoxical trinity – composed of primordial violence, hatred, and enmity, which are to be regarded as a blind natural force; of the play of chance and probability within which the creative spirit is free to roam; and of its element of subordination, as an instrument of policy, which makes it subject to pure reason."[51]

Unpacking that: war is the interaction of a "paradoxical trinity"—first, there is the violence inherent in human nature; second, there is the fight or struggle itself; third, there is the pursuit of rational self-interest by states. Although Herberg-Rothe uses "paradoxical trinity" in his quote from Clausewitz, he says that "wondrous trinity" is the better translation.[52] The combination of nature, struggle, and reason does make for a "wondrous trinity." Yet, it's paradoxical that ruthless violence and pure reason co-exist in human nature. According to Clausewitz, the violence of war must be ruthless, "for in such dangerous things as war, the errors which proceed from a spirit of benevolence are the worst."[53] That's what makes war so weird—unrestrained violence that's both rational and natural.

Thomas Hobbes didn't find it weird at all. He thought that war "of every man against every man" is the natural condition of mankind. Without a strong king, there is no place for anything but continual fear and the danger of violent death, so that life is "solitary, poor, nasty, brutish and short."[54] Hobbes was naïve to put his faith in kings. He was also mistaken in his dim view of human nature.

Thucydides (whom Hobbes admired) followed Aristotle (whom Hobbes hated) in thinking that there is more to human nature than primordial violence.[55] Socrates and Plato agreed with Aristotle that mankind is essentially communal. They thought that, in between man's passion and his reason, there is something called "*thumos*."[56] This is often interpreted as spiritedness.[57] It's interesting that Clausewitz was strangely poetic when describing the second element of his trinity (the fight or struggle itself) as: "the play of chance and probability within which the creative spirit is free to roam."[58] There is no easy English translation of *thumos*. It does mean fight or struggle in the Clausewitz sense, but there's more to it. *Thumos* also signifies an intuitive reaction to injustice, though often a violent one. It has to do with honor, which Hobbes dismissed as "vain-glory," but the Greeks did not because they associated honor with justice.[59] Perhaps Clausewitz was alluding to *thumos* in his lyrical reference to the fight or struggle as a roaming creative spirit influenced by chance and probability.

If we were to dismiss Hobbes as a Grinch, accept the Greek view that man is communal, and interpret *thumos* as a spirited fight or struggle in the cause of justice, this would leave us with a much more optimistic view of human nature. It wouldn't reconcile the "trinity"—human nature, struggle, and reason. It would only show us that the violence in human nature is a force that is neither entirely good nor entirely bad. We'd then be back to reason and its role in warfare. For the Greeks, there was something transcendental about reason. Clausewitz simply equated reason with politics, even though the political response to violence is not always rational, though often it is. Defensive war is nearly always thought of as reasonable—even preemptive war is sometimes considered reasonable. Usually, it's only the aggressor who is thought unreasonable—at least at the outset of a war.

What if we were to assume that a nation would always take a rational, long-term, and enlightened view of its own interests? Would it respond to violence by going to war? Sometimes it would. Opposing violence with violence can be entirely rational. What if *every* nation were to act with the same broad, enlightened view of its interests—would any nation ever start a war, knowing that it would be starting a cycle of violence? Maybe—because it's possible to be both rational and mistaken.

Even if reason were enough to avert war, we'd still have to acknowledge that we aren't always ruled by reason. We're not entirely rational—we're not even supposed to be. As the Ancient Greeks said, we're communal, not because they said so but because evolution dictates that our survival is the interplay of competition and cooperation. Even if you take the Hobbesian view that competition is the default setting, it's still clear that we wouldn't have come this far without cooperation—and cooperation requires altruism, while reason doesn't. In every society, there is altruism—disinterested and selfless concern for the well-being of others. Instinctively, we try to be better than reason requires of us. We try to be ethical. This is because the human experience is not about individual lives. It's not just about the here and now of any one person or group. It's about humanity as a whole—human survival. Humanity is compelled to continue—that's its evolutionary purpose. So, don't take life too personally. It's not so much about you, it's more about the species!

In the evolutionary balancing act, the primordial violence that is part of human nature is on the competition side of the scale, while altruism is on the cooperation side. The problem is that the scales don't balance. We became very good at violence. It evolved technologically, while altruism didn't. We haven't been able to make anything in the service of altruism that is nearly as effective as a Satan missile.

Ironically, the wars of the future may be fought over the most communal interest of all—the quality of life on Earth. Resource depletion, environmental degradation, and climate change are part of a cluster of existential threats to humanity. The onset is uneven. Those most acutely affected are already beginning to move to places less affected. Their numbers will increase. Immigration is already a polarizing political issue. There's a risk that parochial interests will trump humanity's overall interest, leading to wars over water, arable land, and other resources.

We don't have a sense of our species as a single community, even in the face of serious threats to its survival. The limits in our nature that turn distance, time, and large numbers into abstractions that defeat empathy also make the idea of a global community too abstract for us to engage with. We'd need to show altruism on a scale that seems beyond us. Is that where reason comes back into play? Our faculty of reason evolved in order to help us deal with abstractions— like what to do when the next major war could so easily result in our extinction. Reason ought to be able to turn existential threats like this into a cause for cooperation that transcends our bounded sense of altruism. It ought to be able to provide a rationale for the protection of our most vital common interest—survival. What if it isn't enough? Then we'd be left with the Clausewitz trinity. Would the trinity be "wondrous" enough to save us from extinction, or would it be "paradoxical" enough to wipe out the only species on Earth endowed with reason, a sense of justice, and an innate longing for immortality?

[1] Brian Fung, "Bill Gates Told New Grads to Read this Book. Now it's Surging on Amazon," *Washington Post*, May 15, 2017, https://www.washingtonpost.com/news/the-switch/wp/2017/05/15/bill-gates-told-new-grads-to-read-this-book-now-its-surging-on-amazon/?utm_term=.f16c852153b2.

[2] Steven Pinker, *The Better Angels of Our Nature: Why Violence Has Declined* (New York: Viking Books, 2011).

[3] Dan Heching, "The Better Angels of Our Nature Hits No. 1 on Amazon Following Bill Gates Tweet," *Entertainment Weekly*, May 16, 2017, http://ew.com/books/2017/05/16/steven-pinker-the-better-angels-of-our-nature-bill-gates/.

[4] Pasquale Cirillio and Nassim Nicholas Taleb, "What Are the Chances of a Third World War?" Real World Risk Institute Working Paper Series, n.d., http://www.fooledbyrandomness.com/longpeace.pdf.

[5] From a letter to the editor dated June 8, 1891, the *National Observer* (U.K.), June 13, 1891, p. 93-94 under the heading "National Pensions."

[6] Michael Balter, "The Seeds of Civilization," *Smithsonian Magazine*, May 2005, https://www.smithsonianmag.com/history/the-seeds-of-civilization-78015429/ .

[7] Nassim Nicholas Taleb, *Fooled by Randomness: The Hidden Role of Chance in Life and the Markets* (Penguin Books, 2009).

[8] Cirillio and Taleb, "What Are the Chances."

[9] Steven Pinker, "Fooled by Belligerence: Comments on Nassim Taleb's 'The Long Peace is a Statistical Illusion,'" n.d., https://stevenpinker.com/files/comments_on_taleb_by_s_pinker.pdf.

[10] Plus over 70 pages of "Notes and References."

[11] Pinker, *Better Angels*, Chapter 5 "The Long Peace."

[12] "The Cuban Missile Crisis, October 1962," Office of the Historian, Department of State, United States of America, n.d., https://history.state.gov/milestones/1961-1968/cuban-missile-crisis.

[13] "About Steven Pinker," Department of Psychology, Harvard University (biography and curriculum vitae), https://stevenpinker.com/biocv.

[14] Abraham Lincoln, "First Inaugural Address," (March 4, 1861), available at *The Avalon Project*, Yale Law School, http://avalon.law.yale.edu/19th_century/lincoln1.asp.

[15] Ed Douglas, "Steven Pinker: The Mind Reader," *Guardian*, November 6, 1999, quoting Pinker's statement: "I never outgrew my conversion to atheism at 13…," https://www.theguardian.com/books/1999/nov/06/1.

[16] Pinker, *Better Angels*, Preface, Chapter 8 "Inner Demons" and Chapter 9 "Better Angels."

[17] *Stanford Encyclopedia of Philosophy*, "Kant and Hume on Morality," March 26, 2008, as revised on July 28, 2016, https://plato.stanford.edu/entries/kant-hume-morality/.

[18] *Stanford Encyclopedia of Philosophy*, "Kant and Hume."

[19] Herbert A. Simon, *Reason in Human Affairs* (Stanford: Stanford University Press, 1983), Chapter 1.

[20] Pinker, *Better Angels*, Chapter 4 "The Humanitarian Revolution" – Pinker endorses the views of the philosopher, Peter Singer, expressed in Peter Singer, *The Expanding Circle: Ethics, Evolution and Moral Progress* (Princeton University Press, 1981).

[21] Jeremy Rifkin, *The Empathetic Civilization: The Race to Global Consciousness in a World in Crisis* (Penguin Group, 2009).

[22] As of November 28, 2017, there were 3,502: https://www.amazon.com/s/ref=nb_sb_noss?url=search-aliaspercent3Dstripbooks&field-keywords=emphathy.

[23] Paul Bloom, *Against Empathy: The Case for Rational Compassion* (London: Bodley Head, 2016).

[24] Spencer Kornhaber, "Empathy: Overrated?" *Atlantic*, July 3, 2015, quoting Paul Bloom, *Against Empathy*, https://www.theatlantic.com/health/archive/2015/07/against-empathy-aspen-paul-bloom-richard-j-davidson/397694/.

[25] According to the *Online Etymological Dictionary*, "empathy" was "coined [in] 1858 by German philosopher Rudolf Lotze": https://www.etymonline.com/word/empathy.

[26] *English Oxford Living Dictionaries*, s.v. "empathy," https://en.oxforddictionaries.com.

[27] Bloom is an advocate of "rational compassion."

[28] Jack Weatherford, *Genghis Khan and the Making of the Modern World* (New York: Three Rivers Press, Crown Publishing Group, 2004).

[29] Peter F. Drucker, *Post Capitalist Society* (Routledge, 2011), Chapter 1, 20.

[30] Eisenhower, "Farewell Radio and Television Address."

[31] Praveen Duddu, "The 10 Longest Range Intercontinental Ballistic Missiles (ICBM)," *Army Technology*, November 3, 2013, http://www.army-technology.com/features/feature-the-10-longest-range-intercontinental-ballistic-missiles-icbm/.

[32] Rakesh Krishnan Simha, "Satan Scare: Why the US Is Going Ballistic over a Russian Missile," *Russia Beyond*, May 23, 2014, https://www.rbth.com/blogs/2014/05/23/satan_scare_why_the_us_is_going_ballistic_over_a_russian_missile_35461.

[33] Simha, "Satan Scare."

[34] Evan Andrews, "10 Things You May Not Know About Genghis Khan," *History.com*, April 29, 2104, http://www.history.com/news/history-lists/10-things-you-may-not-know-about-genghis-khan.

[35] Erich Maria Remarque, *The Black Obelisk, A Novel* (Random House, 2013), Kindle edition.

[36] Remarque, *Black Obelisk*, 141.

[37] WashingtonsBlog, "America Has Been at War 93 Percent of the Time – 222 Out of 239 Years – Since 1776," *World News Daily Information Clearing House*, February 23, 2015, http://www.informationclearinghouse.info/article41086.htm.

[38] Max Roser, "War and Peace," *OurWorldInData.org,* n.d., https://ourworldindata.org/war-and-peace/; "Wars Involving the United States," *Histropedia* http://histropedia.com/timeline/1fjqtpg9bg0t/Wars-involving-the-United-States.

[39] Between 1898 and 1934, in a series of occupations and police and military actions, the United States intervened in several Central American and Caribbean countries to protect the commercial interests of American owners of banana plantations, in particular, United Fruit.

These became known as the "Banana Wars." For more information see: Peter Chapman, *Bananas: How the United Fruit Company Shaped the World* (New York: Canongate Books, 2008). See also: Lester D. Langley, *The Banana Wars: United States Intervention in the Caribbean, 1898-1934,* rev. ed. (Langham, MD: Scholarly Resources, 2001).

[40] George Heymont, "Looking Back 100 Years," *Huffington Post*, September 13, 2015, as updated on December 6, 2017, https://www.huffingtonpost.com/george-heymont/looking-back-100-years_b_8129840.html; Max Roser, "War and Peace."

[41] Adam Withnall, "Global Peace Index 2016: There Are Now Only 10 Countries in the World that Are Actually Free From Conflict," *Independent*, June 8, 2016, http://www.independent.co.uk/news/world/politics/global-peace-index-2016-there-are-now-only-10-countries-in-the-world-that-are-not-at-war-a7069816.html.

[42] "Global Peace Index 2017," *Vision of Humanity*, n.d., http://visionofhumanity.org/indexes/global-peace-index/.

[43] MENA stands for Middle East and North Africa.

[44] "Global Peace Index 2016," Institute for Economics & Peace (2016), Executive Summary, 3, https://reliefweb.int/sites/reliefweb.int/files/resources/GPIpercent202016percent20Report_2.pdf.

[45] General Carl von Clausewitz, *On War*, translated by Colonel J.J. Graham in 1874 (1832, rev. ed. Project Gutenberg, 2006), Book I, Chapter I, paragraph 24, https://www.gutenberg.org/ebooks/1946.

[46] Clausewitz, *On War*, Book II, Chapter II, paragraph 15.

[47] Lucas Baur, "Machiavelli and Sun Tzu: Comparisons on their Art of War," *Liberty and Security*, May 21, 2014, https://libertyandsecurity.wordpress.com/2014/05/21/machiavelli-and-sun-tzu-comparisons-on-their-art-of-war/.

[48] Baur, "Machiavelli and Sun Tzu."

[49] Mao Zedong, "Protracted War" (Series of lectures, Yenan Association for the Study of the War of Resistance against Japan, May 26 to June 3, 1938), "War and Politics," para 64, https://www.marxists.org/reference/archive/mao/selected-works/volume-2/mswv2_09.htm.

[50] Andreas Herberg-Rothe, "Clausewitz's 'Wondrous Trinity' as a Coordinate System of War and Violent Conflict," *International Journal of Conflict and Violence* 3, No. 2 (2009): 204-219.

[51] Herberg-Rothe, "Clausewitz's 'Wondrous Trinity,'" 208—the part in italics is the quote from Clausewitz and Herberg-Rothe's citation is: "(Clausewitz 1984, 88–89; 1980, 213)."

[52] Herberg-Rothe, "Clausewitz's 'Wondrous Trinity,'" 208, footnote 7.

[53] Clausewitz, *On War*, Book I, Chapter I, paragraph 3.

[54] Hobbes, *Leviathan,* XIII.9.

[55] Jonathan Wensveen, "Human Nature in Hobbes and Thucydides" (Master thesis, Carleton University, Ottawa, Ontario, 2003), https://curve.carleton.ca/system/files/etd/531746aa-265a-45e0-9e46-7246253f17e9/etd_pdf/9b3abf1b2f0595779560cee42182245f/wensveen-humannatureinhobbesandthucydides.pdf.

[56] Socrates (an alias), "Tradition of Thumos," *Classical Wisdom Weekly*, June 23, 2014, http://classicalwisdom.com/tradition-thumos/.

[57] Wensveen, "Human Nature"; Jessica Moss, "Shame, Pleasure and the Divided Soul," essay, Oxford Studies in Ancient Philosophy, XXIX (2005), http://www.nyu.edu/gsas/dept/philo/faculty/moss/Shame,Pleasureandth eDividedSoul.pdf.

[58] Herberg-Rothe, "Clausewitz's 'Wondrous Trinity,'" 208.

[59] Wensveen, "Human Nature," 8.

Chapter 9

ABOUT REALITY:

The Real Snafu

Age-otori is a Japanese word that means the feeling of looking worse after a haircut. We all know that feeling, but we don't have a single word for it in English. What if we did?

Beyonce: "Hey, girl, s'up?"

Lady Gaga: "I'm hairfuct."

Beyonce: "I feel ya, girl. Stick a hat on that thing."

If "hairfuct" were a real word, we would have grown up using it. It would be a part of our "vocabulary of emotions." The bigger that vocabulary, the better able we are to "construct" our emotions and learn to deal with them. So says Lisa Feldman Barrett, a professor of psychology at Northeastern University in Boston.

Age-otori is lifted from Barrett's 2017 book *How Emotions Are Made*.[1] She goes on to claim that we've been looking at reality all wrong, that it's more subjective than we might think, and that subjectivity itself is fluid—influenced by the way our emotions change over time and affected by our "social reality." What's "social reality"?

Barrett explains that "the dividing line between biology and culture is porous"—one affects the other.[2] She gives an example: if you're Russian, a rainbow has seven colors. If you're American, it has only six. In Russian, there are two distinct words for the color we call blue. So, Russians are taught to think of them as two different colors, not different shades of the same color. These color "concepts," built around language and culture, become wired into Russian brains, she says, so they see seven colors in a rainbow, while we see six.[3] This is one of the ways in which their social reality is different from ours. Is it really so different?

We use the language of colors to talk about the tiny band of the electromagnetic radiation spectrum we can see—the wavelengths from about 400 to 700 nanometers.[4] Russians don't see any more, or any less, of that band than we do. So, would it be confusing to talk to a Russian about colors? It wouldn't be like talking to a bird about colors, if birds could talk.

Man:	"Wow, what a beautiful blue sky!"
Eagle:	"Yeah. Hey—look at that dazzling trail of mouse pee down there."
Man:	"I don't see any mouse pee."
Eagle:	"Sorry, dude, it's in the ultra-violet range. I forgot you guys don't see much. Let's just stick to talking sports."

As an example of how our vocabulary of emotions is enriched by words, Barrett uses "schadenfreude." It means the malicious joy we take in the misfortune of others.[5] The word came into English from German around the mid-1800s, but it only became popular in the 1990s.[6] It's a compound word from *schaden* (damage or harm) and *freude* (joy).[7] In German, new concepts can be created almost at will by making word combinations like this. Germans do it all the time.[8] According to Barrett, those of us who use "schadenfreude" have a richer emotional vocabulary, and this serves to enrich our emotions, which in turn affects our "reality."

The role language plays in shaping our reality is only part of Barrett's thesis (we'll come back to it). Her main insight is that the brain creates its own reality by making predictions, not only from the language it hears but from every bodily sensation. It uses these predictions to make the body act in the moment. It also builds a database of experiences to guide future actions—our inner Google.

There are two sources of sensations: internal, from organs, tissues and hormones;[9] and external, from the senses. The brain uses internal sensations to predict what the body needs to keep it alive. Externally—"What we see, hear, touch, taste, and smell, are all simulations of the world, not reactions to it... Through prediction, your brain constructs the world you experience. It combines bits and pieces of your past and estimates how likely each bit applies in your current situation."[10] As Barrett said in a 2017 interview: "Basically, your brain is processing internal and external sensations all the time, and it's making meaning out of them. That's what an emotion is."[11] All of this occurs automatically, below the level of consciousness. If it were deliberative, it would be too slow.

Emotions also drive actions we think of as reflexive, like "fight-or-flight" responses. But sometimes the brain's predictions are wrong. For example, sometimes the eyes see what the brain expects them to see, not what's really there. In the heat of the moment, a cop actually sees a man with a gun, while his Bodycam[12] sees a teenager with a cell phone. It may only be after the gun is fired that the cop's brain corrects its prediction. Only then he sees the cell phone and the teenager—who might be dead or wounded.

Prediction errors don't happen only in reflexive situations. They happen in every aspect of our lives. Daniel

Kahneman has spent his career studying perception errors. He's a psychologist, winner of the Nobel Memorial Prize in Economics, and Professor Emeritus at Princeton University. In 2011, he wrote a book called *Thinking, Fast and Slow*.[13] If he'd consulted Barrett about the title, she might have suggested *Feeling Fast, Thinking Slow* because the brain's automatic prediction system isn't what we usually think of as thinking. Anyway, Kahneman's book did very well.

Barrett cites a (now famous) 2011 study that Kahneman quotes in his book. It's about Israeli judges who spend their days hearing parole applications. On average, they approve only thirty-five percent of requests. Even though the order of applicants is random, approvals spike to sixty-five percent after lunch. But, during the two hours before lunch, the approval rate drops steadily. Just before lunch, it's near zero. The judges experience their internal sensations not as hunger but as evidence for their parole decisions. Without them knowing it, their bodily sensations (reactions to levels of blood sugar) shape their perceptions. On the way home from work, do these judges wonder why all the bad guys show up just before lunch and all the good guys just after? Maybe not—they're probably hungry again.[14]

Barrett's "constructed emotions," operating below the surface of consciousness are what Kahneman calls "System 1." He calls slow, conscious thinking "System 2."[15] It doesn't matter what you call them, they're in an uneasy marriage.

System 1 is doing stuff that System 2 doesn't know about, but System 2 thinks it's in control. They may live in the same body, but they're not talking to each other. It gets weirder. System 1 can even fool System 2—with metaphors.

In his course *Being Human*, Robert Sapolsky, a professor of biology and neurology at Stanford University, talks about the way System 1 tricks the conscious mind (System 2). [16]

You step into an elevator on your way to interview a job candidate. There's someone else in the elevator. She has an unwieldy bundle of files under one arm—a cup of coffee in her other hand. She asks you to hold the coffee cup. She gets off on the 10th floor—you hand it back to her. You get off on the 11th floor and go to the interview. If the coffee cup was warm against your hand, you are more likely to think that the job candidate has a warm personality. If it was iced coffee, you're more likely to find the candidate cold. If the chair you sit on during the interview is soft, you're more likely to think of the candidate as cooperative and agreeable. A hard chair would lead you to find him an inflexible hard-ass. [17]

Sapolsky explains that the warm-or-cold, soft-or-hard sensations change your body's "affect." Affect isn't an emotion, it's more like a background setting: pleasant versus unpleasant, and calm versus aroused. System 1 continually adjusts your affect as you go about your day. Sensations from the warm coffee cup and the soft chair tilt the balance towards a pleasant and calm affect. System 2 senses the positive shift, but not its cause. It misreads it as something to do with the candidate because that's where its focus lies. So, unless the candidate does something odd, System 2 is going to find him warm and agreeable. And System 1 won't know that it fooled System 2 with sensory metaphors.

It seems that we don't always know why we do the things we do, or why we make the decisions we make, even though we might think we do. There's also a sense in which we have misconceptions about who we really are.

French philosophers are fond of categorical statements. René Descartes said: "I think, therefore I am."[18] What if he'd said: "I eat, therefore I am?" Sure enough, one of his compatriots, Jean Anthelme Brillat-Savarin, said something similar in 1826: "Tell me what you eat, and I will tell you who you are."[19] Although he didn't mean it literally, Brillat-Savarin was onto something.

There's a part of the body that weighs about the same as the brain. It's self-contained and has a vital function, so it fits the definition of an organ. It's the microbiota. There are scientists who call it "the forgotten organ." One of them is Emeran Mayer M.D., a research director at UCLA. In 2016, he published a book, *The Mind-Gut Connection*.[20]

We are not single organisms. Each of us is a "supraorganism." The other parts of "you" have more cells, and vastly more genes, than the part you generally think of as 'you.'[21] Sure—but this is just about digestion, right? Nope. The microbiota is part of our "second brain."[22] The other part is the gut, a sensory organ with a surface area the size of a basketball court that's sprinkled with a hundred million nerve cells. The microbes of the microbiota—there are about a hundred trillion of them—coat the gut. This is where we make ninety-five percent of our serotonin, a neurotransmitter that not only facilitates the peristaltic reflex in the gut but also influences pain sensitivity, appetite, and... mood.[23]

Mayer sums it up this way: "As the prominent microbiome expert David Relman, of Stanford University, expressed it: 'The human microbiota is a fundamental component of what it means to be human.' In addition to their indispensable role in helping us digest large parts of our diet, it is becoming clear that gut microbes have an extensive and wholly unexpected influence on the appetite-control systems and emotional operating systems in our brain, on our behavior, and even on our minds. These invisible creatures in our digestive system have a word to say when it comes to how we feel, how we make our gut-based decisions, and how our brain develops and ages."[24]

Our microbiome is part of a crowd that's been around a lot longer than we have, and they have much better connections. As Mayer says, they have a "shared biological communication system to all the other microbiomes in the soil, the air, the oceans, and the microbes living in symbiosis with almost all other living creatures."[25] What if you were to mess with your microbiome? Would that change who you are? According to researchers at McMaster University, if you swap the microbiome of a mouse from a timid breed with that of a mouse from a gregarious breed, the timid mouse becomes gregarious.[26] No one's going to make a swap between John McEnroe and the Dalai Lama, but the result might be interesting.

The idea of "self" was a problem before we knew we were supraorganisms. Part of it has to do with the way we grow and age. We're a bit like the Buddhist Temple of Horyu-ji in Japan, which is one of the world's oldest wooden structures. The Temple dates back to 609 A.D. It's not entirely clear how many times it's been rebuilt or how much of the original wood survived. [27] We begin as part of someone else, just as trees are the "mother" of the Temple. During the third trimester in the womb, we begin to have some level of awareness. The wood for the Temple is being milled. Somewhere between two and four months after birth, our awareness moves up a level. The wood moves to the site of the Temple. By the time we're eighteen months old, we've moved up again. Construction of the Temple has begun. At around three years old, we move up yet again and, by the age of five, we reach the fifth, and highest, level of self-awareness.[28] The Temple is finished but not decorated. As we mature, our emotions and experiences color our sense of self.

We've been changing since birth. Most of our body's cells have been replacing themselves, except those in the brain's cerebral cortex, which are not replaced (they just gradually die off).[29] The Temple is expanded, repaired, and renovated. That's where the comparison ends. We die. The Temple survives. But which Temple is it that survives—which "self" is it that dies? Is there just one "self"?

Philippe Rochat is a professor in the Department of Psychology at Emory University. His research suggests that there are "five levels of self-awareness that unfold early in life" (that's the title of a paper he wrote in 2003).[30] He concludes that "as adults, we are constantly oscillating in our levels of awareness: from dreaming or losing awareness about ourselves during sleep, to being highly self-conscious in public circumstances or in a state of confusion and dissociation as we immerse ourselves in movies or novels. In fact, each of these oscillating states of self-awareness can be construed as constant transition between the five levels emerging early in life."[31]

Not only do we change physiologically as we go through life, but our sense of self evolves and then oscillates. So, what is this "self" thing anyway?

For Buddhists, the answer is easy. It's an illusion that eats. Just kidding! It's hard to understand the "self/no-self" idea in Buddhism, and there's more than one interpretation of it. If Barrett is right that reality is subjective and that our biological boundaries are "porous," Buddhism seems like a grander version of that premise, coupled with a theory that the subjective self can dissolve into some kind of "oneness." According to Alfred Kaszniak, a professor and Head of Psychology at the University of Arizona, "experienced Buddhist meditators report that the practice of calmly and mindfully observing the mental continuum results in a shift in the sense of self, and what was once thought to comprise a stable, permanent self is eventually seen to be impermanent and interdependent. Self-focus is said to fall away as this realization deepens."[32]

Barrett argues that the sense of self differs from culture to culture. She says: "The human brain evolved, in the context of human cultures, to create *more than one kind of mind*. People in Western cultures, for example, experience thoughts and emotions as fundamentally different and sometimes in conflict. At the same time, Balinese and Ilongot cultures and, to a certain extent, cultures guided by Buddhist philosophy, do not make hard distinctions between thinking and feeling."[33] In the West, do we really experience thoughts as "fundamentally different" from emotions? Don't they sometimes shade into each other? If, as Barrett says, we construct our emotions, could we deconstruct our blend of thoughts and emotions as Buddhists and other meditators are said to do? If we could do this, where would the self go? Where does it go when we're given a general anesthetic?

Western thinkers from the Ancient Greeks onward have had a hard time working out where the self is, never mind where it goes when it's changed by meditation or medication. David Hume, a moral philosopher of the 17th-century Scottish Enlightenment, wrote: "I may venture to affirm... that (persons) are nothing but a bundle or collection of different perceptions, which succeed each other with an inconceivable rapidity, and are in perpetual flux and movement."[34] This came to be known as the "bundle theory."[35] It's been remarkably persistent, but where does it take us? What turns this bundle into a self? Maybe we should look to science for an answer.

For scientists, the self is about theories of consciousness. According to neuroscientist Christof Koch, the two theories of consciousness that the neuroscience community takes most seriously are "global workplace theory" and "integrated information theory."[36] Koch favors the second. Michael Graziano, another neuroscientist, says that they are both part of the same family of ideas, which holds that consciousness arises when a sufficiently large network of neural circuits synchronizes long enough to command attention and guide action.[37] Graziano says that this thesis satisfies our intuition but it doesn't really explain consciousness. He has his own idea, which he calls "attention schema theory."[38] According to Graziano, "the brain constructs packets of information, virtual models, that describe things in the world. Anything useful to monitor and predict, the brain can construct a model of it. These simulations change continuously as new information comes in, and they're used to guide ongoing behavior. For example, the visual system constructs rich, detailed models of the objects in the visual world; a desk, a car, another person. But the brain doesn't just model concrete objects in the external world. It also models its own internal processes. It constructs simulations of its own cognition. And those simulations are never accurate. They contain incomplete, sometimes surreal information. The brain constructs a distorted, cartoon sketch of itself and its world. And this is why we're so certain that we have a kind of magic feeling inside us."[39] Graziano's idea resonates with Barrett's idea about emotions. He concedes that we need to learn more. He believes that, in fifty years, scientists will be able to build a device capable of having the subjective experience of, say, the color blue.[40] In the meantime, we have an extra-sensory "magic feeling" that tells us when consciousness is "on," but not when it's "off." We're sometimes slightly spooked when it's been off for a while and then suddenly comes back on, such as when we step out of a car and realize we have no memory of having driven it. We drove skillfully enough to avoid an accident but without paying conscious attention.

We think of our conscious self as being inside our head, but there is no place in the brain where it lives. Maybe the self is something that we can only express as an idea—at least until science can tell us more. This brings us back to the system for expressing ideas, language, and Barrett's theory about how language affects our reality.

If each of us were an island in the universe, we might not need a self. But we're not islands. We're part of a system within a network of systems. As Barrett says, the self needs the context of "social reality," just as a word needs context to give it meaning. The word "run" has no sense of self, but it does have an essence, which is in its sound and the symbols we use to write it. Even though it's a short word, it has a range of meanings. It needs other words in order to tell us what meaning it will take. I can *run* to a store that's *run* as a franchise. I can *run* up an account there until I *run* out of money, and then *run* from the law before they *run* me in. The same simple word has several meanings. They all depend on the context provided by the surrounding words.

Even more important than context is a shared idea of what a word means. The better the consensus about its meaning, the easier it is for the word to work with other words in order to convey its meaning. Maybe that's why we evolved a sense of self. Maybe, like language, this sense helps us work together for the good of our social context— our tribe or our community. Barrett says that language helps us construct our emotions by giving us agreed-on mental labels for emotions. Maybe the self is constructed in a similar way. For this to work, we need to be able to read the labels.

How easy is it to do this?

Take the "emotion words"—"guilt" and "shame." *Thesaurus.com* lists them as synonyms.[41] Yet, Brené Brown, once an obscure professor at the University of Houston's Graduate College of Social Work, shot to fame and fortune by explaining the difference between their meanings. Brown's 2010 TED Talk, "The Power of Vulnerability," has been viewed more than thirty million times.[42] Now she's a best-selling author. Brown says that, if you come to work with a hangover and you feel guilty about it, you're focusing on your behavior. You can deal with it and move on. If, instead, it makes you feel like you're a bad person, then you're focusing on who you are, not what you did. That's shame. Brown says her research shows that "shame is highly, highly correlated with addiction, depression, suicide, bullying, aggression, violence, eating disorders. And, if that doesn't get your attention enough, guilt is inversely correlated with those outcomes, meaning the more guilt you're able to use and the more you're able to focus on behavior rather than self, the less likely it is that you'll experience those outcomes."[43] In psychological terms, guilt and shame are diametric opposites—antonyms, not synonyms.

If there's enough confusion about the meanings of common emotion words like guilt and shame to make Brown rich and famous, then knowing the word "schadenfreude" may not enrich our emotions by much, far less help us deal with them. I feel guilty for saying that Brown's fame rests on her explanation of the difference between guilt and shame. She's smart and funny and she has lots of other interesting things to say. Yet, she calls herself a "shame researcher."[44] The shame–guilt space is her sweet spot. So, my exaggeration was only a small one. Even so, I am feeling some guilt about it—not shame. Had she not explained the difference, I'm not sure I would have had the right label for how I feel. (Should I add a winking emoticon here?)

If most of us agree on the meaning of schadenfreude, then using that word is a useful way of conveying the feeling it represents. If we don't, it just ends up in the fossil record— the dictionary. Language is less abstract than the sense of self because we can hear it or see it written down, yet it's still elusive. It involves an endless, complex, and subliminal social negotiation about how and when the meaning of a word changes, and whether we keep using it. *Global Language Monitor* estimates that a new English word is born every ninety-eight minutes.[45] Most of them die in childhood. Those that survive change their meanings over time. "Awful" used to be "awesome," "nice" used to be "silly" and "silly" used to be "blessed."[46]

Are we any nearer to understanding our sense of self? Is it just an abstraction mediated by language, which is itself only slightly less abstract, as well as being highly dependent on context and changing social understandings?

What about our sense of place? What about our sense of time? Are they any easier to understand than our sense of self?

In the 5th century B.C., the earth was a disc at the center of a bigger disc, floating on an ocean. Today, it is a cosmic mote. It rotates around a speck in an expanding universe, larger than we can imagine, or it might be part of a multiverse, stranger than we can imagine. Back in the 5th century B.C., the gods made everything. Today, they make nothing. We didn't fall off the earth when it stopped being flat and started rotating. Nothing changed when the gods went out of business. We didn't shrink when the universe expanded. And, if time is another of our illusions, George Clooney will still advertise Omega watches.[47] Seriously, though, could time be an illusion?

Our conceptions about the world keep changing. From the time of Anaxagoras in the 5th century B.C., our study of physics could be regarded as a history of preconceptions about matter, space, and time that were gradually revealed to be misconceptions—until we ran out of preconceptions in 1905 when Einstein showed that space and time are entwined.[48] We had no preconception about a fourth dimension called space-time. Then, in the mid-1920s, the microscopic world suddenly acquired a different set of rules than those of the macroscopic world, courtesy of Heisenberg and Schrödinger.[49] Now subatomic particles are also waves.

They can be in two places at once, and they can communicate across vast distances faster than the speed of light.[50] This is quantum mechanics. Forty years after Heisenberg and Schrödinger discovered it, Richard Feynman, winner of the Nobel Prize for Physics, admitted: "I think I can safely say that nobody understands quantum mechanics."[51] So, we certainly didn't have any preconceptions about it.

Weird as it is, quantum mechanics works. It underpins the technology of the Information Age.[52] Weirder still is that, although Einstein's general theory of relativity contradicts quantum mechanics, they both work.[53] If they could be unified into a "theory of everything," physics would be complete. In his 1979 inaugural address as Lucasian Professor at Cambridge, Stephen Hawking, an English physicist, announced a fifty percent chance that there'd be a "theory of everything" by end of the century.[54] There wasn't. But, if physicists do come up with such a theory, Julian Barbour, another English physicist, says that time will end.[55] Time is a crucial concept shared by Newtonian physics, relativity, and quantum mechanics. And, when they are unified, time will be revealed as an illusion, Barbour believes. The very different equations of Newton, Einstein, and Heisenberg and Schrödinger work whether time "flows" backwards or forwards. So, mathematical time must be something different from the time we experience. As Barbour notes, Newton called the time we experience "relative" or "apparent" time, implying that, in some interval of "true" time, the universe could do an infinite number of things without in any way changing that interval.[56]

The nature of time has always been puzzling. In the 4th century A.D., Saint Augustine recognized that he couldn't explain it. He mused: "How can the past and future be, when the past no longer is, and the future is not yet? As for the present, if it were always present and never moved on to become the past, it would not be time, but eternity."[57] For Barbour, eternity is a collection of all possible configurations of particles in the cosmos. These configurations exist outside of time. He calls each of them a "now." Barbour takes his inspiration from Ernst Mach, who said in 1883: "It is utterly beyond our power to *measure* the changes of things by *time*...time is an abstraction at which we arrive by means of the changes of things; made because we are not restricted to any one *definite* measure, all being interconnected."[58] In other words, time is just one way of conceptualizing change or motion. If Barbour is right, then there is no motion either. Every possible configuration of the cosmic system exists "now," so that we must be in a simultaneous, static multiverse. Barbour concedes that "writing about the nature of time is a hard task. Unlike the Emperor dressed in nothing, time is nothing dressed in clothes. I can only describe the clothes."[59] Physicists working to reconcile quantum mechanics and general relativity agree that there is a "problem of time."[60] But not many of them are ready to give up on time, though it may just be a matter of time—whatever that is.

If we are just tiny, easily confused, supraorganic chemical casseroles in a timeless, static multiverse, what the hell are we doing here? Whoever answers that question can take the rest of the day off.

The bit of the cosmos we can see is beautiful and weird—weird beyond our understanding. Yet, the whole thing has rules. We can detect patterns in it. That has to mean something, doesn't it? Yes. It means we've adapted to detect patterns. If we weren't good at this, we wouldn't have survived as long as we have. But the patterns keep changing. For Newton, the cosmos was mechanical. For Einstein, it was relative. And for Schrödinger, it was probabilistic. We keep searching for meaning in the patterns. This invites us to view probability through a prism, breaking it into a plausible spectrum of stories about "self," about society, about history, and about destiny. Some believe the patterns we "see" are pre-determined. Others believe they follow from our acts of will. These are just stories about probability. But probability has no story. We have some choices about our actions, but they are limited—more so than we like to believe. Our limited choices, interacting with the many things about which we have no choice, mean that our lives follow paths that are neither willed nor fated—just more or less probable.

So, what is reality, really? Nothing happens if you ignore this question. The cops don't show up at your house and ask you why you haven't thought about it. Yet, everything we do involves tacit assumptions about reality that matter in the real world—when we see things that aren't there, do things without knowing why, confuse feelings with thoughts, and hear, say, read, or write things that are misunderstood. Our awareness flutters like the wings of a Lorenz butterfly,[61] while electrochemical impulses dance beneath its surface—and we die a different supraorganism from the one that was born. Our biological reality is a miracle. At least for now, our psychological reality is a paradox—you might even call it a snafu.

---

[1] Lisa Feldman Barrett, *How Emotions Are Made: The Secret Life of the Brain* (Macmillan, 2017), Kindle edition.

[2] Barrett, *How Emotions Are Made*, Chapter 13.

[3] Barrett, *How Emotions Are Made*, Chapter 7.

[4] "Why Is Human Vision Restricted to 400-700 nm?" *Biology, StackExchange*, n.d., https://biology.stackexchange.com/questions/35337/why-is-human-vision-restricted-to-400-700-nm.

[5] *Online Etymology Dictionary*, s.v. "schadenfreude," https://www.etymonline.com.

[6] Jane Hu, "A Joyful & Malicious History of 'Schadenfreude,'" *Awl*, October 20, 2011, https://www.theawl.com/2011/10/a-joyful-malicious-history-of-schadenfreude/.

[7] *Online Etymology Dictionary*, s.v. "schadenfreude."

[8] Johnson (blog), "The Long and the Short of It," *Economist*, June 21, 2010, https://www.economist.com/blogs/johnson/2010/06/short_and_long_words.

[9] This is called "interoception," a word Barrett uses a lot in her book.

[10] Barrett, *How Emotions Are Made*, Chapter 4.

[11] Ben Dickinson, "You're More in Control of Your Emotions than You Think (Says New Brain Science)," *Elle*, February 18, 2017, http://www.elle.com/life-love/a42863/how-emotions-are-made/.

[12] "Bodycam" is the trademark and name of a video camera worn on the body. It is made by Pro-Vision, http://www.bodycameras.com.

[13] Daniel Kahneman, *Thinking, Fast and Slow* (New York: Farrar, Straus and Giroux, 2011).

[14] During the study, the judges had several meal breaks and the results were consistent for periods before and after all meal breaks. They didn't go home for dinner. (Poetic license)

[15] Kahneman, *Thinking*, 13.

[16] Robert Sapolsky, "Being Human: Life Lessons from the Frontiers of Science," *Great Courses*, Course No. 1686, n.d., https://www.thegreatcourses.com/courses/being-human-life-lessons-from-the-frontiers-of-science.html.

[17] This is adapted from some of the situations that Sapolsky describes in his course.

[18] The phrase originally appeared in French, "Je pense, donc je suis," in Descartes' *Discourse on Method*, published in 1637. It often appears in Latin ("cogito, ergo sum").

[19] Jean Anthelme Brillat-Savarin, *The Physiology of Taste: Or Meditations on Transcendental Gastronomy* (1825), M.F.K Fisher, trans. (New York: Vintage Classics, 2011).

[20] Emeran Mayer, M.D., *The Mind Gut Connection: How the Hidden Conversation Within Our Bodies Impacts Our Mood, Our Choices, and Our Overall Health* (New York: Harper Wave, 2016).

[21] Mayer, *The Mind Gut Connection*, 18.

[22] This is the title of a 1999 book by Michael D. Gershon, M.D. (published by Harper Perennial) that Mayer refers to in his book.

[23] Mayer, *The Mind Gut Connection,* 23.

[24] Mayer, *The Mind Gut Connection,* 102.

[25] Mayer, *The Mind Gut Connection,* 18.

[26] Mayer, in *The Mind Gut Connection,* refers to this study in passing. There is a more comprehensive reference to it in Giulia Enders and David Show, trans., *Gut: The Inside Story of Our Body's Most Underrated Organ* (Brunswick, VIC, AU: Scribe, 2015), Kindle.

[27] "Horyuji Temple," Architecture, Japan Atlas, n.d., http://web-japan.org/atlas/architecture/arc19.html.

[28] Philippe Rochat, "Five Levels of Self-Awareness as they Unfold Early in Life," *Consciousness and Cognition* 12 (2003): 717-31, available at *Science Direct, Elsevier*, February 27, 2003, http://www.psychology.emory.edu/cognition/rochat/Rochat5levels.pdf.

[29] Pelletier, TC., "Do We Replace Our Cells Every 7 or 10 years?" *Ask a Naturalist.com,* August 10, 2010, http://askanaturalist.com/do-we-replace-our-cells-every-7-or-10-years/.

[30] Rochat, "Five levels," 728.

[31] Rochat, "Five levels," 728.

[32] Alfred W. Kaszniak, "Empathy and Compassion in Buddhism and Neuroscience," *WGBH, PBS*, March 17, 2010, http://www.pbs.org/thebuddha/blog/2010/Mar/17/empathy-and-compassion-buddhism-and-neuroscience-a/.

[33] Barrett, *How Emotions Are Made*, Chapter 13 (emphasis in the original).

[34] Jeff Speaks, "Hume on Identity over Time and Persons," Handout, PHIL 20208, October 3, 2006, page 1, quoting David Hume, https://www3.nd.edu/~jspeaks/courses/2006-7/20208/hume-personal-identity.pdf.

[35] *Encyclopaedia Britannica*, s.v. "Bundle Theory," https://www.britannica.com/topic/bundle-theory.

[36] Christof Koch, *The Quest for Consciousness: A Neurobiological Approach* (Englewood, CO: Roberts, 2004). Koch is the Chief Scientific Officer at the Allen Institute for Neuroscience in Seattle.

[37] Michael Graziano, "Most Popular Theories of Consciousness Are Worse than Wrong," *Atlantic*, March 9, 2016, https://www.theatlantic.com/science/archive/2016/03/phlegm-theories-of-consciousness/472812/. Graziano is a professor of Psychology and Neuroscience at Princeton University.

[38] Taylor W. Webb and Michael S.A. Graziano, "The Attention Schema Theory: A Mechanistic Account of Subjective Awareness," *Frontiers in Psychology*, April 23, 2015, https://www.frontiersin.org/articles/10.3389/fpsyg.2015.00500/full.

[39] Graziano, "Most Popular Theories."

[40] Graziano, "Most Popular Theories."

[41] *Thesaurus.com*, s.v. " guilt" and "shame," http://www.thesaurus.com.

[42] As of November 29, 2017, the number is 32,130,673, https://www.ted.com/talks/brene_brown_on_vulnerability.

[43] Brené Brown, *The Power of Vulnerability: Teachings on Authenticity, Connection, and Courage,* narrated by Brené Brown (Sounds True, 2013) audiobook, Chapter 12.

[44] Brown, *The Power of Vulnerability*, Chapter 1.

[45] "The Number of Words in the English Language," *Global Language Monitor*, http://www.languagemonitor.com/top-words-of-the-year/no-of-words/.

[46] You can find these examples in: John McWhorter, *Words on the Move: Why English Won't and Can't Sit Still (Like, Literally)* (New York: Henry Holt, 2016), 61, 65, 75, 77, 84 and 110.

[47] "All About the Ambassadors of Omega Watches," https://oemgaambassadors.weebly.com.

[48] Richard Panek, "The Year of Albert Einstein," *Smithsonian Magazine*, June 2005, https://www.smithsonianmag.com/science-nature/the-year-of-albert-einstein-75841381/.

[49] "Erwin Schrödinger and Werner Heisenberg devise a quantum theory, January 27, 1926," *CERN Timelines*, https://timeline.web.cern.ch/events/erwin-schrödinger-and-werner-heisenberg-devise-a-quantum-theory.

[50] Robert Coolman, "What is Quantum Mechanics?" *Live Science*, September 26, 2014, https://www.livescience.com/33816-quantum-

mechanics-explanation.html; Karl Tate, "How Quantum Entanglement Works (Infographic)," *Live Science*, April 8, 2013, https://www.livescience.com/28550-how-quantum-entanglement-works-infographic.html.

[51] Richard Feynman, Robert B. Leighton and Matthew Sands, *The Feynman Lectures on Physics, Volume III (Quantum Mechanics) 1964*, revised and extended edition (Boston, MA: Addison-Wesley, 2005), Chapter 6.

[52] John Matson, "What is Quantum Mechanics Good for?" *Scientific American*, November 2, 2010, https://www.scientificamerican.com/article/everyday-quantum-physics/.

[53] "A list of Inconveniences between Quantum Mechanics and (General) Relativity?" *Physics. StackExchange*, n.d., https://physics.stackexchange.com/questions/387/a-list-of-inconveniences-between-quantum-mechanics-and-general-relativity.

[54] Stephen Hawking, *Is the End in Sight for Theoretical Physics: An Inaugural Lecture, 1979* (Cambridge: Cambridge University Press, 1980).

[55] Julian Barbour, *The End of Time* (Oxford University Press, 1999), Chapter 1.

[56] Julian Barbour, "The Nature of Time," March 2009, https://arxiv.org/pdf/0903.3489.pdf.

[57] St. Augustine, *The Confessions of Saint Augustine*, Trans. E. B. Pusye (Edward Bouverie) (AD 401, Project Gutenberg, 2002), Book Eleven, Chapter XIV. https://www.gutenberg.org/ebooks/3296.

[58] Ernst Mach and Thomas J. McCormack, trans., *The Science of Mechanics: A Critical and Historical and its Development*, (The Open Court Publishing Co, 4th ed., 1919), 224, https://archive.org/details/scienceofmechani005860mbp.

[59] Barbour, "The Nature of Time."

[60] Natalie Wolchover, "Quantum Gravity's Time Problem," *Quanta Magazine*, December 2, 2016, https://www.quantamagazine.org/quantum-gravitys-time-problem-20161201/.

---

[61] Edward Norton Lorenz (1938-2008), an American theoretical meteorologist, used the metaphor of a butterfly flapping its wings to illustrate that small disturbances in a complex weather system can be magnified as they interact with other elements of the system. In a lecture he gave in December 1972, he said: "a butterfly flapping its wings in Brazil can produce a tornado in Texas." See: José Manuel Sánchez Ron, "When Lorenz Discovered the Butterfly Effect," *Open Mind*, May 22, 2015, https://www.bbvaopenmind.com/en/when-lorenz-discovered-the-butterfly-effect/.

Chapter 10

REFLECTIONS ON THE 'ACCELERATED AGE':

Is snafu as good as it gets?

This question about snafu is really a question about the future—a place we can't go. But we can go to the past. As William Faulkner said: "The past is never dead. It's not even past."[1] So, let's go there. It might have an answer or, at least, a clue.

In January 1976, Gerald Ford delivered to Congress the annual "Economic Report of the President." In it, he wrote: "The sharpest recession in the post-World War II period hit bottom last spring, and a substantial recovery is now under way."[2] He was right, but it didn't help him. In November, Ford lost the Presidency to an outsider—Jimmy Carter. Under Carter, Presidential politics began a brief experiment with truth and introspection. The experiment peaked less than three years later, soon after the onset of the Second Oil Shock.[3]

On July 15, 1979, President Carter appeared on national television. He said: "Ten days ago I had planned to speak to you again about a very important subject—energy. For the fifth time I would have described the urgency of the problem and laid out a series of legislative recommendations to the Congress. But as I was preparing to speak, I began to ask myself the same question that I now know has been troubling many of you. Why have we not been able to get together as a nation to resolve our serious energy problem?"[4] Carter went on to warn of "a fundamental threat to American democracy."[5] "The threat is nearly invisible in ordinary ways. It is a crisis of confidence. It is a crisis that strikes at the very heart and soul and spirit of our national will. We can see this crisis in the growing doubt about the meaning of our own lives and in the loss of a unity of purpose for our Nation."[6]

This was stern stuff, yet initial reactions to the speech were positive, "with eighty-five percent of the public voicing a favorable view of it. Carter's anemic approval ratings jumped eleven percent overnight."[7] But within just two days, Carter asked his entire Cabinet to resign, later accepting five resignations.[8] This spooked the American public. His aura of command vanished. The speech acquired the tag "malaise," even though Carter hadn't used that word.[9] As Kevin Mattson, author of the 2009 book *What the Heck Are You Up to, Mr.*

President?, told an interviewer: "It's from then on that Carter had a really difficult time at bouncing back and being seen on the part of the American people as a strong and significant leader—especially a leader that could take America through solving the energy crisis."[10] In November, Edward Kennedy and Ronald Reagan announced they'd run for the presidency. They used the malaise speech to mock Carter. A year later, Reagan took the presidency.

Many remember Carter's speech as a turning point—the prelude to a swing to political conservatism and neoliberal economics. It was. Some dismiss it as an over-reaction to the immediate disruptions of the Second Oil Shock.[11] It wasn't. Carter talked about changes that had "come upon us gradually over the last generation."[12] The speech sounded like a lament—a dirge for the end of an era. This was fitting. An era did end around that time or, perhaps it ended back in 1976 when voters first looked to Carter to try to change things. How long was that era? Was it just a generation, or could it have been longer?

The Industrial Revolution began in England around 1750.[13] In the United States, it began later—because the English were secretive about their new technologies—but not much later. Samuel Slater, the "Father of the American Industrial Revolution," had his mechanized cotton mill running in Rhode Island by 1790.[14]

Sixty or seventy years on, the Industrial Revolution

reached a tipping point with the widespread use not only of coal but other fossil fuels: petroleum and natural gas. And the U.S. was in the vanguard. The start of the "Oil Age" isn't precise. There were discoveries in Western Pennsylvania as early as 1859.[15] Whenever it started, the U.S. became its epicenter, especially after the 1901 strike near Beaumont in Texas, which marked the beginning of large-scale oil production.[16] Meanwhile, Thomas Edison had conquered darkness with the first commercial installation of incandescent electric lights in 1880.[17] Two years later, the world's first commercial electric power plant went into service—Edison's coal-fired plant at Pearl Street in Manhattan.[18]

By 1900, fossil fuels made up eighty percent of primary energy use in the U.S.[19] By then, they were also widely used in the U.K., Europe, and elsewhere. This was the inflection point of an exponential surge in the energy intensity of human activity. Crude oil has almost twice the energy density of coal—natural gas has a quarter more than crude oil.[20] A barrel of crude oil is roughly the energy equivalent of 25,000 hours of human work.[21] Fossil fuels were a game-changer for humanity.

Robert Gordon, a professor at Northwestern University and author of the 2016 book *The Rise and Fall of American Growth*, divides the Industrial Revolution into parts: "IR1" and "IR2."[22] As he puts it: "The first (IR1) with its main inventions between 1750 and 1830 created steam engines, cotton spinning, and railroads. The second (IR2) was the most important, with its three central inventions of electricity, the internal combustion engine, and running water with indoor plumbing, in the relatively short interval of 1870 to 1900. Both revolutions required about 100 years for their full effects to percolate through the economy. During the two decades 1950-70, the benefits of IR2 were still transforming the economy, including air-conditioning, home appliances, and the interstate highway system. After 1970, productivity growth slowed markedly, most plausibly because the main ideas of IR2 had by and large been implemented by then."[23]

This slowdown of growth coincided with other changes. Domestic oil production peaked and, in 1973, the U.S. became a net importer of oil, and the cost of extracting oil began to rise.[24] High inflation, and a falling dollar, meant that most other commodity prices rose.[25] Wages, having risen in the post-war boom, ate into profits, and U.S. corporations began offshoring manufacturing to countries with low labor costs. This began a period of wage stagnation in the U.S. that hasn't yet ended.[26] Producers began having to bear pollution and other costs, which they'd previously been able to "externalize" to the rest of society. Rachel Carson's account of the effects of pesticides in her 1962 book *Silent Spring* launched the environmental movement that led directly to the creation of the Environmental Protection Agency in 1970.[27] And Ralph Nader's 1965 book *Unsafe At Any Speed* exposed the cynicism behind "planned obsolescence," leading to statutory protections for consumers.[28] These things hit the bottom line of U.S. producers.

Carter sensed the shift. He thought it had to do with energy. Energy had enabled America to make so much stuff, but: "We've learned that piling up material goods cannot fill the emptiness of lives which have no confidence or purpose."[29] Energy had made agriculture and industry profligate, and this had damaged the environment and depleted resources. "We will protect our environment... I'm proposing a bold conservation program to involve every State, county, and city and every average American in our energy battle."[30] Carter made connections between energy, materialism and conservation. He talked too about a "loss of confidence, that" "the erosion of our confidence in the future is threatening to destroy the social and the political fabric of America."[31]

The connections weren't entirely obvious. It would have taken more speeches and new programs to make them clearer. But Carter missed his chance. The July Cabinet sackings dented his credibility. In November, the Iran Hostage Crisis blindsided him, wrecking the rest of his Presidency. His "window of opportunity" to steer the country's course for a new era slammed shut.[32] Materialism marched on. Conservation stalled. Energy consumption rose even though manufacturing, as a share of GDP, continued to decline from its 1970 high.[33] The price of oil rose, too. Although it fell when the Second Oil Shock[34] ended in 1980, it soon began to trend upwards.[35]

Carter used strong language. It was almost apocalyptic. It seemed out of proportion, even for a generational change. What he was really mourning was a decoupling of progress from values. For Carter, this was profound. He grew up in rural Georgia in a deeply religious family. The first on his father's side to graduate high school, he studied engineering, then served in the Navy, where he continued his studies and graduated in the top ten percent of his class at Annapolis. After ten years, he returned to Georgia to rescue the family farm after his father died.[36] In the Navy, he'd served under Admiral Rickover, the pioneer not only of the nuclear navy but also civilian nuclear power.[37] Carter occasionally boasted that, while in the Navy, he'd been a nuclear physicist.[38] It wasn't such a big exaggeration, given his role at the birth of America's nuclear industry. He knew about energy. And he understood the complexities of American history and values. He knew the history of the energy stolen from African slaves in the pre-Industrial South. He also knew firsthand that the Civil War hadn't solved as much as Lincoln had hoped it would, and that repayments had to be made to African Americans. In order to gain the political power to do this, he was willing to resort to subterfuge, and he courted segregationists in his run for Governor of Georgia. So much so that the Atlanta Constitution Journal called him an "ignorant, racist, backward, ultra-conservative, red-necked South Georgia peanut farmer."[39] Yet, as Governor, "he reportedly raised the number of Georgia blacks on state boards and agencies from just three to a staggering fifty-three. Under his leadership, almost half, forty percent, of public servants in influential positions were African American."[40] The first President elected from the Deep South since 1844, Carter won votes from four out of five African Americans.[41]

Here was a complicated and clever man talking about things he understood, using powerful language. It's just possible that the change he felt was more than generational; it's possible that it was part of something deeper. Maybe the era that was ending had started much earlier than he thought. Maybe it had started with the United States itself—an era of two hundred years from 1776 to 1976. Of course, this is far too neat. History doesn't have a narrative for those two hundred years. Carter might not have had one either. Even so, those two hundred years were exceptional. In fact, they were unique in human history—just as the United States was, and is, unique.

In 1776, there were two and a half million people in the thirteen colonies.[42] The Constitution hadn't been written yet. There wasn't even a framework for how politics would work in the new republic.[43] Most Americans worked on farms or as independent artisans.[44] The great cities and factories were still to come. Making Americans pay taxes was something the British did—and would regret. There were few corporations, and they had little influence on George Washington and the other Founding Fathers.

In 1976, the U.S. was home to around 218 million people—more than eighty-seven times as many as there were in 1776.[45] It covered an area more than ten times the size of the original colonies.[46] It was vast and rich—with more navigable rivers and waterways and more and better farmland than any other country on Earth. It had abundant natural resources. It enjoyed a temperate climate.[47] Geographically isolated from its enemies, it had, in any case, no reason to fear them, because it was armed to the teeth.

In those two hundred years, the United States went from a precarious, fledgling republic to an economic and military colossus that dominated the world. In doing so, it illustrated just how unusual those two hundred years were, coinciding as they did with the greatest technological revolution in human history—one made possible by a fossil-energy endowment built up over eons, and "liberated" during those years.

In January 1976, just days before President Ford delivered his Economic Report to Congress, the first supersonic passenger jet—Concorde—made its maiden flights.[48] In April, Steve Jobs and Steve Wozniak started Apple.[49] Later in the year, IBM shipped its first laser printer.[50] NASA announced that its Viking 1 Lander had arrived on

Mars and, a few months on, it unveiled the first space shuttle, Enterprise.[51] Mao Zedong died.[52] An American panel warned that chlorofluorocarbons (CFCs) were damaging the ozone layer.[53] And, of course, on July 4th, the United States celebrated its "birthday"—two hundred years of independence from Britain.

Concorde made its last flight in 2003, a casualty of high fuel costs and noise pollution.[54] Apple became the most valuable company in the world in May 2017.[55] IBM stopped making printers.[56] The space shuttle was retired in 2012. Today, spending on NASA, as a percentage of the Federal Budget, is about half what was in 1976.[57] China transformed its economy beyond recognition after Mao died, with people moving to cities at ten times the rate and a hundred times the scale of Britain in the Industrial Revolution.[58] CFCs are banned and the hole in the ozone layer has shrunk, but we've become aware of a much greater problem called Climate Change.[59]

Professor Gordon identified a third Industrial Revolution—the computer and Internet revolution (IR3). IR3 began around 1960. It reached its climax in the dot.com era of the late 1990s. But, he says, "Many of the inventions that replaced tedious and repetitive clerical labor with computers happened a long time ago, in the 1970s and 1980s. Invention since 2000 has centered on entertainment and communication devices that are smaller, smarter, and more capable, but do not fundamentally change labor productivity or the standard of living in the way that electric light, motor cars, or indoor plumbing changed it."[60] Gordon is selling IR3 short. One day artificial intelligence may end work altogether. It may have other far-reaching effects on the way we live and the way we govern ourselves (though some call this IR4). But he is right about IR1 and IR2. They changed the world profoundly—especially IR2 and the energy revolution that powered it. So did the American Revolution. As Gordon points out, many of the original and spin-off inventions of IR2 could happen only once—urbanization, transportation speed, and the freedom of women from domestic drudgery.[61] The same is true of America, its natural endowments, and the spectacular use it made of them. All this could happen only once. America can never grow again as it did in those two hundred years, and there are no new Americas.

If history has eras, they surely don't start and end at precise times. Nonetheless, we look for patterns. We try to make smooth curves out of jagged lines and neat paths out of random walks—as I've just done with those two hundred years. What was the point of that, and what does it have to do with the question posed at the start of this chapter?

Snafu is a word born out of an acronym: "situation normal, all fucked up." But what's "normal"? Snafu is a word invented in wartime, and we like to think that war isn't "normal." Inside snafu, "normal" is meant sarcastically—

normal for wartime—in other words, anything but normal. Those two hundred years were anything but normal—in a special sense. What made them abnormal was energy—first coal, then oil and gas, and later nuclear power. This era was the historical equivalent of "jump drive" for humanity—a speed faster than the limit. When a situation is anything but normal, it's more likely to get all fucked up. That's my argument. This was an abnormal era: abnormal in energy intensity, abnormal in its rate of economic growth. I call it the 'Accelerated Age.'

When Carter spoke in 1979, people were being murdered waiting in line at gas stations. In Los Angeles, someone attacked a pregnant woman in a gas line.[62] Even a short interruption to the flow of energy can get ugly. Carter worried about our relationship with energy—what we were doing with it, what it was doing to us. He worried about the connection between energy, materialism, and sustainability. He worried about growth without purpose and principle. This is the aspect of the Accelerated Age that is now outmoded—the pursuit of growth for its own sake and at any cost. Just as we're changing our sources of energy—because we must—we will also have to change what we do with energy. The conventional wisdom holds that our purpose is to produce and consume. It was always an empty purpose. Now it has run up against physical limits that we can't change or ignore. This much is already clear: it isn't a prediction. After about 1976, when growth began to slow and we began to make ever greater efforts to revive it, we cut corners—bent morality, social justice, and economic equity until they broke. The limits to growth were becoming clear to Carter in 1979. It was already clear to him that growth for its own sake was an empty purpose, just as it was clear to another clever man who might have become President eight years before him. It would be hard to express that emptiness better than Robert Kennedy did in March 1968.

"Our Gross National Product, now, is over $800 billion a year, but that Gross National Product—if we judge the United States of America by that—that Gross National Product counts air pollution and cigarette advertising, and ambulances to clear our highways of carnage. It counts special locks for our doors and the jails for the people who break them. It counts the destruction of the redwood and the loss of our natural wonder in chaotic sprawl. It counts napalm and counts nuclear warheads and armored cars for the police to fight the riots in our cities. It counts Whitman's rifle and Speck's knife, and the television programs which glorify violence in order to sell toys to our children. Yet, the gross national product does not allow for the health of our children, the quality of their education or the joy of their play. It does not include the beauty of our poetry or the strength of our marriages, the intelligence of our public debate or the integrity of our public officials. It measures neither our wit nor our courage, neither our wisdom nor our learning, neither our compassion nor our devotion to our country, it measures everything in short, except that which makes life worthwhile. And it can tell us everything about America except why we are proud that we are Americans."[63]

In defiance of the conventional wisdom, Kennedy and Carter dared to say that economic growth isn't the same as human progress—that some of what we call growth is not only empty but also harmful. The initial reaction to Carter's speech suggests that many Americans thought so too. But, in 1980, when, as Presidential candidate, Ronald Reagan offered them a smiley fake reality, it was easier for them to fall back on the conventional wisdom than it would have been to make the kind of sacrifices that Carter's prognosis involved. When he became President, Reagan's "sugar hit" of tax cuts for the rich, deficit spending on the military, and deregulation of the financial sector worked just long enough to make him a legend. And the fall of the Soviet Union burnished his legacy. After Reagan, politicians were afraid to say that the party was over. Even now, it would be political suicide to admit that supercharged growth isn't coming back. The Global Financial Crisis of 2007 to 2009 served as a warning that America can't borrow its way back to high growth. The warning wasn't heeded—politicians doubled-down and borrowed more. But the Accelerated Age won't repeat. And a cynical populist can't bring it back by resurrecting Reaganomics and building walls. Objective reality can't be dismissed as fake news.

At the very base of objective reality are the three resources that sustain human life: air, land and water—they're not growing. They're part of a complex system that involves many other elements—a system that we still don't fully understand. Looking at one of these resources in isolation doesn't give us anything like a complete picture of how the exponential growth of the Accelerated Age affected it. Let's take a look at one of them anyway.

Everybody loves water. About forty percent of us live within sixty miles or so of a coast.[64] At the start of the Accelerated Age, Adam Smith wrote about water's "paradox of value,"[65] that "nothing is more useful than water; but it will purchase scarce any thing; scare anything can be had in exchange for it."[66] That's because it was so abundant. It's no less abundant now than it was then. All the water we have was delivered about four and a half billion years ago—it's all still here. Most of it is seawater. The rest—about three percent—is mostly locked up in glaciers and ice caps, or far below the ground. The part we can use easily—about 1.2 percent—is at or near the surface.[67] About a fifth of this is in a single lake, Lake Baikal in Siberia—now badly fouled by phosphates from detergents and other wastewater runoff.[68] Although water is still abundant, the paradox of value no longer holds. Even though markets around the world routinely mispriced water, it was much more valuable at the end of the Accelerated Age than it was at the beginning, when Smith wrote. There are several reasons for this.

For a start, at the end of the Accelerated Age, there were more people using water. During those two hundred years, world population grew from just over 900 million to just under 4.2 billion.[69] As the inventions of IR2 moved outwards from Europe and America, improvements in agricultural productivity and public health meant that more people survived longer—long enough to have more children, who also survived and had children. The annual rate of population growth increased after 1800, from a historical rate well below one percent to a peak rate of 2.1 percent in 1962.[70] After that, the rate began to decline.[71]

During the Accelerated Age, we also changed the way we used water, and we found new uses for it. Agricultural use became more intensive. Again, the new energy abundance, powering the new technologies of IR2, was revolutionizing. They enabled mechanization, irrigation, and fertilization on a scale previously unimaginable. They allowed food to be transported in huge quantities over vast distances. Industry, transportation, and commerce developed new and concentrated uses for water. Even domestic use increased significantly. Behind all these uses, lay energy. It takes eight gallons of water to make one gallon of gasoline.[72] And every other primary source of energy in the Accelerated Age required lots of water.

Politicians, the law, and markets were slow to allocate responsibility for water. So, around 1860, we found a new meaning for an old word—"pollution."[73] More than two million tons of sewage and industrial and agricultural waste are discharged into the world's water every day.[74] More people die from unsafe water than from all forms of violence, including war.[75] Much of this pollution is in the service of another "industry" that grew during the Accelerated Age—waste. Most of the water we use is for agriculture, typically seventy percent—more in developing countries.[76] The cost is often subsidized by governments, yet a third to a half of all the food it produces is thrown away, and with it, the water used to produce it.[77] It's the same with manufactured goods, like clothing—eighty-five percent of which ends up in landfills.[78]

To cap off the Accelerated Age, we damaged the Earth's natural water cycle by heating the atmosphere with greenhouse gases from all those fossil fuels we burned. We changed the patterns of evaporation, condensation, and precipitation. Now we have droughts in some places, storm surges in others, and rising sea levels everywhere.[79] All of us who live near a coast, and all the farming and industry in low-lying areas, are at risk of inundation.[80]

Meanwhile, Nestlé, Coca-Cola, PepsiCo, and others sell bottled water for thousands of times what it costs at the tap, while their plastic containers end up in oceans and landfills.[81] Other corporations grab water rights and run privatized water systems because water is now big business[82]—so big that the wars of the future might be fought over it.[83] According to the United Nations Environment Program: "158 of the world's 263 trans-boundary water basins lack any type of cooperative management framework."[84]

As it was with water, so it was with air and land—the two other bedrock resources we depend on. It was similar too for other, less critical, resources. The "warp speed" growth of the Accelerated Age damaged all our vital resources. The combined costs and consequences of that damage are incalculable because the whole web of life on this planet is now under threat.

Yet, some things did start to change in the 1970s, thanks in part to the Oil Shocks.[85] Water use was one of them. Charles Fishman, author of the 2012 book *The Big Thirst*,[86] points out: "In the last 30 years, the U.S. has more than doubled its GDP, and added 70 million new people, and reduced total water use... We use less water to produce an economy of $13 trillion than we did to produce an economy of $6 trillion... Most of it comes in efficiency from power generation and farming. Farmers, overall, use 15% less water than they did in 1980, but produce 70% more food. That's an increase in farm-water-productivity of 100%."[87]

So, there is hope. But we're still addicted to fast growth, even though it comes at a price we can no longer afford.

In 1992, 1,575 of the world's most prominent scientists

(including 99 of the 196 Nobel laureates then living) sent the world's government leaders a report called "World Scientists' Warning to Humanity." In it, they said: "A great change in our stewardship of the Earth and the life on it is required, if vast human misery is to be avoided."[88] They expressed concern about "ozone depletion, freshwater availability, marine life depletion, ocean dead zones, forest loss, biodiversity destruction, climate change, and continued human population growth."[89]

Twenty-five years later, in November 2017, the scientists issued a "Second Notice," in which they said: "Since 1992, with the exception of stabilizing the stratospheric ozone layer, humanity has failed to make sufficient progress in generally solving these foreseen environmental challenges, and alarmingly, most of them are getting far worse... Especially troubling is the current trajectory of potentially catastrophic climate change due to rising GHGs [Greenhouse Gases] from burning fossil fuels, deforestation, and agricultural production – particularly from farming ruminants for meat consumption. Moreover, we have unleashed a mass extinction event, the sixth in roughly 540 million years, wherein many current life forms could be annihilated or at least committed to extinction by the end of this century."[90] This time, 15,364 scientists from 184 countries signed the report.[91]

Climate Change is an existential threat, as are the contamination and depletion of our natural resources. We are the only species that has some choice about its fate. In the Accelerated Age, we chose rapid growth at any price—this was the conventional wisdom of the Age. We're now coming to regret that choice. But it's not too late to change it, even though our numbers are still growing, while the resources we depend on are not.

Seven times during his speech, Carter used the word "conservation" or "conserve."[92] He was right. Unless we conserve what we have and make better use of it, we won't survive. Carter's concern about our relationship with energy was timely. The connection he tried to make between "energy" and "purpose" is one that no longer needs an explanation. It's now obvious that the only "purpose" we need to connect with "energy" is the purpose of sustaining life on Earth. What better purpose could there be? Can we do this?

We'd have to end the age of fossil fuels, redefine growth, and change the conventional wisdom. We'd have to regrow the systems we damaged in the Accelerated Age. There are sufficient, alternative energy sources. And there are better ways to use energy. The energy intensity we got used to in the Accelerated Age might not even have to decline. We would also need to make better use of the other kind of energy the Accelerated Age liberated—the creative energy of the intellect.

All this is a way of answering the opening question. Snafu isn't as good as it gets. The Accelerated Age fueled the creative energy we can now use to do better. Its snafus gave us the reason to do better. This isn't only about surviving. We can use our creative energy to thrive, not just survive. There are other lessons we can learn from the snafus of the Accelerated Age. One of them is embedded in the word snafu itself. During World War II, ordinary soldiers used snafu to reassure themselves that war is organized madness that should never be allowed to seem "normal." For them, snafu contained the implicit assertion that they could do a better job of bringing the madness to an end than those in authority. That's the main lesson of snafu. Thanks to the Accelerated Age—the social, political, and technological revolutions that came out of it—ordinary people have the means to bring to an end the other thing that came out of the Accelerated Age—the madness of growth without purpose or principle. We can do this if those in authority won't.

---

[1] William Faulkner, *Requiem for a Nun* (Random House, 1951), Act 1, scene 3.

[2] Gerald R. Ford, "Annual Message to the Congress: The Economic Report of the President," (January 18, 1977). Online by Gerhard Peters and John T. Woolley, *The American Presidency Project*. http://www.presidency.ucsb.edu/ws/?pid=5570. The President's message, together with the "Annual Report of the Council of Economic Advisers," is printed in the "Economic Report of the President, Transmitted to the Congress January 1977" (Government Printing Office) available at (http://www.presidency.ucsb.edu/economic_reports/1976.pdf.

[3] See generally: Verleger Jr., "The U.S. Petroleum Crisis."

[4] Carter, "Malaise Speech," paragraph 3.

[5] Carter, "Malaise Speech," paragraph 7.

[6] Carter, "Malaise Speech," paragraph 9

[7] William F. Grover and Joseph G. Peschek, *The Unsustainable Presidency: Clinton, Bush, Obama, and Beyond* (New York: Pearson Educational Inc., 2014), Chapter One, "Competing Narratives and Political Prospects."

[8] Samuel Walker, *Presidents and Civil Liberties from Wilson to Obama: A Story of Poor Custodians* (Cambridge University Press, 2012), 375.

[9] Kevin Mattson, "Examining Carter's 'Malaise Speech,' 30 Years Later," NPR Books, July 12, 2009, https://www.npr.org/templates/story/story.php?storyId=106508243.

[10] Mattson, "Examining Carter's 'Malaise Speech.'" See also: Kevin Mattson, *What The Heck Are You Up To, Mr. President?* (Bloomsbury, 2009).

[11] See generally: Verleger Jr., "The U.S. Petroleum Crisis."

[12] Carter, "Malaise Speech," paragraph 16.

[13] This is the date used by Robert Gordon in *The Rise and Fall of American Growth* (Princeton University Press, 2016).

[14] President Andrew Jackson called Slater the "Father of the American Manufactures." Slater is also known as the "Founder of the American Industrial Revolution." So the "Father of the American Industrial Revolution" is a mash of those two titles. See: *New World Encyclopedia*, s.v. "Samuel Slater," http://www.newworldencyclopedia.org.

[15] "First American Oil Well," American Oil & Gas Historical Society, n.d., https://aoghs.org/petroleum-pioneers/american-oil-history/.

[16] "Spindletop Oilfield," Texas State Historical Association, n.d., https://tshaonline.org/handbook/online/articles/dos03.

[17] "Edison's Electric Light and Power System – Initial Commercialization of Direct-Current (D.C.) Applications," *Engineering and Technology History Wiki*, http://ethw.org/Edisonpercent27s_Electric_Light_and_Power_System.

[18] "Milestones: Pearl Street Station, 1882," *Engineering and Technology History Wiki*, http://ethw.org/Milestones:Pearl_Street_Station,_1882.

[19] U.S Energy Information Administration, "Fossil Fuels Have Made Up at Least 80% of U.S. Fuel Mix Since 1900," *Today in Energy*, July 2, 2015, https://www.eia.gov/todayinenergy/detail.php?id=21912#.

[20] *Energy Education Encyclopedia*, s.v. "Energy Density," http://energyeducation.ca/encyclopedia/Energy_density.

[21] Luis de Sousa et al., "What is a Human Being Worth (in Terms of Energy)?" The Oil Drum: Europe, July 20, 2008, http://www.theoildrum.com/node/4315.

[22] Robert Gordon, "Is U.S. Economic Growth Over?" Gordon also identified a third part, IR3, which I discuss in this chapter.

[23] Gordon, "Is U.S. Economic Growth Over?" 1.

[24] Energy Information Administration, "U.S. Net Imports"; "Crude Oil Prices – 70 Year Historical Trend."

[25] Robert Mundell, "Commodity Prices, Exchanges Rates and the International Monetary System," *FAO Corporate Document Repository*, http://www.fao.org/docrep/006/Y4344E/y4344e04.htm.

[26] Mishel, Gould and Bivens, "Wage Stagnation in Nine Charts"; DeSilver, "For Most Workers."

[27] Rachel Carson, *Silent Spring* (Boston, MA: Houghton Mifflin, 1962); Eliza Griswold, "How 'Silent Spring' Ignited the Environmental Movement," *New York Times Magazine*, September 21, 2012, http://www.nytimes.com/2012/09/23/magazine/how-silent-spring-ignited-the-environmental-movement.html.

[28] Ralph Nader, *Unsafe at Any Speed* (New York: Grossman Publishers, 1965); Lily Rothman, "This Book Has Kept American Drivers Safe for

50 Years," *Time*, November 30, 2015, http://time.com/4124987/50-years-unsafe-at-any-speed/.

[29] Carter, "Malaise Speech," paragraph 13.

[30] Carter, "Malaise Speech," part of "Point five."

[31] Carter, "Malaise Speech," paragraph 9.

[32] Mattson, "Examining Carter's 'Malaise Speech.'" Mattson used the expression "window of opportunity."

[33] Mark J. Perry, "Manufacturing's Declining Share of GDP is a Global Phenomenon, and it Something to Celebrate," *U.S. Chamber of Commerce Foundation*, March 22, 2012, https://www.uschamberfoundation.org/blog/post/manufacturing-s-declining-share-gdp-global-phenomenon-and-it-s-something-celebrate/34261.

[34] See generally: Verleger Jr., "The U.S. Petroleum Crisis."

[35] "Crude Oil Prices – 70 Year Historical Trend."

[36] "Biography of Jimmy Carter," *Jimmy Carter Presidential Library and Museum*, n.d., https://www.jimmycarterlibrary.gov/about_us/biography_of_jimmy_carter.

[37] A good source of information about Admiral Hyman Rickover is his obituary in the *New York Times*: John W. Finney, "Rickover, Father of the Nuclear Navy, Dies at 86," *New York Times*, July 9, 1986, http://www.nytimes.com/1986/07/09/obituaries/rickover-father-of-nuclear-navy-dies-at-86.html?pagewanted=all.

[38] For example, in an interview with Neil deGrasse Tyson, "Star Talk," May 28, 2015, http://transcripts.foreverdreaming.org/viewtopic.php?f=277&t=18527.

[39] "Jimmy Carter," *Biography.com*, https://www.biography.com/people/jimmy-carter-9240013.

[40] Nadra Kareem Nittle, "President Jimmy Carter's Record on Civil Rights and Race Relations," *ThoughtCo.*, as updated on August 24, 2015, https://www.thoughtco.com/president-jimmy-carters-civil-rights-record-2834612.

[41] Nittle, "President Jimmy Carter's Record."

[42] J.N. Kish, "U.S. Population 1776 to Present," n.d., https://fusiontables.google.com/DataSource?dsrcid=225439#rows:id=1.

[43] Sitaraman, "Our Constitution Wasn't Built for This," *New York Times*, September 16, 2017, https://www.nytimes.com/2017/09/16/opinion/sunday/constitution-economy.html?_r=0.

[44] Curtis P. Nettels, *The Emergence of a National Economy, 1775–1815. The Economic History of the United States, Volume II* (New York: Holt, Rinehart and Winston, 1962).

[45] Kish, "U.S. Population."

[46] U.S. land area is 3,531,905.43 square miles: "United States – Land area in square miles, 2010 by State," *Index Mundi*, https://www.indexmundi.com/facts/united-states/quick-facts/all-states/land-area#map. Land area of the '13 colonies' is 339,258 square miles. The size ratio is, therefore, 10.41:1: "States Ranked by Size & Population," *ipl2*, http://www.ipl.org/div/stateknow/popchart.html#statesbysize.

[47] See: Zeihan, *The Accidental Super Power*, Chapters 2 to 4 for a good discussion of America's endowments.

[48] Will Coldwell, "Concorde's Maiden Flight Was 40 Years Ago Today," *Guardian*, January 21, 2016, https://www.theguardian.com/travel/2016/jan/21/concorde-40th-anniversary-new-supersonic-flights-club-concorde.

[49] Angelique Richardson and Ellen Terrel, "Apple Computer, Inc.," Library of Congress, *Business Reference Services*, April 2008, https://www.loc.gov/rr/business/businesshistory/April/apple.html; Kimberly Amadeo, "NASA Budget: Current Funding and History," *Balance*, as updated on May 25, 2017, https://www.thebalance.com/nasa-budget-current-funding-and-history-3306321.

[50] "IBM Archives, 1976," The IBM 3800, https://www-03.ibm.com/ibm/history/history/year_1976.html.

[51] "Viking 1 Spacecraft," *NASA*, August 1, 2008, https://www.nasa.gov/50th/favpic/viking1.html; "The Shuttle Enterprise," *NASA*, February 27, 2015, https://www.nasa.gov/multimedia/imagegallery/image_feature_1204.html.

[52] Andrew Glass, "Mao Zedong Dies in Beijing at Age 82, Sept.9, 1976," *Politico*, September 9, 1976, https://www.politico.com/story/2016/09/mao-zedong-dies-in-beijing-at-age-82-sept-9-1976-227742.

[53] The National Academies of Science issued a report affirming the damaging effects of CFCs on stratospheric ozone: "Chlorofluorocarbons and Ozone Depletion," *American Chemical Society*, n.d., https://www.acs.org/content/acs/en/education/whatischemistry/landmarks/cfcs-ozone.html.

[54] Coldwell, "Concorde's Maiden Flight."

[55] Kif Leswing, "Apple Just Broke its Own Record to Become the Most Valuable Publicly Traded Company of All-Time," *Business Insider* (Australia), May 9, 2017, https://www.businessinsider.com.au/apple-becomes-the-most-valuable-publicly-traded-company-of-all-time-2017-5?r=US&IR=T.

[56] China Martens, "IBM to Give up Printing Division," *PCWorld*, February 9, 2007, https://www.pcworld.com/article/128870/article.html.

[57] "NASA Budget as a Percentage of Federal Budget," Center for Lunar Science and Exploration, n.d., https://www.lpi.usra.edu/exploration/multimedia/NASABudgetHistory.pdf; "NASA Budgets: US Spending On Space Travel since 1958 Updated," *Guardian* (Datablog), n.d., https://www.theguardian.com/news/datablog/2010/feb/01/nasa-budgets-us-spending-space-travel.

[58] "Australia in the Asian Century: White Paper," Australian Government (October, 2012), 66, http://www.defence.gov.au/whitepaper/2013/docs/australia_in_the_asian_century_white_paper.pdf.

[59] "Chlorofluorocarbons and Ozone Depletion"; Eric Hand, "Ozone Layer on the Mend, Thanks to Chemical Ban," *Science*, June 30, 2016, http://www.sciencemag.org/news/2016/06/ozone-layer-mend-thanks-chemical-ban.

[60] Gordon, "Is U.S. Economic Growth Over?" 2, point 4.

[61] Gordon, "Is U.S. Economic Growth Over?" 2, points 5 and 1; 12, section 6.

[62] Kevin Mattson, "Why Jimmy Carter's Malaise Speech Should Have Changed America," interviewed by Robert Schlesinger, *U.S. News &*

World Report, July 24, 2009,
https://www.usnews.com/opinion/articles/2009/07/24/why-jimmy-carters-malaise-speech-should-have-changed-america.

[63] Robert F. Kennedy, "Remarks at the University of Kansas, March 18, 1968," *John F. Kennedy Presidential Library and Museum*, https://www.jfklibrary.org/Research/Research-Aids/Ready-Reference/RFK-Speeches/Remarks-of-Robert-F-Kennedy-at-the-University-of-Kansas-March-18-1968.aspx.

[64] "Percentage of Total Population Living in Coastal Areas," United Nations Department of Economic and Social Affairs, n.d. (converted from kilometers to miles), http://www.un.org/esa/sustdev/natlinfo/indicators/methodology_sheets/oceans_seas_coasts/pop_coastal_areas.pdf.

[65] See: *Encyclopaedia Britannica,* s.v. "Diamond-water paradox," https://www.britannica.com/topic/diamond-water-paradox.

[66] Smith, *Wealth of Nations*, 17.

[67] "The Water Cycle: Fresh Water Storage*,"* *United States Geological Survey,* n.d., https://water.usgs.gov/edu/watercyclefreshstorage.html.

[68] Olga Gertcyck, "Pollution 'Crisis' in Lake Baikal," *Siberian Times*, November 20, 2015, http://siberiantimes.com/ecology/casestudy/news/n0494-pollution-crisis-in-lake-baikal/.

[69] "World Population by Year," *Worldometers*, http://www.worldometers.info/world-population/world-population-by-year/.

[70] Max Roser and Esteban Ortiz-Ospina, "World Population Growth," *OurWorldInData.org.*, first published in 2013, as updated in May, 2017, https://ourworldindata.org/world-population-growth/.

[71] Roser and Ortiz-Ospina, "World Population Growth."

[72] "Water Use By Ethanol Compared to Other Industries," East Central Illinois Regional Water Supply Planning Committee, n.d., http://www.rwspc.org/documents/wateruse_otherindustries_0608.pdf.

[73] *Online Etymology Dictionary,* s.v. "pollution," https://www.etymonline.com.

[74] "World Water Assessment Programme," *United Nations Education, Scientific and Cultural Organization* (UNESCO),

http://www.unesco.org/new/en/natural-
sciences/environment/water/wwap/wwdr/wwdr1-2003/.

[75] "Unsafe Water Kills More People than War, Ban Says on World Day," *UN News Centre*, March 22, 2010, http://www.un.org/apps/news/story.asp?NewsID=34150#.WoAzRK2B1 PO.

[76] The United Nations World Water Development Report 2015, *Water For A Sustainable World*, page 11, http://unesdoc.unesco.org/images/0023/002318/231823E.pdf.

[77] Rebecca Smithers, "Almost Half of the World's Food Thrown Away, Report Finds," *Guardian*, January 10, 2013, https://www.theguardian.com/environment/2013/jan/10/half-world-food-waste.

[78] Elizabeth Cline, "Where Does Discarded Clothing Go?" *Atlantic*, July 18, 2014, https://www.theatlantic.com/business/archive/2014/07/where-does-discarded-clothing-go/374613/; Craig Kielburger and Marc Kielburger, "We Shouldn't Be Filling Up our Landfills With Clothing," *Huffington Post* (CA), June 32, 2016, http://www.huffingtonpost.ca/craig-and-marc-kielburger/clothing-waste-canada_b_10634478.html.

[79] "The Consequences of Climate Change," *NASA*, n.d., https://climate.nasa.gov/effects/.

[80] "Climate Impact on Coastal Areas," *United States Environmental Protection Agency,* n.d., https://19january2017snapshot.epa.gov/climate-impacts/climate-impacts-coastal-areas_.html; "Climate Change Around the World," *BBC News*, 6 April, 2007, http://news.bbc.co.uk/2/hi/in_depth/629/629/6528979.stm.

[81] Matthew Boesler, "Bottled Water Costs 2000 Times as Much as Tap Water," *Business Insider* (Australia), July 13, 2013, https://www.businessinsider.com.au/bottled-water-costs-2000x-more-than-tap-2013-7?r=US&IR=T; Karin Klein, "The Invisible High Price of Your Little Bottle of Water," *Los Angeles Times*, July 15, 2015, http://www.latimes.com/nation/la-ol-arrowhead-bottled-water-20140715-story.html.

[82] See: "Water Privatization: Facts and Figures and Corporate Control of Water," *Food & Water Watch*, August 31, 2015, https://www.foodandwaterwatch.org/insight/water-privatization-facts-

and-figures and
https://www.foodandwaterwatch.org/problems/corporate-control-water;
John Vidal, "Water Privatization: A Worldwide Failure," *Guardian*,
January 31, 2015, https://www.theguardian.com/global-
development/2015/jan/30/water-privatisation-worldwide-failure-lagos-
world-bank; Jeneen Interlandi, "The Race to Buy Up The World's
Water," *Newsweek*, 10 August, 2010, http://www.newsweek.com/race-
buy-worlds-water-73893.

[83] "Fierce competition for fresh water may well become a source of
conflict and wars in the future": Kofi Annan, March 2001. For a
comprehensive discussion of this issue, see: Aaron T. Wolf, "Shared
Waters: Conflict and Cooperation," *Annual Review of Environment and
Resources* 32 (2007): 241-69, available online at
http://transboundarywater.geo.orst.edu/publications/abst_docs/wolf_200
7_shared_waters.pdf.

[84] "The Legal Architecture for Transboundary Waters," UN
Watercourses Convention, Online Users Guide, n.d.,
http://www.unwatercoursesconvention.org/importance/the-legal-
architecture-for-transboundary-waters/.

[85] The 1973-1974 and 1979-1980 oil shocks or oil crises.

[86] Charles Fishman, *The Big Thirst: The Secret Life and Turbulent
Future of Water* (New York: Free Press, 2011).

[87] Charles Fishman, "The Big Thirst: The Secret Revolution in U.S.
Water Use," *Fast Company*, April 19, 2011,
https://www.fastcompany.com/1748537/big-thirst-secret-revolution-us-
water-use.

[88] Henry Kendall et al., "World Scientists' Warning to Humanity,"
Union of Concerned Scientists (April 1997),
https://www.ucsusa.org/about/1992-world-
scientists.html#.WoAwE62B2b8.

[89] William Ripple et al., "World Scientists' Warning to Humanity: A
Second Notice," *BioScience* 67, No. 12 (December 2017): 1026–1028
("Second Notice") available at
https://academic.oup.com/bioscience/article/67/12/1026/4605229.

[90] "Second Notice," third paragraph (references omitted).

[91] "Second Notice," supplemental file 2.

---

[92] Carter used "conservation" six times and "conserve" once in Carter, "Malaise Speech."

BIBLIOGRAPHY

Abadi, Mark. "The Obamas Are Getting a Record-Setting Book Deal Worth at Least $60 Million." *Business Insider*, February 28, 2017. http://www.businessinsider.com/obama-book-deal-2017-2.

Abrams, Rachel and Maher Sattar. "Protests in Bangladesh Shake a Global Workshop for Apparel." *New York Times*, January 22, 2017. https://www.nytimes.com/2017/01/22/business/bangladesh-protest-apparel-clothing.html?_r=0.

Alexander, David and Eric Beech, Ed. "Big U.S. Firms Hold $2.1 Trillion Overseas to Avoid Taxes: Study." *Reuters*, October 6, 2015. https://www.reuters.com/article/us-usa-tax-offshore/big-u-s-firms-hold-2-1-trillion-overseas-to-avoid-taxes-study-idUSKCN0S008U20151006.

Alter, Alexandra. "Obamas Make Book Deal with Penguin Random House." *New York Times*, February 28, 2017. https://www.nytimes.com/2017/02/28/business/media/obama-book-deal-penguin-random-house.html.

Amadeo, Kimberly. "NASA Budget: Current Funding and History." *Balance*, as updated on May 25, 2017. https://www.thebalance.com/nasa-budget-current-funding-and-history-3306321.

———. "Subprime Mortgage Crisis, Its Timeline and Effect." *Balance*, January 11, 2018. https://www.thebalance.com/subprime-mortgage-crisis-effect-and-timeline-3305745.

———. "The S&P 500 and How It Works." *Balance*, June 29, 2017. https://www.thebalance.com/what-is-the-sandp-500-3305888.

———. "U.S. Debt by President: By Dollar and Percent." *Balance*, November 2, 2017. https://www.thebalance.com/us-debt-by-president-by-dollar-and-percent-3306296.

American Chemical Society. "Chlorofluorocarbons and Ozone Depletion." *American Chemical Society*, n.d. https://www.acs.org/content/acs/en/education/whatischemistry/landmarks/cfcs-ozone.html.

American Civil Liberties Union. "In for a Penny: The Rise of America's New Debtors' Prisons." October 2010. www.aclu.org/files/assets/InForAPenny_web.pdf.

American Oil & Gas Historical Society. "First American Oil Well." https://aoghs.org/petroleum-pioneers/american-oil-history/.

Americans for Tax Fairness. "Whopper of a Tax Dodge: How Burger King's Inversion Could Shortchange America." December 2014. https://americansfortaxfairness.org/files/Whopper-Tax-Dodge.pdf.

Anderson, Joel. "A Look at German Inflation: A National Coin Week Exhibit, 1914-1924." n.d. http://www.joelscoins.com/exhibger2.htm.

Andrews, Edmund L. "Greenspan Concedes Error on Regulation." *New York Times*, October 23, 2008. http://www.nytimes.com/2008/10/24/business/economy/24panel.html.

Andrews, Evan. "10 Things You May Not Know About Genghis Khan." *History.com*, April 29, 2014. http://www.history.com/news/history-lists/10-things-you-may-not-know-about-genghis-khan.

Anesi, Chuck. *Fascism: The Ultimate Definition*. October 2008. http://www.anesi.com/Fascism-TheUltimateDefinition.htm.

Arendt, Hannah. *Eichmann in Jerusalem: A Report on the Banality of Evil*. London: Penguin Books, 2006. Kindle.

Aron Salomon (Pauper) v A. Salomon and Company, Limited, by original appeal, and A. Salomon and Company, Limited v Aron Salomon, by cross appeal, [1897] AC 22.

Askew, Anne. "The Origins of Behaviour in the Philosophy of Plato." PhD dissertation. University of Adelaide, Australia, April 1975. https://digital.library.adelaide.edu.au/dspace/bitstream/2440/20614/1/09pha835.pdf.

Australian Government. "Australia in the Asian Century: White Paper." October, 2012. http://www.defence.gov.au/whitepaper/2013/docs/australia_in_the_asian_century_white_paper.pdf.

Avakian, Talia. "The 10 Strangest Things that Have Been Used as Money Around the World." *Business Insider*, April 20, 2016. https://www.businessinsider.com.au/alternative-forms-of-currency-2016-4?r=US&IR=T#/#rai-stones-1.

Babones, Salvatore. "U.S. Income Distribution: Just How Unequal." *Inequality.org*. February 14, 2012. https://inequality.org/research/unequal-americas-income-distribution/.

Bacon, Katie. "The Dark Side of the Gilded Age." *Atlantic*. June 2007. https://www.theatlantic.com/magazine/archive/2007/06/the-dark-side-of-the-gilded-age/306012/.

Bailyn, Bernard, Robert Dallek, David Brion Davis, David Herbert Donald, John L. Thomas and Gordon S. Wood. *The Great Republic: A History of the American People*. Lexington, MA: D.C. Heath, 1985.

Bakshian, Aram, Jr. "The Wrong Cure for a Real Crisis." *Washington Times*, June 14, 2017. https://www.washingtontimes.com/news/2017/jun/14/book-review-the-crisis-of-the-middle-class-constit/.

Balter, Michael. "The Seeds of Civilization." *Smithsonian Magazine*. May 2005. https://www.smithsonianmag.com/history/the-seeds-of-civilization-78015429/.

Barbour, Julian. *The End of Time*. Oxford University Press, 1999.

Barrett, Lisa Feldman. *How Emotions Are Made: The Secret Life of the Brain*. Macmillan, 2017. Kindle.

Barrison, Steven. "Opinion: Study Shows Walmart Kills Small Biz." *New York Daily News* May 4, 2011. http://www.nydailynews.com/new-york/brooklyn/study-proves-walmart-super-stores-kill-local-small-businesses-article-1.140129.

Baur, Lucas. "Machiavelli and Sun Tzu: Comparisons on their Art of War." *Liberty and Security*, May 21, 2014. https://libertyandsecurity.wordpress.com/2014/05/21/machiavelli-and-sun-tzu-comparisons-on-their-art-of-war/.

BBC News. "Climate Change Around the World." April 6, 2007. http://news.bbc.co.uk/2/hi/in_depth/629/629/6528979.stm.

Bergin, Tom. "Special Report: How Starbucks Avoids UK Taxes." *Reuters*, October 15, 2015. https://www.reuters.com/article/us-britain-starbucks-tax/special-report-how-starbucks-avoids-uk-taxes-idUSBRE89E0EX20121015.

Beschloss, Michael. "The Ad that Helped Reagan Sell Good Times to an Uncertain Nation." *New York Times*, May 7, 2016. https://www.nytimes.com/2016/05/08/business/the-ad-that-helped-reagan-sell-good-times-to-an-uncertain-nation.html.

Better Explained. "Understanding the Pareto Principle (The 80/20 Rule)." https://betterexplained.com/articles/understanding-the-pareto-principle-the-8020-rule/.

Bilmes, Linda J. "Iraq and Afghanistan: The US$6 Trillion Bill for America's Longest War Is Unpaid." *Conversation*, May 25, 2017. https://theconversation.com/iraq-and-afghanistan-the-us-6-trillion-bill-for-americas-longest-war-is-unpaid-78241.

Blinder Alan S. and Jeremy B. Rudd, "The Supply-Shock Explanation of the Great Stagflation Revisited." National Bureau of Economic Research, Working Paper 14563 (December 2008). http://www.nber.org/papers/w14563.pdf.

Block, Fred and Margaret R. Somers. *The Power of Market Fundamentalism: Karl Polanyi's Critique*. Cambridge, MA: Harvard University Press, 2014. Kindle.

Bloom, Paul. *Against Empathy: The Case for Rational Compassion*. London: Bodley Head, 2016.

Boesler, Matthew. "Bottled Water Costs 2000 Times as Much as Tap Water." *Business Insider (Australia)*, July 13, 2013. https://www.businessinsider.com.au/bottled-water-costs-2000x-more-than-tap-2013-7?r=US&IR=T.

Bosshart, David. *Cheap?: The Real Cost of Living in a Low Price, Low Wage World*. London: Kogan Page, 2006.

Boucoyannis, Deborah "Contrary to Popular and Academic Belief, Adam Smith Did Not Accept Inequality as a Necessary Trade-Off for a More Prosperous Economy." *British Politics and Policy* (blog), February 18, 2014. http://blogs.lse.ac.uk/politicsandpolicy/adam-smith-and-inequality/.

Branfman, Fred. "America Keeps Honoring One of its Worst Mass Murderers: Henry Kissinger." *Alternet*, April 16, 2013. https://www.alternet.org/news-amp-politics/america-keeps-honoring-one-its-worst-mass-murderers-henry-kissinger.

Brillat-Savarin, Jean Anthelme. *The Physiology of Taste: Or Meditations on Transcendental Gastronomy* (1825). M.F.K Fisher, trans. New York: Vintage Classics, 2011.

Brook, Yaron. "The Morality of Moneylending: A Short History." *Objective Standard*, January 22, 2014. https://www.theobjectivestandard.com/issues/2007-fall/morality-of-moneylending/.

Brown, Brené. *The Power of Vulnerability: Teachings on Authenticity, Connection, and Courage*. Narrated by Brené Brown. Sounds True, 2013. Audiobook.

Browning, Lynnley, Laura Davison and Matthew Townsend. "Apple Among Giants Due for Foreign Tax Bill Under House Plan." *Bloomberg*, November 3, 2017, https://www.bloomberg.com/news/articles/2017-11-02/house-bill-would-tax-offshore-corporate-profit-at-up-to-12.

Broushaki, F et al. "Early Neolithic Genomes from the Eastern Fertile Crescent." *Science* 10.1126/science.aaf7943 (2016). http://science.sciencemag.org/content/early/2016/07/13/science.aaf7943.full.

Bryan, Michael. "The Great Inflation 1965-1982." *Federal Reserve History.* https://www.federalreservehistory.org/essays/great_inflation.

Burwell v. Hobby Lobby (previously Sebelius v. Hobby Lobby Stores), 573 U.S. _ (2014).

Bush, George W. "Address to a Joint Session of Congress and the American People." September 20, 2001. https://georgewbush-whitehouse.archives.gov/news/releases/2001/09/20010920-8.html.

———. "Portraits of Courage: A Commander in Chief's Tribute to America's Warriors." *Bush Centre,* n.d. http://www.bushcenter.org/exhibits-and-events/exhibits/2017/portraits-of-courage-exhibit.html.

Buzan, Barry and George Lawson. "The Global Transformation: The Nineteenth Century and the Making of Modern International Relations." *International Studies Quarterly* 57, No. 3 (October 2013): 620-634. LSE Research Online. http://eprints.lse.ac.uk/44894/.

C-Span. "Gen, Mattis Agrees That The National Debt Is Our Biggest National Security Threat." User created clip of Defense Secretary Confirmation Hearing. *C-Span,* January 12, 2017. https://www.c-span.org/video/?c4645271/gen-mattis-agrees-debt-biggest-security-threat.

Carnegie, Andrew. "The Gospel of Wealth." Carnegie Corporation of New York, 2017. https://www.carnegie.org/media/filer_public/0a/e1/0ae166c5-fca3-4adf-82a7-74c0534cd8de/gospel_of_wealth_2017.pdf.

Carson, Rachel. *Silent Spring.* Boston, MA: Houghton Mifflin, 1962.

Carter, Jimmy. "Address to the Nation on Energy and National Goals: The 'Malaise Speech'." (Oval Office, Washington DC, July 15, 1979). Online by Gerhard Peters and John T. Woolley, *The American Presidency Project.* http://www.presidency.ucsb.edu/ws/?pid=32596.

———. Interview by Neil deGrasse Tyson. *Star Talk.* May 28, 2015. http://transcripts.foreverdreaming.org/viewtopic.php?f=277&t=18527.

Center for Lunar Science and Exploration. "NASA Budget as a Percentage of Federal Budget." n.d. https://www.lpi.usra.edu/exploration/multimedia/NASABudgetHistory.pdf.

Center on Budget and Policy Priorities. "Policy Basics: Where Do Federal Tax Revenues Come From?" September 5, 2017. https://www.cbpp.org/research/federal-tax/policy-basics-where-do-federal-tax-revenues-come-from.

CERN. "Erwin Schrödinger and Werner Heisenberg devise a quantum theory, January 27, 1926." *CERN Timelines.* https://timeline.web.cern.ch/events/erwin-schrödinger-and-werner-heisenberg-devise-a-quantum-theory.

Chapman, Peter. *Bananas: How the United Fruit Company Shaped the World.* New York: Canongate Books, 2008.

Chartbook of Economic Inequality. "Economic Inequality in USA." https://www.chartbookofeconomicinequality.com/inequality-by-country/usa/.

Churchill, Winston and Richard Langworth, ed. *Churchill by Himself: The Definitive Collection of Quotations.* New York: PublicAffairs, 2008.

Cirillio, Pasquale and Nassim Nicholas Taleb. "What Are the Chances of a Third World War?" Real World Risk Institute Working Paper Series, n.d. http://www.fooledbyrandomness.com/longpeace.pdf.

Citizens United v. Federal Election Commission, 558 U.S. 310 (2010).

Clausewitz von, Carl. *On War*, translated by Colonel J.J. Graham in 1874. 1832, Project Gutenberg, rev.ed., 2006. https://www.gutenberg.org/ebooks/1946.

Cleary, Siobhan, Stefano Alderighi, Richard Fenner, Anthony Miller and Sylvie Somerville. "The Role of Stock Exchanges in Fostering Economic Growth and Sustainable Development." Joint Report, World Federation of Exchanges and United Nations Conference on Trade and Development (UNCTAD) (September 2017). http://unctad.org/en/PublicationsLibrary/WFE_UNCTAD_2017_en.pdf.

Clements, Jeffrey D. *Corporations Are Not People: Why They Have More Rights than You Do and What You Can Do About It.* San Francisco: Berrett-Koehler Publishers, 2012.

Cline, Elizabeth L. *Overdressed: The Shockingly High Cost of Cheap Fashion*. New York: Penguin Group, 2013.

———. "Where Does Discarded Clothing Go?" *Atlantic*, July 18, 2014. https://www.theatlantic.com/business/archive/2014/07/where-does-discarded-clothing-go/374613/.

CNN Wire Staff, "Mullen: Debt Is Top National Security Threat." *CNN*, August 27, 2010. http://edition.cnn.com/2010/US/08/27/debt.security.mullen/index.html.

Coates, John C. IV "Corporate Speech and the First Amendment: History, Data, and Implications." *Constitutional Commentary* 30, No. 2 (Summer 2015). https://papers.ssrn.com/sol3/papers.cfm?abstract_id=2566785.

Coldwell, Will. "Concorde's Maiden Flight Was 40 Years Ago Today." *Guardian*, January 21, 2016. https://www.theguardian.com/travel/2016/jan/21/concorde-40th-anniversary-new-supersonic-flights-club-concorde.

Collman, Ashley. "Barack Obam-AIR! New Photos Show Former President Kite-Surfing and Horsing Around with Billionaire Buddy Richard Branson. *Daily Mail*, February 7, 2017. http://www.dailymail.co.uk/news/article-4199624/New-photos-Barack-Obama-kite-surfing-Richard-Branson.html#ixzz4zJJjPrux.

Compania General De Tabacos De Filipinas v. Collector of Internal Revenue, 275 U.S. 87.

Companies Act 1862 (25 & 26 Vict. C.89).

Congressional Budget Office. Cost estimate. The Reconciliation Recommendations of the Senate Committee on Finance (November 2017). https://www.cbo.gov/publication/53348.

———. *Trends in the Distribution of Household Income between 1979 and 2007* (October, 2011). https://www.cbo.gov/publication/42729.

Consumer Federation of America. "How Payday Loans Work." PayDay Loan Consumer Information, n.d. http://www.paydayloaninfo.org/facts.

Coolman, Robert. "What is Quantum Mechanics?" *Live Science*, September 26, 2014. https://www.livescience.com/33816-quantum-mechanics-explanation.html.

Cornell University Law School. "*Citizens United v. Federal Election Commission* (08-205)."
https://web.archive.org/web/20170124175326/https://www.law.cornell.edu/supct/cert/08-205.

Croft, Jane and Kate Burgess. "UK Nationalizes Bradford & Bingley." *Financial Times*, September 29, 2008.
https://www.ft.com/content/1e5b888c-8c06-11dd-8a4c-0000779fd18c.

Darwin, Charles. *On the Origin of Species*. John Murray, 1859.

———. *The Descent of Man, and Selection in Relation to Sex*. John Murray, 1871.

Day, Matt. "How Microsoft Moves Profits Offshore to Cut Its Tax Bill." *Seattle Times*. Last modified December 12, 2015.
https://www.seattletimes.com/business/microsoft/how-microsoft-parks-profits-offshore-to-pare-its-tax-bill/.

Denning, Steve. "The Origins of 'The World's Dumbest Idea': Milton Friedman." *Forbes*, June 26, 2013.

Department of State, United States of America. "The Cuban Missile Crisis, October 1962." Office of the Historian, n.d.
https://history.state.gov/milestones/1961-1968/cuban-missile-crisis.

Department of State, United States of America. "Nixon and the End of the Bretton Woods System, 1971-1973." Office of the Historian, n.d.
https://history.state.gov/milestones/1969-1976/nixon-shock.

Department of the Treasury. "Gross External Debt Position: By Sector 1/ as of December 31, 2016" June 30, 2016.
http://ticdata.treasury.gov/Publish/deb2a2016q4.html.

DeSilver, Drew. "For Most Workers, Real Wages Have Barely Budged for Decades." *Pew Research Center*, October 9, 2014.
http://www.pewresearch.org/fact-tank/2014/10/09/for-most-workers-real-wages-have-barely-budged-for-decades/.

———. "U.S. Income Inequality, on Rise for Decades, Is Now Highest since 1928." *Pew Research Center,* December 5, 2013.
http://www.pewresearch.org/fact-tank/2013/12/05/u-s-income-inequality-on-rise-for-decades-is-now-highest-since-1928/.

Desjardins, Jeff. "All of the World's Money and Markets in One Visualization." *The Money Project*, December 17, 2015. http://money.visualcapitalist.com/all-of-the-worlds-money-and-markets-in-one-visualization/?link=mktw

Devlin, Hannah. "Oldest Known Human Fossil outside of Africa Discovered in Israel." *Guardian*, January 26, 2018. https://www.theguardian.com/science/2018/jan/25/oldest-known-human-fossil-outside-africa-discovered-in-israel.

Dickinson, Ben. "You're more in Control of Your Emotions than You Think (Says New Brain Science)." *Elle*, February 18, 2017. http://www.elle.com/life-love/a42863/how-emotions-are-made/.

Dobbs, Michael "Gorbachev Resignation Ends Soviet Era." *Washington Post,* December 26, 1991. https://www.washingtonpost.com/archive/politics/1991/12/26/gorbachev-resignation-ends-soviet-era/00444c16-0fe3-4b35-96df-e514956ee354/?utm_term=.2209167221d0.

Dodge v. Ford Motor Company, 170 N.W. 668 (Mich. 1919).

Dole, Charles E. "Pinto Verdict Lets US Industry Off Hook." *Christian Science Monitor*, March 14, 1980. https://www.csmonitor.com/1980/0314/031435.html.

Douglas, Ed. "Steven Pinker: The Mind Reader." *Guardian*, November 6, 1999. https://www.theguardian.com/books/1999/nov/06/1.

Drucker, Jesse and Simon Bowers. "After a Tax Crackdown, Apple Found a New Shelter for its Profits." *New York Times*, November 6, 2017. https://www.nytimes.com/2017/11/06/world/apple-taxes-jersey.html.

Drucker, Peter F. *Post Capitalist Society*. Abingdon, Oxon: Routledge, 2011.

Duddu, Praveen. "The 10 Longest Range Intercontinental Ballistic Missiles (ICBM)." *Army Technology*, November 3, 2013. http://www.army-technology.com/features/feature-the-10-longest-range-intercontinental-ballistic-missiles-icbm/.

Dumond, Dwight Lowell. *America in Our Time 1896-1946*. New York: H. Holt, 1947.

East Central Illinois Regional Water Supply Planning Committee. "Water Use by Ethanol Compared to Other Industries." http://www.rwspc.org/documents/wateruse_otherindustries_0608.pdf.

Economist. "Crash Course: The Origins of the financial crisis." September 7, 2013. https://www.economist.com/news/schoolsbrief/21584534-effects-financial-crisis-are-still-being-felt-five-years-article.

———. "The Long and the Short of." Johnson (blog). June 21, 2010. https://www.economist.com/blogs/johnson/2010/06/short_and_long_wo rds.

———. "They Pretend to Pay Us, We Pretend to Work." August 26, 1999. http://www.economist.com/node/234594.

———. "Why the Decline in the Number of Listed American Firms Matters." Schumpeter, April 22, 2017. https://www.economist.com/news/business/21721153-company-founders-are-reluctant-go-public-and-takeovers-are-soaring-why-decline.

Eisenhower, Dwight D. "Farewell Radio and Television Address to the American People." (Washington DC, January 17, 1961). Online by Gerhard Peters and John T. Woolley, *The American Presidency Project.* http://www.presidency.ucsb.edu/ws/?pid=12086.

Elite Readers. "12 Unusual Objects Used as Money." n.d. https://www.elitereaders.com/12-unusual-objects-used-money/.

Enders, Giulia and David Show, trans. *Gut: The inside Story of Our Body's Most Underrated Organ.* Brunswick, VIC, AU: Scribe, 2015. Kindle.

Energy Information Administration (U.S.). "U.S. Net Imports of Crude Oil and Petroleum Products." Petroleum & Other Liquids, n.d. https://www.eia.gov/dnav/pet/hist/LeafHandler.ashx?n=pet&s=mttntus2 &f=a.

———. "Fossil Fuels Have Made Up at Least 80% of U.S. Fuel Mix Since 1900." *Today in Energy*, July 2, 2015. https://www.eia.gov/todayinenergy/detail.php?id=21912#.

Engineering and Technology History Wiki. "Edison's Electric Light and Power System – Initial Commercialization of Direct-Current (D.C.) Applications." http://ethw.org/Edisonpercent27s_Electric_Light_and_Power_System.

————. "Milestones: Pearl Street Station, 1882."
http://ethw.org/Milestones:Pearl_Street_Station,_1882.

EPA. "Climate Impact on Coastal Areas." *United States Environmental Protection Agency,* n.d. https://19january2017snapshot.epa.gov/climate-impacts/climate-impacts-coastal-areas_.html.

Erich Maria Remarque, *The Black Obelisk, A Novel.* Random House, 2013. Kindle.

European Commission. "State Aid: Ireland Gave Illegal Tax Benefits to Apple Worth Up to €13 Billion." Press Release, August 30, 2016. http://europa.eu/rapid/press-release_IP-16-2923_en.htm.

Farabaugh, Kane. "Former President Bush Honors Veterans with Portraits of Courage." *VOA,* March 4, 2017. https://www.voanews.com/a/president-george-bush-portraits-of-courage/3748579.html.

Faulkner, William. *Requiem for a Nun.* Random House, 1951.

Fernández Campbell, Alexia. "The Cost of Corporate Tax Avoidance." *Atlantic,* April 14, 2016. https://www.theatlantic.com/business/archive/2016/04/corporate-tax-avoidance/478293/.

Feynman, Richard, Robert B. Leighton and Matthew Sands, *The Feynman Lectures on Physics, Volume III (Quantum Mechanics) 1964.* Revised and extended edition. Boston, MA: Addison-Wesley, 2005.

Finney, John W. "Rickover, Father of the Nuclear Navy, Dies at 86." *New York Times,* July 9, 1986. http://www.nytimes.com/1986/07/09/obituaries/rickover-father-of-nuclear-navy-dies-at-86.html?pagewanted=all.

Fioretti, Julia and Tom Bergin. "EU Says Ireland Swapped Apple Tax Deal for Jobs." *Reuters,* September 30, 2014. https://www.reuters.com/article/us-apple-ireland-tax/eu-says-ireland-swapped-apple-tax-deal-for-jobs-idUSKCN0HP0QT20140930.

Fishman, Charles. "The Big Thirst: The Secret Revolution in U.S. Water Use." *Fast Company,* April 19, 2011. https://www.fastcompany.com/1748537/big-thirst-secret-revolution-us-water-use.

————. *The Big Thirst: The Secret Life and Turbulent Future of Water.* New York: Free Press, 2011.

Flanagan, Mike. "The Flanarant – Factory Safety Isn't the Biggest Risks to Bangladeshi Workers." *Just-style*, 13 July 2017. https://www.just-style.com/comment/the-flanarant-factory-safety-isnt-the-biggest-risk-to-bangladesh-workers_id131173.aspx.

Fleming, Michael J. and Asani Sarkar. "The Failure Resolution of Lehman Brothers." *Federal Reserve Bank of New York Economic Policy Review* (December 2014): 175-206. https://www.newyorkfed.org/medialibrary/media/research/epr/2014/141 2flem.pdf.

Food & Water Watch. "Water Privatization: Facts and Figures and Corporate Control of Water." August 31, 2015. https://www.foodandwaterwatch.org/insight/water-privatization-facts-and-figures and https://www.foodandwaterwatch.org/problems/corporate-control-water.

Ford, Gerald R. "Annual Message to the Congress: The Economic Report of the President." (January 18, 1977). Online by Gerhard Peters and John T. Woolley, *The American Presidency Project.* http://www.presidency.ucsb.edu/ws/?pid=5570.

Ford, Henry. *My Life and Work.* In collaboration with Samuel Crowther. Garden City: Doubleday, Page, 1922.

Fox, Justin. "The Real Story Behind Those 'Record' Corporate Profits." *Harvard Business Review*, November 24, 2010. https://hbr.org/2010/11/the-real-story-behind-those-re.html.

Francis, Norton et al. *The Tax Policy Centre's Briefing Book: A Citizens' Guide to the Fascinating (Though Often Complex) Elements of the Federal Tax System* (Tax Policy Center, 2016). http://www.taxpolicycenter.org/briefing-book/how-does-current-system-international-taxation-work.

Frey, Thomas. "The Complexity Disease." *Futurist Speaker*, April 14, 2008. http://www.futuristspeaker.com/business-trends/the-complexity-disease/.

Friedman, Milton. "A Friedman Doctrine – The Social Responsibility of Business is to Increase its Profits." *New York Times Magazine*, September 13, 1970. https://timesmachine.nytimes.com/timesmachine/1970/09/13/22353570 2.html?action=click&contentCollection=Archives&module=LedeAsset &region=ArchiveBody&pgtype=article&pageNumber=379.

———. "Work and Consumption in an Era of Unbalanced Technological Advance." *Journal of Evolutionary Economics* 27, No. 2 (2017).

Fung, Brian. "Bill Gates Told New Grads to Read this Book. Now it's Surging on Amazon." *Washington Post*, May 15, 2017. https://www.washingtonpost.com/news/the-switch/wp/2017/05/15/bill-gates-told-new-grads-to-read-this-book-now-its-surging-on-amazon/?utm_term=.f16c852153b2.

Galbraith, John Kenneth. *The Affluent Society*, rev. ed. London: Penguin Books, 1999.

Gallarotti, Giulio M. "The Advent of the Prosperous Society: The Rise of the Guardian State and Structural Changes in the World Economy." *Review of International Political Economy* 7, No. 1 (Spring, 2000): 1-52.

Garcia-Bernardo, Javier, Jan Fichtner, Frank W. Takes and Eelke M. Heemskerk. "Uncovering Offshore Financial Centers: Conduits and Sinks in the Global Corporate Ownership Network." *Scientific Reports* 7, Article No. 6246 (2017). http://www.nature.com/articles/s41598-017-06322-9.

Gardner, Matthew, Robert S. McIntryre and Richard Phillips. "The 35 Percent Corporate Tax Myth: Corporate Tax Avoidance by Fortune 500 Companies, 2008 to 2015." Institute on Taxation and Economic Policy, March 2017. https://itep.org/wp-content/uploads/35percentfullreport.pdf.

Gertcyck, Olga. "Pollution 'Crisis' in Lake Baikal." *Siberian Times*, November 20, 2015. http://siberiantimes.com/ecology/casestudy/news/n0494-pollution-crisis-in-lake-baikal/.

Ghizoni, Sandra Kollen. "Nixon Ends Convertibility of US Dollars to Gold and Announces Wage/Price Controls, August 1971." *Federal Reserve History*, November 22, 2013. https://www.federalreservehistory.org/essays/gold_convertibility_ends.

Glass, Andrew. "Mao Zedong Dies in Beijing at Age 82, Sept.9, 1976." *Politico*, September 9, 1976. https://www.politico.com/story/2016/09/mao-zedong-dies-in-beijing-at-age-82-sept-9-1976-227742.

Global Language Monitor. "The Number of Words in the English Language." n.d. http://www.languagemonitor.com/top-words-of-the-year/no-of-words/.

Goldberg, Eleanor. "You're Probably Going to Throw Away 81 Pounds of Clothing This Year: And 95 Percent of It Could Be Reused or Recycled." *Huffington Post* (Australia), September 6, 2016. http://www.huffingtonpost.com.au/entry/youre-likely-going-to-throw-away-81-pounds-of-clothing-this-year_us_57572bc8e4b08f74f6c069d3.

Gordon, Colin. "Wolves of Wall Street: Financialization and American Inequality." *Dissent*, April 17, 2014. https://www.dissentmagazine.org/online_articles/wolves-of-wall-street-financialization-and-american-inequality.

Gordon, Robert J. "Is U.S. Economic Growth Over? Faltering Innovation Confronts the Six Headwinds." National Bureau of Economic Research, Working Paper No.18315 (August 2012). http://www.nber.org/papers/w18315.

———. *The Rise and Fall of American Growth*. Princeton, NJ: Princeton University Press, 2016.

Graeber, David. "A Practical Utopian's Guide to the Coming Collapse." *Baffler*, No. 22 (April 2013). https://thebaffler.com/salvos/a-practical-utopians-guide-to-the-coming-collapse.

———. *Debt: The First 5,000 Years*, rev. ed. New York: Melville House Publishing, 2014.

Graziano, Michael. "Most Popular Theories of Consciousness Are Worse than Wrong." *Atlantic*, March 9, 2016. https://www.theatlantic.com/science/archive/2016/03/phlegm-theories-of-consciousness/472812/.

Greco, Thomas H. Jr. *Money: Understanding and Creating Alternatives to Legal Tender*. White River Junction, VT: Chelsea Green Publishing, 2001.

Greenfield, Kent. *The Failure of Corporate Law: Fundamental Flaws and Progressive Possibilities*. Chicago, IL: University of Chicago Press, 2006.

Greenhouse, Linda. "Reversal of Fortune for Bill Clinton and Kenneth Starr." *New York Times*, September 1, 2016. https://www.nytimes.com/2016/09/01/opinion/the-president-the-prosecutor-and-the-wheel-of-fortune.html.

Greenspan, Alan. *The Age of Turbulence: Adventures in a New World.* London: Penguin Books, 2008.

Griswold, Eliza. "How 'Silent Spring' Ignited the Environmental Movement." *New York Times Magazine*, September 21, 2012. http://www.nytimes.com/2012/09/23/magazine/how-silent-spring-ignited-the-environmental-movement.html.

Gross, Michael. "The Complicated Origins Of Our Species." *Current Biology* 24, No. 8 (April 2014). *Science Direct.* http://www.sciencedirect.com/science/article/pii/S096098221400390X.

Grossman, Andrew L. "Is the Tax Code Really 70,000 Pages Long? No, Not Even Close,*" Slate*, April 2014. http://www.slate.com/articles/news_and_politics/politics/2014/04/how-long-is-the-tax-code-it-is-far-shorter-than-70,000-pages.html.

Grover, William F. and Joseph G. Peschek. *The Unsustainable Presidency: Clinton, Bush, Obama, and Beyond.* New York: Pearson Educational, 2014.

Guardian. "NASA Budgets: US Spending On Space Travel since 1958 Updated." Datablog. n.d. https://www.theguardian.com/news/datablog/2010/feb/01/nasa-budgets-us-spending-space-travel.

Guerrera, Francesco. "Welch Condemns Share Price Focus." *Financial Times*, March 12, 2009. https://www.ft.com/content/294ff1f2-0f27-11de-ba10-0000779fd2ac.

Hagen, Lisa. "Clinton Manager 'Reticent' to Comment on Report Clinton Floated Drone Strike against WikiLeaks." *Hill,* October 3, 2016. http://thehill.com/blogs/ballot-box/hillary-clinton-drone-strike-wikileaks-julian-assange.

Haines, Michael R. "Population of Europe: The Demographic Transition and After." *Encyclopedia of European Social History.* http://www.encyclopedia.com/international/encyclopedias-almanacs-transcripts-and-maps/population-europe-demographic-transition-and-after.

Hamblin, Dora Jane. "Has the Garden of Eden Been Located at Last?" *Smithsonian Magazine* 18, No. 2 (May 1987).

Hamdani, Khalil and Lorraine Ruffing. *United Nations Centre on Transnational Corporations: Corporate Conduct and the Public Interest.* Abingdon, Oxon: Routledge, 2015.

Hand, Eric. "Ozone layer on the Mend, Thanks to Chemical Ban."
Science, June 30, 2016.
http://www.sciencemag.org/news/2016/06/ozone-layer-mend-thanks-chemical-ban.

Harding, Luke. "What We Know About Russia's Interference in the US
Election." *Guardian*, December 17, 2016.
https://www.theguardian.com/us-news/2016/dec/16/qa-russian-hackers-vladimir-putin-donald-trump-us-presidential-election.

Hartman, Mitchell. "How Much Money Is there in the World?"
Marketplace, October 30, 2017.
https://www.marketplace.org/2017/10/30/world/how-much-money-there-world.

Hawking, Stephen. *Is the End in Sight for Theoretical Physics: An
Inaugural Lecture, 1979*. Cambridge: Cambridge University Press,
1980.

Heath, Joseph. *Morality, Competition, and the Firm: The Market
Failures Approach to Business Ethics*. New York: Oxford University
Press, 2014.

Heching, Dan. "The Better Angels of Our Nature Hits No. 1 on Amazon
Following Bill Gates Tweet." *Entertainment Weekly*, May 16, 2017.
http://ew.com/books/2017/05/16/steven-pinker-the-better-angels-of-our-nature-bill-gates/

Henley, Jon. "Sweden Leads the Race to Become Cashless Society."
Guardian, June 5, 2016.
https://www.theguardian.com/business/2016/jun/04/sweden-cashless-society-cards-phone-apps-leading-europe.

Herberg-Rothe, Andreas. "Clausewitz's 'Wondrous Trinity' as a
Coordinate System of War and Violent Conflict." *International Journal
of Conflict and Violence* 3, No. 2 (2009): 204-219.

Heymont, George. "Looking Back 100 Years." *Huffington Post*,
September 13, 2015, as updated on December 6, 2017.
https://www.huffingtonpost.com/george-heymont/looking-back-100-years_b_8129840.html.

Hobbes, Thomas. *Leviathan or The Matter, Forme and Power of a
Common-Wealth Ecclesiastical and Civil*. 1651. Project Gutenberg
2009. https://www.gutenberg.org/ebooks/3207.

Hofstadter, Richard. "The Myth of the Happy Yeoman." *American Heritage* 7, No. 3 (April 1956). https://www.americanheritage.com/content/myth-happy-yeoman.

Horn, Heather. "Pope Francis's Theory of Economics." *Atlantic*, November 26, 2013. https://www.theatlantic.com/business/archive/2013/11/pope-franciss-theory-of-economics/281865/.

House of Commons Public Accounts Committee (U.K.). "The Nationalisation of Northern Rock." June 1, 2009. https://publications.parliament.uk/pa/cm200809/cmselect/cmpubacc/394/394.pdf.

Hu, Jane. "A Joyful & Malicious History of 'Schadenfreude.'" *Awl*, October 20, 2011. https://www.theawl.com/2011/10/a-joyful-malicious-history-of-schadenfreude/.

Hudson, Michael. "How America Will Get Europe to Finance its 2002-03 Oil War with Iraq." *Michel Hudson: On Finance, Real Estate and the Powers of Neoliberalism*, November 25, 2002. http://michael-hudson.com/2003/03/press-release-super-imperialism/.

———. *Super Imperialism: The Economic Strategy of American Empire*. London: Pluto Press, 2nd ed., 2003.

Humer, Caroline and Ransdell Pierson. "Obama's Inversion Curbs Kill Pfizer's $160 Billion Allergan Deal." *Reuters*, April 5, 2016. https://www.reuters.com/article/us-allergan-m-a-pfizer/obamas-inversion-curbs-kill-pfizers-160-billion-allergan-deal-idUSKCN0X21NV.

Hunnicutt, Benjamin Klein. "The New Deal and the End of Shorter Hours." Paper presented at the Social Science History Association meetings, 1988.

———. *Work without End: Abandoning Shorter Hours for the Right to Work*. Philadelphia, PA: Temple University Press, 1988.

Hylton, Wil S. "Alan Greenspan Takes a Bath." *GQ*, March 2, 2005. https://www.gq.com/story/alan-greenspan-budget-federal-reserve.

Inequality.org. "Income Inequality in the United States." n.d. https://inequality.org/facts/income-inequality/.

Ingraham, Christopher. "The Richest 1 Percent Now Owns more of the Country's Wealth than at any Time in the Past 50 Years." *Washington Post*, December 6, 2017. https://www.washingtonpost.com/news/wonk/wp/2017/12/06/the-richest-1-percent-now-owns-more-of-the-countrys-wealth-than-at-any-time-in-the-past-50-years/?utm_term=.c55b70acb68f.

Institute for Economics & Peace. "Global Peace Index 2016." (2016). https://reliefweb.int/sites/reliefweb.int/files/resources/GPIpercent20201 6percent20Report_2.pdf.

Interlandi, Jeneen. "The Race to Buy Up The World's Water." *Newsweek*, 10 August, 2010. http://www.newsweek.com/race-buy-worlds-water-73893.

Iyengar, Rishi. "This Is How Long Your Business Will Last, According to Science." *Time*, April 2, 2015. http://time.com/3768559/company-mortality-rate-survival-study/.

Japan Atlas. "Horyuji Temple." Architecture. n.d. http://web-japan.org/atlas/architecture/arc19.html.

Jimmy Carter Presidential Library and Museum. "Biography of Jimmy Carter." n.d. https://www.jimmycarterlibrary.gov/about_us/biography_of_jimmy_car ter.

Johnston, David Cay. *Perfectly Legal: The Covert Campaign to Rig Our Tax System to Benefit the Super Rich – And Cheat Everybody Else*. London: Penguin Group, 2003.

Joint Stock Companies Act 1844 (7& 8 Vict. C110).

Kahneman, Daniel. *Thinking, Fast and Slow*. New York: Farrar, Straus and Giroux, 2011.

Kalecki, Michał, Jerzy Osiatyński, Ed., and Chester Adam Kisiel, trans. *Collected Works of Michal Kalecki: Volume I Capitalism: Business Cycles and Full Employment*. Oxford: Clarendon Press, 1990.

——. "Political Aspects of Full Employment." *Political Quarterly* 14, No. 4 (October 1943), 322-31.

Kaszniak, Alfred W. "Empathy and Compassion in Buddhism and Neuroscience." *WGBH, PBS*, March 17, 2010. http://www.pbs.org/thebuddha/blog/2010/Mar/17/empathy-and-compassion-buddhism-and-neuroscience-a/.

Kendall, Henry et al. "World Scientists' Warning to Humanity." Union of Concerned Scientists (April 1997). https://www.ucsusa.org/about/1992-world-scientists.html#.WoAwE62B2b8.

Kennedy, Gavin. "Adam Smith and the Invisible Hand: From Metaphor to Myth (June 2007)." *Journal of the American Institute for Economic Research* 6, No 2 (May 2009): 239-63. https://econjwatch.org/file_download/252/2009-05-kennedy-watchpad.pdf?mimetype=pdf.

———. "The Origins of the Word 'Capitalism.'" *Adam Smith's Lost Legacy Blog*, January 14, 2009. https://adamsmithslostlegacy.blogspot.com.au/2009/01/free-capitalist-13-january-here-carries.html.

Kennedy, John F. "Special Message to the Congress on Taxation." (Congress, Washington DC, April 20, 1961). Online by Gerhard Peters and John T. Woolley, *The American Presidency Project*. http://www.presidency.ucsb.edu/ws/?pid=8074.

———. "Address of President-Elect John F. Kennedy Delivered to a Joint Convention of the General Court of the Commonwealth of Massachusetts." (The State House, Boston, January 9, 1961), John F. Kennedy Presidential Library and Museum. https://www.jfklibrary.org/Asset-Viewer/ohJztSnpV06qFJUT9etUZQ.aspx.

———. "Remarks at the University of Kansas, March 18, 1968." John F. Kennedy Presidential Library and Museum. https://www.jfklibrary.org/Research/Research-Aids/Ready-Reference/RFK-Speeches/Remarks-of-Robert-F-Kennedy-at-the-University-of-Kansas-March-18-1968.aspx.

Keynes, John Maynard. "Economic Possibilities for Our Grandchildren." In *Essays in Persuasion*. New York: W. W. Norton, 1963.

———. *The General Theory of Employment, Interest and Money*. New York: Harcourt, Brace, 1936.

Kielburger, Craig and Marc Kielburger. "We Shouldn't Be Filling Up our Landfills With Clothing." *Huffington Post* (CA), June 32, 2016. http://www.huffingtonpost.ca/craig-and-marc-kielburger/clothing-waste-canada_b_10634478.html.

Kish, J.N. "U.S. Population 1776 to Present." n.d. https://fusiontables.google.com/DataSource?dsrcid=225439#rows:id=1.

Klein, Karin. "The Invisible High Price of Your Little Bottle of Water." *Los Angeles Times*, July 15, 2015. http://www.latimes.com/nation/la-ol-arrowhead-bottled-water-20140715-story.html.

Kleinbard, Edward D. "Stateless Income." *Florida Tax Review* 11, No. 9 (2011). https://www.sbs.ox.ac.uk/sites/default/files/Business_Taxation/Docs/WP1208.pdf.

Koch, Christof. *The Quest for Consciousness: A Neurobiological Approach*. Englewood, CO: Roberts, 2004.

Kornhaber, Spencer. "Empathy: Overrated?" *Atlantic*, July 3, 2015. https://www.theatlantic.com/health/archive/2015/07/against-empathy-aspen-paul-bloom-richard-j-davidson/397694/.

Krugman, Paul. "Who was Milton Friedman?" *New York Review of Book* 54, No. 2 (February 2007). http://www.nybooks.com/articles/2007/02/15/who-was-milton-friedman/.

Lam, Bourree. "2015: A Merger Bonanza." *Atlantic*, January 9, 2016. https://www.theatlantic.com/business/archive/2016/01/2015-mergers-acquisitions/423096/.

———. "How Much Wealth and Income Does America's 1 Percent Really Have?" *Atlantic*, March 12, 2016. https://www.theatlantic.com/business/archive/2016/03/brookings-1-percent/473478/.

Langely, Lester D. *The Banana Wars: United States Intervention in the Caribbean, 1898-1934,* rev. ed. Langham, MD: Scholarly Resources, 2001.

Law Teacher. "Lifting the Corporate Veil." n.d. https://www.lawteacher.net/free-law-essays/business-law/article-on-lifting-of-the-law-essays.php.

Leswing, Kif. "Apple Just Broke its Own Record to Become the Most Valuable Publicly Traded Company of All-Time." *Business Insider* (Australia), May 9, 2017. https://www.businessinsider.com.au/apple-becomes-the-most-valuable-publicly-traded-company-of-all-time-2017-5?r=US&IR=T.

Liaquat, Ahamed. *Lords of Finance: The Bankers Who Broke the World*. London: Windmill Books, 2009.

Lincoln, Abraham. "First Inaugural Address." (March 4, 1861), available at *The Avalon Project*, Yale Law School. http://avalon.law.yale.edu/19th_century/lincoln1.asp.

Lindert, Peter H. and Jeffrey G. Williamson. "American Incomes 1774 – 1860." National Bureau of Economic Research, Working Paper No. 18396 (September 2012). http://www.nber.org/papers/w18396.

Long, Heather. "How an Unequal Tax Cut Grew More Unequal." *Washington Post*, December 1, 2017. https://www.washingtonpost.com/business/economy/as-tax-bill-evolved-benefits-for-corporations-and-the-wealthy-grew/2017/12/01/17f1478e-d6c0-11e7-b62d-d9345ced896d_story.html?utm_term=.ba62a1163a90.

———. "The Senate Just Passed a Massive Tax Bill. Here's What Is in It," *Washington Post*, November 30, 2017. https://www.washingtonpost.com/news/wonk/wp/2017/11/30/what-is-in-the-senates-massive-tax-bill-and-what-could-change/?utm_term=.00fa85a0b714.

Lowrey, Annie. "The 7 Myths of the GOP Tax Bill." *Atlantic*, December 1, 2017. https://www.theatlantic.com/business/archive/2017/12/the-7-myths-of-the-gop-tax-bill/547322/.

Lynn, Barry C. "America's Monopolies Are Holding Back the Economy." *Atlantic*, February 22, 2017. https://www.theatlantic.com/business/archive/2017/02/antimonopoly-big-business/514358/.

Mach, Ernst and Thomas J. McCormack, trans. *The Science of Mechanics: A Critical and Historical and its Development*. The Open Court Publishing Co, 4th ed. 1919. e-Book. https://archive.org/details/scienceofmechani005860mbp.

Macrotrends. "Crude Oil Prices – 70 Year Historical Trend." n.d. http://www.macrotrends.net/1369/crude-oil-price-history-chart.

Mandelbrot, Beniot and Richard L Hudson. *The (Mis)behavior of Markets: A Fractal View of Risk, Ruin, and Reward*. New York: Basic Books, 2004.

Manjoo, Farhad. "State of the Art, Tech's Frightful Five: They've Got Us." *New York Times*, May 10, 2017. https://www.nytimes.com/2017/10/18/technology/frightful-five-start-ups.html?_r=0.

Mark, Joshua J. "Great Pyramid of Giza." *Ancient History Encyclopedia*, December 19, 2016. https://www.ancient.eu/Great_Pyramid_of_Giza/.

Martens, China. "IBM to Give up Printing Division." *PCWorld*, February 9, 2007. https://www.pcworld.com/article/128870/article.html.

Martens, Pam and Russ Martens, "Warren: Citigroup, Morgan Stanley, Merrill Lynch Received $6 Trillion Backdoor Bailout from Fed." *Wall Street on Parade*, March 4, 2015. http://wallstreetonparade.com/2015/03/warren-citigroup-morgan-stanley-merrill-lynch-received-6-trillion-backdoor-bailout-from-fed/.

Martin, Justin. *Greenspan: The Man Behind Money*. Cambridge, MA: Perseus Publishing, 2001.

Matson, John. "What is Quantum Mechanics Good for?" *Scientific American*, November 2, 2010. https://www.scientificamerican.com/article/everyday-quantum-physics/.

Mattson, Kevin. "Examining Carter's 'Malaise Speech,' 30 Years Later." NPR Books, July 12, 2009. https://www.npr.org/templates/story/story.php?storyId=106508243.

———. "Why Jimmy Carter's Malaise Speech Should Have Changed America." Interview by Robert Schlesinger. *U.S. News & World Report*, July 24, 2009. https://www.usnews.com/opinion/articles/2009/07/24/why-jimmy-carters-mailaise-speech-should-have-changed-america.

Mayer, Emeran M.D. *The Mind Gut Connection: How the Hidden Conversation Within Our Bodies Impacts Our Mood, Our Choices, and Our Overall Health*. New York: Harper Wave, 2016.

McGinn, Dan. "$1 billion for Obama's Library? Stop this Presidential Trend." *Chicago Tribune*, May 9, 2016. http://www.chicagotribune.com/news/opinion/commentary/ct-obama-presidential-library-chicago-perspec-0510-jm-20160509-story.html.

McWhorter, John. *Words on the Move: Why English Won't and Can't Sit Still (Like, Literally)*. New York: Henry Holt, 2016.

Meltzer, Allan H. "Origins of the Great Inflation." *Federal Reserve Bank of St. Louis Review* 87, No. 2, part 2 (March/April 2005): 145-75. https://files.stlouisfed.org/files/htdocs/publications/review/05/03/part2/Meltzer.pdf.

Mishel, Lawrence and Jessica Schieder. "CEO Pay Remains High Relative to the Pay of Typical Workers and High-Wage Earners." *Economic Policy Institute,* July 20, 2017. http://www.epi.org/publication/ceo-pay-remains-high-relative-to-the-pay-of-typical-workers-and-high-wage-earners/.

Mishel, Lawrence, Elise Gould and Josh Bivens. "Wage Stagnation in Nine Charts." *Economic Policy Institute*, January 6, 2015. http://www.epi.org/publication/charting-wage-stagnation/.

Moss, Jessica. "Shame, Pleasure and the Divided Soul," *Oxford Studies in Ancient Philosophy*, 29 (2005): 137-170.

Mundell, Robert. "Commodity Prices, Exchanges Rates and the International Monetary System." *FAO Corporate Document Repository*. http://www.fao.org/docrep/006/Y4344E/y4344e04.htm.

Murphy, Brett. "Shell Games: How Trucking Companies that Cheat Drivers Dodge Penalties." *USA Today*, October 26, 2017. https://www.usatoday.com/pages/interactives/news/rigged-shell-games-how-trucking-companies-that-cheat-drivers-dodge-penalties/.

Mussolini Benito and Giovanni Gentile. "The Doctrine of Fascism." (1932). World Future Fund. http://www.worldfuturefund.org/wffmaster/Reading/Germany/mussolini.htm.

Nader, Ralph. *Unsafe At any Speed*. New York: Grossman Publishers, 1965.

NASA. "The Consequences of Climate Change." n.d. https://climate.nasa.gov/effects/.

National Observer (U.K.). A letter to the editor dated June 8, 1891, the *National Observer* (U.K.), June 13, 1891. p. 93(-94) under the heading "National Pensions."

Nettels, Curtis P. *The Emergence of a National Economy, 1775–1815. The Economic History of the United States, Volume II*. New York: Holt, Rinehart and Winston, 1962.

New York Times. "Compiled by DuPre Jones." October 28, 1973. http://www.nytimes.com/1973/10/28/archives/the-sayings-of-secretary-henry-language-negotiation-humility-the.html.

———. "Let Them Eat Credit," Schott's Vocab: A Miscellany of Modern Words and Phrases (blog), July 6, 2010. https://schott.blogs.nytimes.com/2010/07/06/let-them-eat-credit/.

Nittle, Nadra Kareem. "President Jimmy Carter's Record on Civil Rights and Race Relations." *ThoughtCo.,* as updated on August 24, 2015. https://www.thoughtco.com/president-jimmy-carters-civil-rights-record-2834612.

Noble Holcomb B. and Douglas Martin. "John Kenneth Galbraith, 97, Dies; Economist Held a Mirror to Society." *New York Times,* April 30, 2016. http://www.nytimes.com/2006/04/30/obituaries/30galbraith.html.

Oil Drum: Europe. "What is a Human Being Worth (in Terms of Energy)?" Blogroll, July 20, 2008. http://www.theoildrum.com/node/4315.

O'Rourke, P.J. *On the Wealth of Nations: Books that Changed the World.* New York: Atlantic Monthly Press, Grove/Atlantic, 2007.

Opensecrets.Org. "Lobbying Spending Database | Opensecrets." n.d. https://www.opensecrets.org/lobby/top.php?indexType=i.

Oxfam. "Broken at the Top: How America's Dysfunctional Tax System Costs Billions in Corporate Tax Dodging," Oxfam Media Briefing, Oxfam America, April 2016. https://www.oxfamamerica.org/static/media/files/Broken_at_the_Top_4.14.2016.pdf.

Panek, Richard. "The Year of Albert Einstein." *Smithsonian Magazine,* June 2005. https://www.smithsonianmag.com/science-nature/the-year-of-albert-einstein-75841381/.

Parry, Simon. "The True Cost of Your Cheap Clothes: Slave Wages for Bangladeshi Factory Workers." *Post Magazine,* June 11, 2016. http://www.scmp.com/magazines/post-magazine/article/1970431/true-cost-your-cheap-clothes-slave-wages-bangladesh-factory.

Patel, Jugal K. and Alicia Parlapiano. "The Senate's Official Scorekeeper Says the Republican Tax Plan Would Add $1 Trillion to the Deficit." *New York Times,* December 1, 2017. https://www.nytimes.com/interactive/2017/11/28/us/politics/tax-bill-deficits.html.

PBS NewsHour. "Apple CEO Tim Cook at Senate Hearings (part 2)." YouTube video. 21:52, May 21, 2013. https://www.youtube.com/watch?v=hRmLm6tYNhQ.

———. "Apple CEO Tim Cook Testifies at Senate Hearing." YouTube video. 37:11, May 21, 2013. https://www.youtube.com/watch?v=Lx6YINOfjaQ.

Pelletier, TC. "Do We Replace Our Cells Every 7 or 10 years?" *Ask a Naturalist.com,* August 10, 2010. http://askanaturalist.com/do-we-replace-our-cells-every-7-or-10-years/.

Perry, Mark J. "Manufacturing's Declining Share of GDP is a Global Phenomenon, and it Something to Celebrate." *U.S. Chamber of Commerce Foundation*, March 22, 2012. https://www.uschamberfoundation.org/blog/post/manufacturing-s-declining-share-gdp-global-phenomenon-and-it-s-something-celebrate/34261.

Physicians for Social Responsibility. *Body Count: Casualty Figures After 10 Years of the "War on Terror" Iraq, Afghanistan, Pakistan.* IPPNW, March 2015. https://www.ippnw.de/commonFiles/pdfs/Frieden/Body_Count_first_international_edition_2015_final.pdf.

Picker, Leslie. "Tyco Merger Will Shift Johnson Controls' Tax Liability Overseas." *New York Times,* January 25, 2016. https://www.nytimes.com/2016/01/26/business/dealbook/johnson-controls-to-combine-with-tyco-in-tax-inversion-deal.html.

Piketty, Thomas and Arthur Goldhammer, trans. *Capital in the Twenty-First Century*. Cambridge: Harvard University Press, 2014.

Pinker, Steven. "Fooled by Belligerence: Comments on Nassim Taleb's 'The Long Peace is a Statistical Illusion.'" n.d. https://stevenpinker.com/files/comments_on_taleb_by_s_pinker.pdf.

———. *The Better Angels of Our Nature: Why Violence Has Declined.* New York: Viking Books, 2011.

Pittman, Genevra. "Half a Million Die from Smoking Yearly in U.S." *Reuters*, April 1, 2011. https://www.reuters.com/article/us-smoking-deaths/half-a-million-die-from-smoking-yearly-in-u-s-idUSTRE72U4E220110331.

Plato, *The Republic of Plato,* translated into English with Introduction, Analysis, Marginal Analysis, and Index, by B. Jowett, M.A. The Third

Edition revised and corrected throughout. Oxford: Clarendon Press, 1888. e-Book. http://oll.libertyfund.org/titles/598.

Polanyi, Karl. *The Great Transformation: The Political and Economic Origins of Out Time*. Boston, MA: Beacon Press, 1944.

Porter, Andrew, James Kirkup and Gordon Rayner. "Financial Crisis: HBOS and RBS 'to Be Nationalised' in £50 Billion State Intervention." *Telegraph*, October 12, 2008. http://www.telegraph.co.uk/finance/financialcrisis/3185120/Financial-crisis-HBOS-and-RBS-to-be-nationalised-in-50-billion-state-intervention.html.

Purkiss, Jessica and Jack Serle. "Obama's Covert Drone War in Numbers: Ten Times More Strikes than Bush." *The Bureau of Investigative Journalism*, January 17, 2017. https://www.thebureauinvestigates.com/stories/2017-01-17/obamas-covert-drone-war-in-numbers-ten-times-more-strikes-than-bush.

Quora. "How Many Companies Exist in the World?" n.d. https://www.quora.com/How-many-companies-exist-in-the-world.

Rajan, Raghuram G. *Fault Lines: How the Hidden Fractures Still Threaten the World Economy*. Princeton, NJ: Princeton University Press, 2010.

Reagan, Ronald. "Election Eve Address 'Vision for America.'" (November 3, 1980). Online by Gerhard Peters and John T. Woolley, *The American Presidency Project*. http://www.presidency.ucsb.edu/ws/?pid=85199.

Reid, T.R. *A Fine Mess: A Global Quest for a Simpler, Fairer, and More Efficient Tax System*. London: Penguin Press, 2017.

———. "Now Is the Perfect Time to Think About Taxes – T.R. Reid on A Fine Mess." Interview by Chris Schluep. *Omnivoracious, Amazon Book Review*, April 18, 2007. https://www.amazonbookreview.com/post/8b29d081-3613-4a87-a44e-892be6670456/now-is-the-perfect-time-to-think-about-taxes-t-r-reid-on-a-fine-mess.

Reisinger, Don. "Apple's New 'Spaceship' Headquarters Cost this Much, Study Says." *Fortune*, October 6, 2017. http://fortune.com/2017/10/06/apple-park-build-cost/.

Richardson, Angelique and Ellen Terrel. "Apple Computer, Inc." Library of Congress, *Business Reference Services*, April 2008. https://www.loc.gov/rr/business/businesshistory/April/apple.html.

Rifkin, Jeremy. *The Empathetic Civilization: The Race to Global Consciousness in a World in Crisis.* London: Penguin Group, 2009.

———. *The European Dream.* Cambridge, UK: Polity Press, 2004.

Rimkus, Ron. "Financial Scandals, Scoundrels & Crises: Enron Corporation." *CFA Institute*, December 7, 2016. https://www.econcrises.org/2016/12/07/enron-corporation-2001/.

Ripple, William J., Christopher Wolf, Thomas M. Newsome, Mauro Galetti, Mohammed Alamgir, Eileen Crist, Mahmoud I. Mahmoud, William F. Laurance, and 15,364 scientist signatories from 184 countries. "World Scientists' Warning to Humanity: A Second Notice" *BioScience* 67, No. 12, (December 2017): 1026–1028. https://academic.oup.com/bioscience/article/67/12/1026/4605229.

Robinson, Joan. "Michal Kalecki: A Neglected Prophet." *New York Review of Books* 23, No. 3 (March, 1976). http://www.nybooks.com/articles/1976/03/04/michal-kalecki-a-neglected-prophet/.

Rochat, Philippe. "Five Levels of Self-Awareness as they Unfold Early in Life." *Consciousness and Cognition* 12 (2003): 717-31. *Science Direct, Elsevier*, February 27, 2003. http://www.psychology.emory.edu/cognition/rochat/Rochat5levels.pdf.

"Ronald Reagan TV Ad: 'It's Morning in America Again'." YouTube video, 0:59, posted by "Andre Morgado," November 12, 2006. https://www.youtube.com/watch?v=EU-IBF8nwSY.

Rosen, Rebecca J. "Can the Country Survive Without a Strong Middle Class?" *Atlantic*, March 21, 2017. https://www.theatlantic.com/business/archive/2017/03/middle-class-constitution/519909/.

Rosenbaum, David E. "The 1992 Campaign: Candidates' Records; Bush and Congress: Rising Feud Produced a Legislative Deadlock." *New York Times*, August 9, 1992. http://www.nytimes.com/1992/08/09/us/1992-campaign-candidates-records-bush-congress-rising-feud-produced-legislative.html?pagewanted=all.

Rosenberg, Yuval. "US Companies Are Dying Faster Than Ever." *Business Insider,* August 6, 2015. http://www.businessinsider.com/us-companies-are-dying-faster- than-ever-2015-8?IR=T.

Roser, Max and Esteban Ortiz-Ospina, "World Population Growth." *OurWorldInData.org.* Last modified in May, 2017. https://ourworldindata.org/world-population-growth/.

Roser, Max. "War and Peace." *OurWorldInData.org,* n.d. https://ourworldindata.org/war-and-peace/.

Rothman, Lily. "This Book Has Kept American Drivers Safe for 50 Years." *Time*, November 30, 2015. http://time.com/4124987/50-years-unsafe-at-any-speed/.

Ruffini, Patrick. "Why Russia's Facebook Ad Campaign Wasn't Such a Success." *Washington Post,* November 3, 2017. https://www.washingtonpost.com/outlook/why-russias-facebook-ad-campaign-wasnt-such-a-success/2017/11/03/b8efacca-bffa-11e7-8444-a0d4f04b89eb_story.html?utm_term=.464441b88c90.

Saez, Emmanuel. "Striking it Richer: The Evolution of Top Incomes in the United States." *Pathways Magazine, Stanford Center for the Study of Poverty and Inequality,* (Winter 2008) as updated on September 3, 2013. https://eml.berkeley.edu//~saez/saez-UStopincomes-2012.pdf.

Sahlins, Marshall. *Stone Age Economics.* Chicago, IL: Aldine Atherton, 1972.

Salisbury, Ian. "This Chart Shows How Much Americans Pay in Taxes vs. the Rest of the World." *Money*, July 19, 2017. http://time.com/money/4862673/us-tax-burden-vs-oecd-countries/.

Samuelson, Paul A. *Economics: An Introductory Analysis.* New York: McGraw Hill Book, 1948.

Sanchez, Yoani. "As They Used to Say in the USSR: We Pretend to Work and They Pretend to Pay Us." *Huffington Post,* n.d. https://www.huffingtonpost.com/yoani-sanchez/as-they-used-to-say-in-th_b_564573.html.

Sánchez Ron, José Manuel. "When Lorenz Discovered the Butterfly Effect." *Open Mind*, May 22, 2015. https://www.bbvaopenmind.com/en/when-lorenz-discovered-the-butterfly-effect/.

Sapolsky, Robert. "Being Human: Life Lessons from the Frontiers of Science." *Great Courses*, Course No. 1686. n.d. https://www.thegreatcourses.com/courses/being-human-life-lessons-from-the-frontiers-of-science.html.

"Sarah Palin 2012 Ad – 'Hopey Changey'." YouTube video, 0:30, posted by "AndersonGOP," April 10, 2011. https://www.youtube.com/watch?v=BEgrrvywXhI.

Schultz, E.J. "Snickers Surging to Top of Global Candy Race." *AdAge*, September 20, 2012. http://adage.com/article/news/snickers-surging-top-global-candy-race/237349/.

SEC. "Securities and Exchange Commission Form 10-K, Annual Report of Microsoft Corporation for the Fiscal Year Ended June 30, 2017." https://www.sec.gov/Archives/edgar/data/789019/000156459017014900/msft-10k_20170630.htm#ITEM5_MARKET_FOR_REGISTRANTS.

——. "Securities and Exchange Commission Form 10-K, GE 2016 Annual Report." https://www.sec.gov/Archives/edgar/data/40545/000004054517000010/ge10k2016.htm.

Shaw William H. and Vincent E. Barry. *Moral Issues in Business*. 8th ed. Belmont, CA: Wadsworth, 2001.

Shelley, Mary. *Frankenstein; or, The Modern Prometheus*. Lackington, Hughes, Harding Mavor & Jones, 1818. Kindle.

Sherman Act, 26 Stat. 209, 15 U.S.C.

Sicilia, David B. "A Brief History of U.S. Unemployment." *Washington Post*, n.d. http://www.washingtonpost.com/wp-srv/special/business/us-unemployment-rate-history/.

Simha, Rakesh Krishnan. "Satan Scare: Why the US Is Going Ballistic over a Russian Missile." *Russia Beyond*, May 23, 2014. https://www.rbth.com/blogs/2014/05/23/satan_scare_why_the_us_is_going_ballistic_over_a_russian_missile_35461.

Simon, Herbert A. *Reason in Human Affairs*. Stanford: Stanford University Press, 1983.

Sitaraman, Ganesh. "Our Constitution Wasn't Built for This." *New York Times*, September 16, 2017. https://www.nytimes.com/2017/09/16/opinion/sunday/constitution-economy.html?_r=0.

———. *The Crisis of the Middle Class Constitution: Why Economic Inequality Threatens our Republic*. New York: Knopf, 2017.

Skidelsky, Robert and Edward Skidelsky. *How Much is Enough? Money and the Good Life*. New York: Other Press, 2012.

Skousen, Mark. "The Perseverance of Paul Samuelson's Economics." *Journal of Economic Perspectives* 11, No. 2 (Spring 1997): 137-152.

Smith, Adam. *An Enquiry into the Nature and Causes of the Wealth of Nations* (1st ed. 1776) edited with an Introduction, Notes, Marginal Summary and an Enlarged Index by Edwin Cannan. London: Methuen, 1904. Kindle. http://oll.libertyfund.org/titles/237.

Smithers, Rebecca. "Almost Half of the World's Food Thrown Away, Report Finds." *Guardian*, January 10, 2013. https://www.theguardian.com/environment/2013/jan/10/half-world-food-waste.

Socrates (an alias), "Tradition of Thumos." *Classical Wisdom Weekly*, June 23, 2014. http://classicalwisdom.com/tradition-thumos/.

Speaks, Jeff. "Hume on Identity over Time and Persons." Handout, PHIL 20208, October 3, 2006. https://www3.nd.edu/~jspeaks/courses/2006-7/20208/hume-personal-identity.pdf.

St. Augustine, *The Confessions of Saint Augustine*. Translated by E. B. Pusye (Edward Bouverie). AD 401. Project Gutenberg, 2002. https://www.gutenberg.org/ebooks/3296.

StackExchange. "A list of Inconveniences between Quantum Mechanics and (General) Relativity?" *Physics,* n.d. https://physics.stackexchange.com/questions/387/a-list-of-inconveniences-between-quantum-mechanics-and-general-relativity.

———. "Why Is Human Vision Restricted to 400-700 nm?" *Biology,* n.d. https://biology.stackexchange.com/questions/35337/why-is-human-vision-restricted-to-400-700-nm.

Stapleton, Sabrina. "How Many Calories Are in a Snickers Bar?" *Livestrong.com*, October 3, 2017. https://www.livestrong.com/article/302359-how-many-calories-are-in-a-snickers-bar/.

Statista. "Non-U.S. Share of Apple's Revenue from 1st Quarter 2006 to 4th Quarter 2017." *The Statistics Portal*, n.d. https://www.statista.com/statistics/263435/non-us-share-of-apples-revenue/.

Stensrude J. *A Dictionary of Ozian Terminology.* n.d. http://www.stensrude.com.

Stevens, Paul. "Bretton Woods: 1944-1971." *Foundation for Economic Education*, May 1, 1973. https://fee.org/articles/bretton-woods-1944-1971/.

Stout, Lynn A. "The Shareholder Value Myth." YouTube video, 3:38, posted by "Rotman School of Management," April 16, 2013. https://www.youtube.com/watch?v=ZzztBF9nprA.

———. "Why We Should Stop Teaching Dodge v. Ford." *Virginia Law & Business Review* 3, No. 1 (Spring 2008). Cornell Law Library, Scholarship@Cornell Law: A Digital Repository, Cornell Law Faculty Publications. http://scholarship.law.cornell.edu/cgi/viewcontent.cgi?article=1826&context=facpub.

Straub, Richard. "The Promise of a Truly Entrepreneurial Society." *Harvard Business Review*, March 25, 2016. https://hbr.org/2016/03/the-promise-of-a-truly-entrepreneurial-society.

Streeck, W, Patrick Camiller, trans. and David Fernbach, trans. *Buying Time: The Delayed Crisis of Democratic Capitalism.* London: Verso, 2 ed. 2017.

Swift, John. "The Soviet-American Arms Race." *History Review*, Issue 63 (March 2009). http://www.historytoday.com/john-swift/soviet-american-arms-race.

Tabuchi, Hiroko. "Walmart to End Health Coverage for 30,000 Part-Time Workers." *New York Times*, October 7, 2014. https://www.nytimes.com/2014/10/08/business/30000-lose-health-care-coverage-at-walmart.html?_r=0.

Talbot, L E. *Critical Company Law.* Abingdon, Oxon: Routledge-Cavendish, 2008.

Taleb, Nassim Nicholas. *Fooled by Randomness: The Hidden Role of Chance in Life and the Markets.* London: Penguin Books, 2009.

Tate, Karl. "How Quantum Entanglement Works (Infographic)." *Live Science*, April 8, 2013. https://www.livescience.com/28550-how-quantum-entanglement-works-infographic.html.

Tax Cuts and Jobs Act 2017 – An Act to Provide for Reconciliation Pursuant to Titles II and V of the Concurrent Resolution on the Budget for Fiscal Year 2018. Public Law No: 115-97.

Tax Foundation. "Federal Tax Revenue by Source, 1934-2018." November 21, 2013. https://taxfoundation.org/federal-tax-revenue-source-1934-2018/.

Telegraph. "Bailing out Britain's Banks: A Timeline." January 19, 2009. http://www.telegraph.co.uk/finance/newsbysector/banksandfinance/4285063/Bail-out-Britains-banks-A-timeline.html.

Teles, Steven M. "Kludgeocracy in America." *National Affairs* No. 17 (Fall, 2013). http://www.nationalaffairs.com/publications/detail/kludgeocracy-in-america.

Texas State Historical Association. "Spindletop Oilfield." n.d. https://tshaonline.org/handbook/online/articles/dos03.

Thomas of Chobham, c.11680-c.1235, *The History of Economic Thought*. http://www.hetwebsite.net/het/profiles/chobham.htm.

Thomasberger, Claus. "Fictitious Ideas, Social Facts and the Double Movement: Polanyi's Framework in the Age of Neoliberalism." (Paper presented at the 13th International Karl Polanyi Conference. "The Enduring Legacy of Karl Polanyi." Concordia University, November 6-8, 2014).

Torres-Spelliscy, Ciara. "The History of Corporate Personhood." *Brennan Center for Justice at New York University School of Law* (blog), April 7, 2014. https://www.brennancenter.org/blog/hobby-lobby-argument.

Trending Top Most. "Top 10 Best Selling Candy Bars Brands in the World." n.d. http://www.trendingtopmost.com/worlds-popular-list-top-10/2017-2018-2019-2020-2021/product/best-selling-candy-bars-brands-world-india-market-usa-famous-expensive-cheapest-reviews/.

Trueman, C.N. "Hyperinflation and Weimar Germany." *History Learning Site*, May 22, 2015. http://www.historylearningsite.co.uk/modern-world-history-1918-to-1980/weimar-germany/hyperinflation-and-weimar-germany/.

Trump, Donald. "Remarks by President Trump on Tax Reform." (St. Charles Convention Center, St. Charles, Missouri, November 30, 2017). The White House, Office of the Press Secretary. https://www.whitehouse.gov/the-press-office/2017/11/30/remarks-president-trump-tax-reform.

Twain, Mark and Charles Dudley Warner. *The Gilded Age: A Tale of Today*. 1873. Project Gutenberg, 2008. https://www.gutenberg.org/ebooks/3178.

UN News Centre. "Unsafe Water Kills More People than War, Ban Says on World Day." March 22, 2010. http://www.un.org/apps/news/story.asp?NewsID=34150#.WoAzRK2B1PO.

UN Watercourses Convention. "The Legal Architecture for Transboundary Waters." Online Users Guide. n.d. http://www.unwatercoursesconvention.org/importance/the-legal-architecture-for-transboundary-waters/.

UNESCO. "World Water Assessment Programme." *United Nations Education, Scientific and Cultural Organisation.* http://www.unesco.org/new/en/natural-sciences/environment/water/wwap/wwdr/wwdr1-2003/.

United Nations Department of Economic and Social Affairs. "Percentage of Total Population Living in Coastal Areas." n.d. http://www.un.org/esa/sustdev/natlinfo/indicators/methodology_sheets/oceans_seas_coasts/pop_coastal_areas.pdf.

United States Census Bureau. "Population, Table 4 'Population: 1790 to 1990.'" n.d. https://www.census.gov/population/censusdata/table-4.pdf.

United States Geological Survey. "The Water Cycle: Fresh Water Storage.*"* n.d. https://water.usgs.gov/edu/watercyclefreshstorage.html.

United States of America and others v. Philip Morris USA, Inc., and others, 9F. Supp. 2d 1 (D.D.C. 2006) Civil Action No. 99-2496 (GK).

Veblen, Thorstein. *The Theory of the Leisure Class: An Economic Study in the Evolution of Institutions*. 1899, Project Gutenberg, 2008. https://www.gutenberg.org/ebooks/3296.

Verleger, Philip K. Jr. "The U.S. Petroleum Crisis of 1979." *Brookings Papers on Economic Growth* 2 (1979). https://www.brookings.edu/bpea-articles/the-u-s-petroleum-crisis-of-1979/.

Vidal, John. "Water Privatization: A Worldwide Failure." *Guardian*, January 31, 2015. https://www.theguardian.com/global-development/2015/jan/30/water-privatisation-worldwide-failure-lagos-world-bank.

Vision of Humanity. "Global Peace Index 2017." n.d. http://visionofhumanity.org/indexes/global-peace-index/.

Walker, Samuel. *Presidents and Civil Liberties from Wilson to Obama: A Story of Poor Custodians.* New York: Cambridge University Press, 2012.

Washington Post. "Evaluating the Success of the Great Society: Lyndon B. Johnson's Visionary Set of Legislation Turns 50." May 17, 2014. http://www.washingtonpost.com/wp-srv/special/national/great-society-at-50/.

WashingtonsBlog, "America Has Been at War 93 Percent of the Time – 222 Out of 239 Years – Since 1776." *World News Daily Information Clearing House*, February 23, 2015. http://www.informationclearinghouse.info/article41086.htm.

Wattles, Jackie. "Walmart Increasing Wages; Union Says It's All Show." *CNN Money*, January 20, 2016. http://money.cnn.com/2016/01/20/news/companies/walmart-pay-raise-wages/index.html.

Weatherford, Jack. *Genghis Khan and the Making of the Modern World.* New York: Three Rivers Press, Crown Publishing Group, 2004.

Webb, Taylor W. and Michael S.A. Graziano. "The Attention Schema Theory: A Mechanistic Account of Subjective Awareness." *Frontiers in Psychology*, April 23, 2015. https://www.frontiersin.org/articles/10.3389/fpsyg.2015.00500/full.

Weinstein, Michael M. "Paul A. Samuelson, Economist, Dies at 94." *New York Times*, December 13, 2009. http://www.nytimes.com/2009/12/14/business/economy/14samuelson.html?pagewanted=all.

Wellhausen, Rachel L. "Recent Trends in Investor-State Dispute Settlement." *Journal of International Dispute Settlement* 7, No. 1 (March, 2016): 117–135.

———. "Investors Have Controversial New Rights to Sue Countries. Here's why this Matters for the U.S." *Washington Post*, November 30, 2015. https://www.washingtonpost.com/news/monkey-cage/wp/2015/11/30/investors-have-controversial-new-rights-to-sue-countries-heres-why-this-matters-for-the-u-s/?utm_term=.83b49a80c09a.

Wensveen, Jonathan. "Human Nature in Hobbes and Thucydides." Master thesis. Carleton University, Ottawa, Ontario, 2003. https://curve.carleton.ca/system/files/etd/531746aa-265a-45e0-9e46-7246253f17e9/etd_pdf/9b3abf1b2f0595779560cee42182245f/wensveen-humannatureinhobbesandthucydides.pdf.

Whaples, Robert. "Hours of Work in U.S. History." *EH.net*. n.d. https://eh.net/encyclopedia/hours-of-work-in-u-s-history/.

———. "The Shortening of the American Work Week: An Economic and Historical Analysis of its Context, Causes, and Consequences." PhD dissertation. University of Pennsylvania, 1990.

Willard, Haley. "10 Things You Didn't Know About Snickers." *Daily Meal*, November 4, 2014. https://www.thedailymeal.com/10-things-you-didnt-know-about-snickers.

Wilson, Megan R. "Lobbying's Top 50: Who's Spending Big." *Hill*, February 7, 2017. http://thehill.com/business-a-lobbying/business-a-lobbying/318177-lobbyings-top-50-whos-spending-big.

Withnall, Adam. "Global Peace Index 2016: There Are Now Only 10 Countries in the World that Are Actually Free from Conflict." *Independent*, June 8, 2016. http://www.independent.co.uk/news/world/politics/global-peace-index-2016-there-are-now-only-10-countries-in-the-world-that-are-not-at-war-a7069816.html.

Wolchover, Natalie. "How Much Would it Cost to Build the Great Pyramid Today?" *Live Science*, February 22, 2012. https://www.livescience.com/18589-cost-build-great-pyramid-today.html.

———. "Quantum Gravity's Time Problem." *Quanta Magazine*, December 2, 2016. https://www.quantamagazine.org/quantum-gravitys-time-problem-20161201/.

Wolf, Aaron T. "Shared Waters: Conflict and Cooperation." *Annual Review of Environment and Resources* 32 (2007): 241-69. http://transboundarywater.geo.orst.edu/publications/abst_docs/wolf_2007_shared_waters.pdf.

Wolff, Edward N. "Household Wealth Trends in the United States, 1962 to 2016: Has Middle Class Wealth Recovered?" NBER Working Paper No. 24085 (November 2017).

Woolley, Suzanne. "Do You Have More Debt than the Average American?" *Bloomberg*, December 15, 2016. https://www.bloomberg.com/news/articles/2016-12-15/average-credit-card-debt-16k-total-debt-133k-where-do-you-fit-in.

Worldometers. "World Population by Year." http://www.worldometers.info/world-population/world-population-by-year/.

Yount, Dave. "Statements that Plato Never Made!" n.d. http://www.mesacc.edu/~davpy35701/text/plato-things-not-said.html.

Zedong, Mao. "Protracted War" (Series of lectures, Yenan Association for the Study of the War of Resistance against Japan, May 26 to June 3, 1938). https://www.marxists.org/reference/archive/mao/selected-works/volume-2/mswv2_09.htm.

Zeihan, Peter. *The Accidental Super Power: The Next Generation of American Preeminence and the Coming Global Disorder*. New York: Hachette Book Group, 2014.

Ziobro, Paul and Michael Calia. "Walgreen Board Wasn't Comfortable with 'Inversion.'" *Wall Street Journal*, August 6, 2014. https://www.wsj.com/articles/walgreen-to-buy-remaining-stake-in-alliance-boots-1407321248.

Zuraw, Lydia. "Critics Say Food Safety Standards Could Be Threatened by U.S./EU Trade Agreement." *Food Safety News*, May 16, 2014. http://www.foodsafetynews.com/2014/05/food-safety-standards-could-be-threatened-in-u-s-eu-trade-agreement/#.WitkGBRgr8M.

ABOUT THE AUTHOR

Peter Deegan was born in Scotland and grew up in Australia. He is a corporate finance, and mergers and acquisitions lawyer. A former partner of an English "Magic Circle" law firm, Deegan has lived and worked in the United Kingdom, the United States, Australia, Hungary, Poland, Russia, Spain, Turkey and the United Arab Emirates. For the last few years he has spent much of his time in China. In the Nineties he took time out from practicing law to develop and produce the feature film, *"Shimmer"* (based on the play by John O'Keefe) for American Playhouse. Deegan is married with three children. *"Snafu"* is his first book.

For more by the author, please visit: www.snafublog.com

Made in the USA
Columbia, SC
19 April 2018